The Encyclopedia of
FINANCIAL PLANNING

What You Need to Know About Money from the Nation's Leading Financial Planners

The Encyclopedia of
FINANCIAL PLANNING

What You Need to Know About Money from the Nation's Leading Financial Planners

Editor, Lisa Holton

The Financial Planning Association (FPA) is the membership association for the financial planning community. FPA is committed to providing information and resources to help financial planners and those who champion the financial planning process succeed. FPA believes that everyone needs objective advice to make smart financial decisions.

FPA Press is the publishing arm of FPA, providing current content and advanced thinking on technical and practice management topics.

Information in this book is accurate at the time of publication and consistent with the standards of good practice in the financial planning community. As research and practice advance, however, standards may change. For this reason, it is recommended that readers evaluate the applicability of any recommendation in light of particular situations and changing standards.

Financial Planning Association
4100 Mississippi Ave., Suite 400
Denver, Colorado 80246-3053

Phone: 800.322.4237
Fax: 303.759-0749
E-mail: fpapress@fpanet.org

www.fpanet.org

ISBN: 0-9753448-7-0
ISBN-13: 978-0-9753448-7-3

Manufactured in the United States of America

A wise man should have money in his head,
but not in his heart.
—Jonathan Swift

Every time you spend money, you're casting a
vote for the kind of world you want.
—Anna Lappe

Money is like a sixth sense without which you
cannot make a complete use of the other five.
—W. Somerset Maugham

About the Editor

Lisa Holton heads The Lisa Company, an Evanston, IL-based writing, editing and research firm founded in 1998. She is a former business editor and reporter for the *Chicago Sun-Times* and a former editor with the *Thomson Corporation*. She has 25 years of experience writing about business and investing topics and has authored or co-written 11 books. Her earlier titles include *How to be a Value Investor* [McGraw-Hill, June 1999] and *The Essential Dictionary of Real Estate* [Barnes & Noble Books, November 2003].

In 2005, she became a contributing writer to the Financial Planning Association on consumer finance and retirement planning issues.

Holton has written for a variety of national magazines and newspapers including the *American Bar Association Journal, Parents, American Demographics, Latina, Working Mother,* the *Boston Globe* and the *Chicago Tribune.* She is also a busy writer for corporations, associations, and universities nationwide.

Lisa is a graduate of Northwestern University's Medill School of Journalism and a former national board member of the Society of American Business Editors and Writers (SABEW.) She is a current member of the American Society of Journalists and Authors, the International Association of Business Communicators and the Society of Midland Authors.

In her spare time, Holton writes short stories and screenplays. Her feature screenplay "The Plant" was a quarterfinalist for the 2002 Nicholl Fellowships in Screenwriting offered by the Academy of Motion Picture Arts and Sciences. She has attended the film program at Chicago's Columbia College and completed film production courses at Chicago Filmmakers Workshop.

A native of Moline, Illinois, Holton grew up in Louisville,

Kentucky, and now considers the Windy City her home. She lives in suburban Evanston.

Acknowledgements

Thanks to Bruce Most, who authored many of the Financial Planning Perspectives on which this book was based, to the planners who agreed to be interviewed, and to Clare Stenstrom, CFP®, June Schroeder, CFP®, and all the Financial Planning Perspectives content reviewers throughout the years.

About FPA

The Financial Planning Association® (FPA®) is the membership organization for the financial planning community. FPA is built around four Core Values—Competence, Integrity, Relationships, and Stewardship. We want as members those who share our Core Values.

FPA's primary aim is to be the community that fosters the value of financial planning and advances the financial planning profession. The FPA strategy to accomplish its objectives involves welcoming all those who advance the financial planning process and promoting the CERTIFIED FINANCIAL PLANNER™ (CFP®) marks as the cornerstone of the financial planning profession. FPA is the heart of financial planning, connecting those who deliver, support, and benefit from it.

FPA was created on the foundation that the CFP marks best represent the promise and the future of the financial planning profession. CFP certification offers the public a consistent and credible symbol of professional competence in financial planning. And FPA benefits the public by helping to ensure that financial planning is delivered through competent and ethical financial planners.

FPA members include individuals and companies who are dedicated to helping people make wise financial decisions to achieve their life goals and dreams. FPA believes that everyone needs objective advice to make smart financial decisions and that when seeking the advice of a financial planner, the planner should be a CFP professional.

FPA is committed to improving and enhancing the professional lives and capabilities of our members. We offer a variety of programs and services to that end.

Table of Contents

Introduction

In recent years, the Financial Planning Association®
(FPA®) has created an extensive archive of information
on financial planning topics. FPA—the organization on
which thousands of financial planning professionals
rely—has drawn from that archive and from up-to-the-
minute observations from its financial planners to
create this book. The book is designed to help you make
smart financial decisions and realize your life's dreams,
whatever your financial situation and whatever your
stage in life.

HOW TO USE THIS BOOK

Use this book in much the same way that you would use
a home medical guide. You would expect a home medical
guide to answer all of your basic questions on health. It
might provide useful statistics to help you put medical
conditions in perspective and anticipate associated risks
and opportunities. The ideal medical guide would help
you stay healthy by providing information on topics such
as exercise, stress, nutrition, weight management, and
high-risk activities.

Similarly, this book will provide you with basic guidance to establish and maintain your *financial health*. It will acquaint you with basic financial terminology and provide you with general guidance on healthy financial practices. You'll learn how to organize your financial information and view your finances the way financial planning professionals do—as a series of interrelated considerations that work together to create financial strength. You'll discover how saving and budgeting combine with topics such as taxes, insurance, investing, retirement planning, estate planning, and your employee benefits to create your whole financial picture. You can use the table of contents to find what you need to know and gather the basic information you'll need to start thinking about the critical financial decisions in your life. For simple questions, you might want to jump to the glossary in the back of the book. There, we also provide a list of valuable Internet resources to aid you as you progress in the financial planning process.

Of course, your home medical guide is no substitute for the diagnosis and treatment you can receive through emergency medical care or regular checkups with your doctor. Similarly, the guidance in this book is not intended to replace the tailored advice a financial planner can give you. When you decide to consult a financial planner, you will find a wealth of information herein about how to select one—someone with whom you can work confidently and comfortably to meet your immediate needs and pursue your long-term goals. You'll also find the information provided in these pages invaluable in helping you prepare for your first meeting with a financial planner. It will help you ask insightful questions and better understand the advice your financial planner gives you.

WHERE TO START

The book is divided into a dozen sections that bundle together related topics according to your general needs, interests, and life stages. I strongly encourage you to read the first section, "What Is Financial Planning?" thoroughly to get an overview of what financial advice is all about. This section will help you put the rest of the information contained in these pages into a useful context. You'll learn why advice is critical, what financial planners are, and how to choose the right one for you.

What you'll discover is that financial planning is a lifelong process that starts with your individual financial circumstances and explores your needs and goals. Goals can range from simply planning your next vacation to funding your children's college education or planning for rewarding retirement years. Your goals will change as you grow older and experience life-changing events—graduation, getting or losing a job, marriage or partnership, raising children, starting a business or transitioning out of a business, dealing with the death of a loved one, caring for aging relatives, etc. Feel free to skip around to the sections, chapters, and topics that appeal to you at your particular stage of life. Whether you're 25, 45, or 65, there's something in this book for you.

Part 2 addresses debt—how to get control of it, whether you're just starting out in life or find yourself burdened with debt as retirement approaches. Learn the facts about bankruptcy and building a new financial life.

You'll find the third section filled with valuable guidance for setting up your financial strategy. Find out what kind of expertise you'll need, how to get started, and how to be prepared in the event of a disaster.

If you're just now embarking on your career, you might want to jump to Part 4: "Financial Planning and Career Building Go Hand-in-Hand." Make the most of your first job and living on your own. Identify the things you need to address as you move on in your career.

If that career leads you to start your own business, you'll find a wealth of information in the fifth section on how to make the transition from employer to employee and on handling the insurance, tax, and retirement considerations unique to business owners.

Parts 6 through 8 address financial planning for families. Perhaps you're planning to start a family. In that case, you'll find invaluable financial guidance on raising children, starting with how to prepare financially for their arrival in Part 6. Today's families are experiencing new stresses and challenges. FPA recognizes that sometimes, relationships don't work out. This book will help you be financially prepared for that possibility. More and more individuals find themselves sandwiched between caring for children and caring for aging adult members of the family. The death of a loved one can be devastating and often imposes harsh financial conditions on surviving family members. This book provides a compassionate financial perspective on these and other important issues to help you meet life's greatest challenges and come through them strong and secure. Learn how to teach your children about money. And in Part 7, find out about ways to prepare well in advance for your children's education—college-financing options that will put you at the head of the class. Are you considering buying your first home or embarking on some other major real estate investment? Look to Part 8 to find out about your financing options.

In Part 9, you'll learn about the various types of insurance, such as life, home, disability, auto, health, and long-term care. How much insurance is enough? You'll find guidelines to help you decide. Let us coach you on how to deal with whatever life throws at you financially, whether expected or unexpected.

How much will you need to save for your retirement? What if you haven't saved enough? How can you stretch your retirement dollars to make them last longer? We answer these and other questions in Part 10: "Funding an Underfunded Retirement."

What about investing? What is wealth management? What do people mean when they talk about stocks, mutual funds, commodities, and government bonds? How do you sort through all of these things to create an investment strategy that effectively addresses your unique needs and goals? These and other concerns are carefully explained in Part 11.

NEXT STEPS IN YOUR FINANCIAL JOURNEY

If you'd like to meet a planner in your area who deals with a particular focus to meet your needs, we invite you to go to www.FPAnet.org/public. That's the Financial Planning Association's Web site, and there you'll find a link to PlannerSearch, a nationwide directory of CERTIFIED FINANCIAL

PLANNER™ professionals in your area who can set you on the right course for the rest of your financial life.

We hope you enjoy the book, and we invite your suggestions for the next edition. Write us at FPAPress@FPAnet.org.

Marvin W. Tuttle, Jr., CAE
Executive Director/CEO
Financial Planning Association®

Part I

What Is Financial Planning?

What Financial Planners Do for People

David Yeske, CFP®

"Financial planners help people live exquisite, fulfilling lives," explains David Yeske, a San Francisco-based financial planner.

"If there was one single best thing that we accomplish, it's allowing people to focus clearly on life goals. When everything around the person suggests that their money situation will never allow them to attain what they really want in life, a planner can help them rise above that and see the possibilities."

Yeske emphasizes that financial planners are not corrections officers. "We help people dream, and if that sounds a little corny, think how you feel when you dream about things you really want. It's positive—it makes you feel good. For many people, the road to that dream isn't going to be immediate or painless, but if people can just remember how it feels to picture themselves with that goal, that's a way to keep them focused."

"Sometimes the first step is letting people believe that with the right amount of work they can achieve things they never had confidence in before," Yeske says. "Personal financial planning is about context, making smart financial decisions that are perfectly suited to you."

1 | Why Advice Is Critical

Frankly, financial advice is everywhere. It's on television, the Internet, in hundreds of publications and newspapers, and just as far away as your Uncle Morty who's always bragging about his stock picks.

But what would happen if you had one person working for you who had access to all the information out there and edited out all the investment noise that doesn't fit you? What would happen if you had someone who created a savings, debt management, and investment plan that conformed to your financial circumstances, your risk tolerance, and your specific goals?

It would probably make life a lot easier.

That's what a financial planner does. A financial planner doesn't take control of your assets (unless you specify that role and they are specifically trained and licensed to take it on); they work with you over the course of a lifetime to review, set and execute goals for your money. They don't set a plan and then say, "Okay, you're set for the next 25 years." These are individuals who sit down with you, set a plan, and review that strategy on a regular basis, whether quarterly or every two to three years, but especially when a major life change occurs.

There are no official surveys or studies that say that working with a financial planner ensures a stronger financial future than not working with one. But as you read this book, it might make sense to consider one.

THE MOST COMMON FINANCIAL MISTAKES MADE BY THOSE WHO FAIL TO PLAN

Financial planning goes far beyond picking places to put your money. First, you have to understand your past behaviors and why they have to change.

Failure to budget. Planning is all about realistic use of resources and making accommodations for the unexpected. Many people never think about classifying or ordering what they spend. Financial planning is a process that forces individuals to really think about what they're spending their money on and whether that expense is genuinely worthwhile.

Losing control of debt. The ease of getting a credit card in this country has long been a fact, but the number of people who are borrowing against home equity is staggering. According to the Federal Reserve, in early 2006, household debt climbed at twice the pace of household income from the beginning of 2000 through 2003, and because of low interest rates, Americans took on $2.3 trillion in new mortgage debt during that period—an increase of nearly 50 percent. Consumer credit, from zero-interest auto loans to the much more expensive debt on credit cards, climbed 33 percent, rising to $2 trillion in 2003 from $1.5 trillion in 2000. This rise in mortgage-related debt is frightening because if homeowners can't pay their debt, they risk losing their homes.

Borrowing from retirement funds. Money in 401(k) and 403(b) accounts is tax-free until you withdraw it, and then it will have to be paid back, usually over a shorter period of time than a traditional mortgage. Even though some people use retirement funds to finance their first home purchase, it's still a bad idea.

Late payment of bills. Credit scores affect virtually everything we do in our financial life—they're checked not only for approvals of home loans and other forms of credit, but for stuff you almost never hear about, like insurance premiums, unpaid parking tickets, and overdue library books. Make sure you're whole and on time with all your bills.

PLANNING TIPS: 14 REASONS YOU MAY NEED A FINANCIAL PLANNER

Consumers often mistakenly believe that financial planners are mainly investment advisers, but the fact is that genuine financial planners provide a broad range of financial advice for a broad range of personal financial situations. The following are 14 reasons or situations where you may want to seek the services of a qualified financial planner.

Organize and manage your finances. Many of us have complex financial lives, yet lack the time, expertise, discipline, and objectivity to put our financial house in order. A planner can examine your overall net worth and financial situation, help you identify your life goals and objectives, and recommend strategies to get the most bang from each dollar you earn and spend so you can achieve your life goals.

Marriage and children. Blending two independent financial lives can be complicated and stressful, particularly if there are conflicting financial personalities or there were previous marriages. It's critical to address such issues as insurance, titling of assets, and delegating money-management duties.

Divorce. Breaking up a marriage is frequently far more financially devastating than the impact of even a long bear market. Simply dividing an estate in half is often a bad decision. A planner can help you and/or your attorney design an equitable settlement that will serve you for the long term.

Receiving a financial windfall. Inheriting a substantial sum of money or winning the lottery commonly brings relatives or product sellers with investment "deals" for you. Running them past a planner can eliminate the inappropriate ones. But windfalls often involve other financial and nonfinancial factors. For example, it may be better to put the money toward debts, or you may want to donate some of it to charity. Inheritance in particular is often fraught with deep emotional issues and family conflicts, so independent advice can be invaluable.

Planning for retirement. Investment decisions are naturally a critical component of retirement planning. But often overlooked are how best to withdraw funds from your nest egg once you retire, and especially *what kind* of retirement you want to live. A planner can help you crystallize your retirement vision, and then design a plan that will help you achieve that vision.

Funding for college. Beyond selecting among a plethora of investment options, other key

Continued on page 14

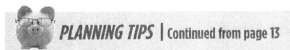

PLANNING TIPS | Continued from page 13

issues include financial aid and tax considerations. Families also should examine closely the trade-off between funding college for their children versus funding their own retirement.

Facing a financial crisis. The loss of a job, a serious illness, a legal problem, or a natural disaster might prompt the seeking of financial advice.

Career advice. Planners can advise you on the financial consequences of a career change, compensation or separation package, stock options, and retirement plans such as deferred compensation and 401(k)s.

Running a business. A planner can help every step of the way, from the business plan and buying the business to setting up a retirement plan for the owner and the employees, and, most often overlooked by owners, creating a realistic succession plan.

Buying and selling a home. A home is typically the largest purchase a family makes, and generates numerous questions a planner can help answer. How much to put down? What type of mortgage? For how long? How much should I borrow? What are the tax ramifications? Should I pay points?

Death of a spouse. All too frequently, the surviving spouse hurriedly and under great stress makes critical long-term financial decisions involving insurance, investments, and retirement plans. Rarely is there a more important time for informed, objective advice. (Much of this stress can be avoided by developing a relationship with a planner as a couple long beforehand!)

Charitable giving. Families blessed with enough discretionary income and assets may want to make substantial donations to one or more favorite charities. But there are many options, some of which can save you more in taxes and thus leave more to the charity.

Insurance. While an insurance agent can always sell you insurance, a financial planner can analyze your insurance needs (many of which people overlook, such as disability and long-term care) in relation to your overall financial circumstances and goals and guide you to buy the amount and type of insurance you should carry.

Estate planning. The terrorist attacks on September 11, 2001, prompted many people to come to planners to discuss wills, living wills, powers of attorney, life insurance, trusts, and other estate planning issues. You'll still need an attorney to draft the documents, but the planner can put those concerns in the context of your financial circumstances and your vision of how you want your estate dispersed, which could save you billable hours with your attorney. ⊠

Inadequate savings for retirement and other expenses. Exactly what people will need to save for their children's college expenses and living expenses in retirement are figures as unique as they are. Planning assistance is perhaps most critical here.

Losing access to tax-deferred savings options. Employees who fail to take advantage of their employers' 401(k) or 403(b) plans are missing out big-time, particularly in companies that match any part of their contributions. The same goes for individuals who qualify for a whole range of IRAs—Roth IRAs, individual IRAs, SEP plans, etc.

Making dumb insurance moves. Insurance isn't an investment; it's a way to protect you against certain catastrophic risks so it is an important part of your financial life. But individuals shouldn't rely solely on the word of brokers when insuring home, life, salary, business, and property—a person's individual situation defines his or her risk scenario, and insurance should be purchased in the amounts and for the time periods that conform to those needs.

FAILURE TO PLAN: A CASE STUDY

The 2001 recession lasted only eight months, but it has had a lasting effect to the date of this book's publication. One of the big reasons is how much was lost by investors who thought the sky was the limit right up until April 2000, when the NASDAQ would begin a decline which at its worst point would shave nearly 80 percent off its all-time high.

While recessions have come and gone since the early 1980s, never in recent memory have so many individual investors suffered critical losses due to their own poor assumptions. Why? Since the early 1980s, Americans have been put in charge of money once managed by corporations and other employers. First there was the creation of the 401(k) retirement savings plan provision in 1978—which benefits adviser Ted Benna lifted out of the arcane language to create today's widespread 401(k) plan. And in the early 1980s, the Reagan administration's bellwether step to popularize the individual retirement account (IRA) gave individual investors the idea that they would potentially see greater results once they became responsible for investing their own retirement nest eggs. Figure 1.1 illustrates the dramatic shift in workers subject to defined contribution plans, like 401(k)s.

What happened? The post 9/11 economic shock and the 2000–2002 recession that followed proved that most investors weren't ready to fly solo.

The move over the last 25 years from defined benefit plans (traditional company-sponsored pension plans) to defined contribution plans (401(k) and 403(b) plans, primarily) has changed everything in the structure of how we save for retirement.

A defined benefit plan provides employees with a guaranteed level of retirement income typically based on the employee's years of service with vesting—or qualification for minimum benefits—at an assigned time in their seniority with the company. Defined contribution plans offer

Figure 1.1: The Switch from Traditional Pension Plans to 401(k)s

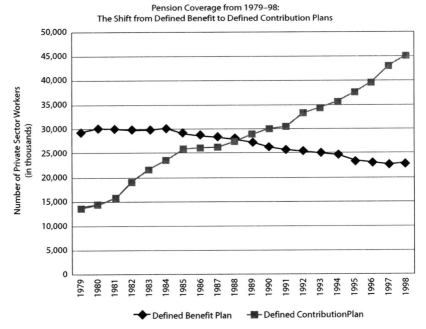

Pension Coverage from 1979–98:
The Shift from Defined Benefit to Defined Contribution Plans

Source: Economic Policy Institute.

employees an opportunity to contribute a share of their income to an individual account. Employers generally contribute directly to such plans or match the contributions of employees with all investment choices left up to the employee.

The shift to defined contribution plans has been dramatic. According to the Federal Reserve, the share of households that had a defined contribution plan rose by 70 percent from 1979 to 1998, while the share of households covered by a traditional defined benefit plan declined simultaneously by 22 percent.

In the early 1980s, it all sounded like a good idea. Companies could save money by offsetting the heavy costs for their traditional plans, and employees, empowered by the reality that they would determine their retirement future and tailor their plans to their specific risk tolerance, would be able to do a much better job than the boss.

Yet today, the retirement outlook for many is shockingly poor. In a 2005 MetLife study, 64 percent of full-time U.S. workers reported they were either behind in their retirement savings goals, or haven't yet started saving. The financial services giant said women were particularly at risk. Twenty-three percent of women said they haven't yet started to save for retirement (compared with 15 percent of men). Among widows, 26 percent said they had no retirement savings goals—70 percent of them said they live paycheck to paycheck.

WHAT TYPES OF PEOPLE HIRE PROFESSIONAL ADVICE?

It's a fact that people with more substantial assets tend to rely more on advisory services because they have more disposable income to pay for them. Yet those who have less are the ones who really need the help.

In a 2003 study, the Economic Policy Institute, a Washington, DC, economic think tank, pointed out how severely various constituencies need financial advice and assistance with their overall financial planning:

- 1988 federal data showed that more than 19 percent of all near-retiree households (households in which the main earner is between the ages of 47 and 64) could expect to retire in poverty. Only 57 percent of these older households can expect to replace half their income in retirement, down from 70 percent in 1989.

- The late 1990s stock market did not raise all boats for workers in 401(k) plans. The boom primarily helped those with accumulated wealth of $1 million or more.

- Women generally have less retirement security than men do. In 2000, 43.2 percent of men over 65 received annuity or pension income compared with 28.5 percent of women. The mean annuity in 2000 was $14,232 for men, and $8,734 for women. (See Figure 1.2.) From 1976 to 1996, pension income levels for women remained stagnant, while men experienced a 13 percent increase.

- African American and Hispanic workers have significantly less retirement security than their white counterparts. The percentage of workers aged 47–64 with expected retirement income below the poverty line—based on 1998 retirement wealth—was 43.1 percent for African

Figure 1.2: Men vs. Women in the Retirement Picture

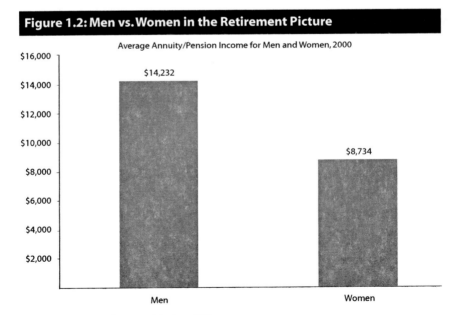

Average Annuity/Pension Income for Men and Women, 2000

Source: Employee Benefits Research Institute, 2002.

American and Hispanic workers and 12.8 percent for non-Hispanic whites. (See Figure 1.3.)

KEEPING EMOTION OUT OF YOUR DECISIONS

Do-it-yourself financial planning has worked for people with the right temperament, ability to learn, and time to focus on their financial life. Timing's also a big factor. It's not for everyone, though, as the American Association for Individual Investors points out in an educational piece entitled, "The Psychology Behind Common Investor Mistakes."[1] It's an interesting view of how the human mind works in decision-making. Most of us can't separate our emotions from our decision-making.

There are six key mistakes the AAII points to in the go-it-alone approach:

- **Overconfidence.** Overconfidence in our own abilities can lower returns. The article points out that in a study of trading at a national discount brokerage, returns averaged 16.4 percent over the period of study, though those accounts that traded the most averaged 11.4 percent in annual returns, significantly less than for an account with average

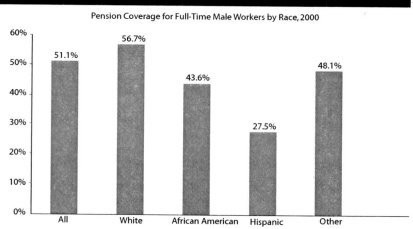

Figure 1.3: How Various Groups Fare

Pension Coverage for Full-Time Male Workers by Race, 2000

Source: Economic Policy Institute.

turnover. Over the same period, the S&P 500 returned 17.9 percent on average. It also points out that men tend to trade more aggressively than women do when left to their own devices.

- **Fear of regret.** When it comes to money, humans tend to obsess about whether they've made the right decision. In stock transactions, as the article points out, individuals who want to avoid the pain of regret often hold losing stocks too long and sell winners too soon.
- **Cognitive dissonance.** We like to believe fully in our decisions, even to the point of shutting out good information from other sources. Call it "investment noise," if you want. The idea is that, at a certain point, an individual with certain preparation or skills will make a decision and then act to screen out all the new or conflicting information. It's why people dump stocks when they hear a frightening news report or hang on to them after a significant run-up, even when the news has started to turn bad.
- **Anchoring.** According to the piece, "The brain uses mental shortcuts to simplify the very complex tasks of information processing and decision-making. Anchoring is the psychologists' term for one shortcut the brain uses." Yet, when you're working full-time, watching the kids, trying to relax, etc., such shortcuts mean you're not developing new ways to think about important things like your investments. This is why it's particularly important to get a second set of eyes on the investment strategy you've chosen.
- **Representativeness.** This is a psychological term that reflects another key danger to our financial life—we assume things with the same qualities are quite alike. "If poor earnings and share price performance has a stock branded as 'bad,' representativeness will tend to delay the reclassification of the stock as ones investors would like to own. On the other hand, 'good' stocks may continue to be classified as such by investors well after the firm's prospects for either earnings or price appreciation have diminished significantly."
- **Myopic risk aversion.** If you were to judge an investment in the stock based on its performance between 2000–2002, you'd never

want to buy a single share. This characteristic refers to a human tendency to fixate on a single "good" quality or "bad" quality of an investment. It's shortsightedness, pure and simple.

What's the point of all this? That it's virtually impossible, given the way most of us have to get through the day, for us to do the best job of research, study, and decision-making in our financial planning. Most of us need an expert second opinion to overcome our own biases and timing issues.

The next chapter will focus on what financial planning is and what financial planners do.

2 | *What Is a Financial Planner?*

A financial planner is a trained professional who advises people on how to maximize their savings, investments, and protect or grow all their other assets.

Financial planners are truly as unique as the clients they serve. We'll cover various strategies for finding the right planner in Chapter 3, but here we'll focus on what they are and what they do.

WHAT A FINANCIAL PLANNER IS NOT

A financial planner is not a substitute for your own final decision-making. Planners serve as guides, editors, and strategists. Sometimes they offer investments you may want to buy, but they need to be licensed to do that. They should begin by asking questions of you—plenty of them. Their purpose is to discover all the goals you have right now—and maybe a few you haven't thought of.

Some of these dreams might include buying a home or business, saving for college education for your children, taking a dream vacation, reducing taxes, or retiring comfortably. Financial planning is the process of wisely managing your finances so that you can achieve your dreams and goals while at the same time helping you negotiate the financial barriers that inevitably arise in every stage of life.

A financial planner can help you:

- Set realistic financial and personal goals
- Assess your current financial health by examining your assets, liabilities, income, insurance, taxes, investments, and estate plan
- Develop a realistic, comprehensive plan to meet your financial goals by addressing financial weaknesses and building on strengths
- Put your plan into action and monitor its progress
- Stay on track to meet changing goals; changing personal circumstances; changing stages of your life; changing products, markets, and tax laws

TYPES OF FINANCIAL PLANNERS

Financial planners come from a variety of backgrounds—college training in accounting, banking, and finance, or career experience in fields unrelated to financial planning in general. It always makes sense to ask for the planner's résumé before you sit down.

There are several major certifications held by financial planners:

- **CERTIFIED FINANCIAL PLANNER™ (CFP) professional.** CFP practitioners have to complete one national exam administered by the Certified Financial Planner Board of Standards in Denver, Colorado. The coursework prior to the exam normally takes two years to complete. Three years of financial planning experience is required before the certification is granted. CFP practitioners abide by a strict code of ethics and have to complete a continuing education requirement each year. This certification is endorsed by the Financial Planning Association (FPA), publisher of this book.
- **Chartered Financial Consultant (ChFC).** The ChFC designation typically requires two years to complete and is granted by the American College in Bryn Mawr, Pennsylvania. After finishing the appropriate coursework, a planner will take a ten-part series of exams. Planners who hold the ChFC designation normally work in

PLANNING TIPS: 7 MYTHS ABOUT FINANCIAL PLANNING

Many people recognize the importance of financial planning today. Yet many still hold misconceptions about who can benefit from financial planning and how it can best benefit them. Here are several of those myths.

Myth #1: Financial planning is just for the wealthy. Financial planning isn't about "getting wealthy"—it's about helping people at all levels of income achieve their short- and long-term financial goals. Anyone who wants to take control of their financial life, make good financial decisions, and achieve financial independence can successfully use financial planning.

Myth #2: Financial planning is just about investing. Sound investing is certainly an important part of most financial planning. It helps people achieve many of their goals. But it is not the only part, and it is not even necessarily the main part. Financial planning takes into account all the varied financial aspects of a person's life: taxes, insurance, retirement, budgeting, estate planning, and life goals. It looks at the various, sometimes competing financial aspects of our lives, and develops strategies and objectives that make those parts work together efficiently.

Myth #3: Financial planning is just about retirement. Most people want to retire someday, and financial planning can help them achieve that goal. But retirement is usually only one of many goals people have in their lives that require money. Families often have children to put through college, a home or new car to buy, a business to buy and run, dream vacations, or the challenges of meeting monthly bills or managing debts. Meanwhile, emergencies and financial crises can divert us from working toward those desired ends. Careful, conscientious financial planning can make many or all of these goals happen.

Myth #4: Financial planning isn't necessary until you're older. The older you get without having done any financial planning, the fewer options you have. For example, for every ten years you delay saving for retirement, you have to save three times as much *a month* in order to end up with the same size retirement nest egg. Parents wishing to put their children through college shouldn't wait until their children are in high school to start saving. Many estate planning tools become useless or less effective if people wait too long or death strikes early.

Continued on page 26

25

PLANNING TIPS | Continued from page 25

Myth #5: Financial planning requires a big plan. Ideally, any important financial decision you make should be done in the context of your overall financial needs and situation. But a qualified, competent financial planner, such as a CERTIFIED FINANCIAL PLANNER™ professional, can help you focus on a specific issue, such as how to roll over an individual retirement account or determine if you have an adequate estate plan.

Myth #6: Financial planning is a one-time effort. Financial planning is a lifetime process. Once a plan is in place, it needs to be periodically reviewed and updated. Financial situations and needs change over the years as children are born, people die, jobs are gained or lost, people are married or divorced, inheritances are received. Investments may need to be adjusted in light of changing markets, economies, and personal needs. And changing tax laws may require adjustments.

Myth #7: I can get along without financial planning. Some people can, but they tend to have a lot of skill and time available to execute their decisions. When people attempt to go it alone, they rarely can see all the possibilities a trained professional can. Ultimately, financial planning is all about taking charge of your financial life. A 2006 survey by the Consumer Federation of America and NationsBank found that households with incomes of less than $100,000—the overwhelming majority of Americans—reported saving and investing double the amount when they had a financial plan than when they didn't. That extra savings and investing is, in many cases, the difference between reaching and not reaching personal goals. ☒

the insurance industry. Many also hold the Chartered Life Underwriter (CLU) designation. Any ChFC who falls into any one of the following categories has to earn 30 hours of continuing education credit every two years:

1. Licensed insurance agent/broker/consultant
2. Licensed security representative/registered investment adviser
3. Financial consultant, attorney, accountant, employee benefits specialist, and any other individual who provides insurance, employee benefits, financial planning, or estate planning advice and counsel to the public

- **Personal Financial Specialist (PFS).** These planners are certified public accountants (CPAs) who have completed an extensive financial planning exam administered by the American Institute of Certified Public Accountants (AICPA). Professionals who hold the PFS are required to have at least three years of financial planning experience before they're allowed to hold the designation. As far as continuing education, they must obtain a combined total of 60 PFS points in personal financial planning business experience and qualified "life-long learning" activities every three years. The PFS point system is described in the PFS Credential Handbook.

- **Registered Financial Consultant (RFC).** To become a RFC, you must have a federal securities license and a state insurance license. There are no exams. The work experience requirement demands at least four years in a related field or an industry designation (CFP®, PFS, etc.). RFCs have higher continuing education requirements each year than other designations.

Planners, like any professionals, tend to specialize, and they may receive continuing education in more than a dozen areas of expertise. CERTIFIED FINANCIAL PLANNER™ professionals alone earn continuing education credits in asset management, employee benefits, commercial real estate, insurance, investment management, estate management, retirement planning, 401(k) administration, and health topics, among others.

HOW PLANNERS ARE REGULATED

Many financial professionals are licensed on the state and federal levels in specific areas such as insurance or securities. However, they are not specifically regulated for their financial planning activities—with the exception of CFP professionals, who are certified by CFP Board.

CFP professionals are held accountable to the CFP Board's Code of Ethics and must also meet its standards requirements. CFP Board has the power to suspend or revoke the rights to use the CFP mark from an individual who violates the Board's standards.

The Securities and Exchange Commission and/or state agencies also have requirements for "investment advisers"—a role that most financial planners fulfill. If a planner is a registered investment adviser, or a representative of an advisory firm, FPA advises consumers to carefully review the Form ADV, a form that planners who register as investment advisers must file with the U.S. Securities and Exchange Commission. The form discloses a planner's experience, education, credentials, licenses, disciplinary history, manner of compensation, and potential conflicts of interest.

WHAT DO PLANNERS CHARGE?

This is one of the top questions individuals ask about planners, and it's not an easy one to answer. Planners set their rates based on their experience, clientele, services offered, and what their local market will bear. But generally, there are five categories of compensation:

- **Fee only.** The planner is compensated entirely from fees for purposes of consultation, plan development, or investment management. These fees may be charged on an hourly or project basis depending on your needs, or on a percentage of assets under management.
- **Commission only.** There is no charge for the planner's advice or preparation of a financial plan. Compensation is received solely from the sale of financial products you agree to purchase in order to implement financial planning recommendations.
- **Combination fee/commission.** A fee is charged for consultation, advice, and financial plan preparation on an hourly, project, or percentage basis. In addition, the planner may receive commissions from the sale of recommended products used to implement your plan.
- **Fee offset.** Commissions from the sale of financial products are offset against fees charged for the planning process.
- **Salary.** Some planners work on a salary and bonus basis for financial services firms.

Can you negotiate what you'll pay? Possibly, if you explain your circumstances in an orderly way and you treat the planner with respect for his or her skills. Demanding lower fees from any professional is delicate business, but like all things in the planning process, it involves give-and-take in a frank discussion that will determine your relationship going forward.

Again, if you've done your research (see Chapter 3) and you realize that the planner you're considering has excellent references and a solid track record, be willing to accept that they're worth the money they're charging.

WHAT RESULTS SHOULD PLANNERS PROVIDE?

Like fees, this is an important question that's also one of the toughest to answer. But actually, the answer lies with you, the client. A financial planner's role is to help you discover the full reach of those goals and then help you make the plan to reach them. No adviser, broker, financial planner, or investment manager can guarantee particular results—if that were true, we'd all be rich.

In Chapter 3, we'll discuss how to hire a financial planner.

3 | *How Do I Hire a Financial Planner?*

You're aiming for a good relationship with a trusted adviser, so selecting a planner doesn't need to be a speedy assignment. Yet many people consult planners when there's an emergency issue or a major life-changing event ahead.

See if any of these situations fit you:

- Graduating college and trying to figure out how to pay off your debt while saving for your first home
- Getting married
- Getting divorced
- Handling an inheritance or some other unexpected windfall
- Planning for the birth or adoption of a child
- Facing a financial crisis such as a serious illness, lay-off, or natural disaster
- Caring for aging parents or a disabled child
- Making sure your money will last during retirement or rolling over a retirement plan
- Coping financially with the death of a spouse or close family member
- Funding education for yourself or your children
- Buying, selling, or transferring ownership of a family business

These are only the major reasons people consider meeting with a financial planner. But, typically, the earlier you do it the better the results for your financial lifetime.

HOW TO CHOOSE THE RIGHT FINANCIAL PLANNER

Here are some tips from the Financial Planning Association (FPA) for finding the right planner to fit your needs:

Trust is key. Choosing a financial planner is as important as choosing a doctor or lawyer. Money is one of the most intimate aspects of our lives, and, consequently, working with a financial planner is a deeply personal relationship. As you go through the process of finding and selecting a planner, keep in mind that trust and comfort will be key factors.

What do you want a planner to do for you? Before you start your search, think about why you want a financial planner. Do you want advice about investments, budgeting or cash flow management, retirement planning, an inheritance, a small business, saving for college, a financial crisis such as a divorce or aging parents, or are you looking for a general financial overhaul? Some planners will be especially strong in one or more of these areas.

Be clear that you are hiring a true planner. Many financial professionals call themselves planners, but in reality, their knowledge and focus are limited to a single area, such as selling stocks or annuities, or doing taxes. A financial planner should be educated and trained to address a wide variety of financial issues. Even if your concern is a specific issue, planning should be done in the context of your overall financial situation. Check his or her references before you agree to sit down together.

Start gathering names. Collect names and information about planners from friends and family, work colleagues, and recommendations from other financial professionals, such as your attorney or accountant. The Financial Planning Association also can provide names of planners in your area or by specialty through PlannerSearch, a referral service. You can reach PlannerSearch via the Internet at www.fpanet.org, or by calling 800.322.4237.

Start screening. From your initial list of names, call for preliminary information. You may find out right away, for example, that a particular planner requires a minimum net worth that you don't meet or a minimum fee that you don't want to pay. Many planners will have a brochure outlining their services and background, but you'll want to dig deeper than that. Ask for their ADV Form, Parts I and II. The Securities and Exchange Commission requires Form ADV for anyone who is a registered investment adviser (RIA), and anyone calling themselves a financial planner should be an RIA. Part I shows any disciplinary history. Check with the local Better Business Bureau and the Certified Financial Planner Board of Standards (888.237.6275, or www.cfp.net) for disciplinary problems.

Determine how they charge. Financial planners charge for their services in a variety of ways: by retainer, by the hour, by a percentage of your assets "under management," by commissions of the products they sell, or a combination. Be clear about how they charge and what services they charge for.

Narrow down possibilities. The initial call and literature should help you identify the best candidates. What is their client base—do they work primarily with high-income or middle-income clients? Do they have a specialty that matches your needs? Do they serve a lot of business owners, retirees, or executives? Are they particularly familiar with stock options?

Check qualifications. What financial planning and other financial designations do they hold? What is their educational background and work experience? Are they licensed to sell certain products, such as securities or life insurance? What professional affiliations do they have, such as membership in the Financial Planning Association, which would imply they are keeping up with the ever-changing field of financial planning? What business arrangements do they have that might present a conflict of interest?

Meet in person. Much of the above information you can gather from your referral source, the initial phone call, and the literature. But ultimately, you'll want to narrow your list of candidates to three to five planners and interview them in person. This interview should clarify questions you still have, but more importantly, go to the heart of your initial concern: do you have a sense of trust and rapport with the planner? Is the person forthright in his or her answers? Does he or she seem focused on your needs, rather than selling products?

WHAT TO ASK A FINANCIAL PLANNER BEFORE YOU MEET

It's important to ask for a written disclosure document mentioned above from the planner, but you'll also want to do more due diligence by phone and eventually in person if this planner looks like a good choice for you. Here are some important questions you'll need to ask before you hire anyone:

- What areas of planning do you specialize in?
- What types of clients do you serve? Are there any minimum net worth or income requirements?
- What is your basic approach to financial planning?
- What financial planning and other financial certifications do you hold, particularly in your specialty?
- What's your educational background and work experience?
- Are you licensed to sell certain financial products, such as life insurance or securities?
- If you're so licensed, are you selling only a particular company's products, and are you likely to advise me beyond those products if there's a better opportunity elsewhere?
- What other services do you provide?
- Do you have a relationship with other professionals (lawyers, accountants, investment advisers)?
- What professional associations do you belong to?
- How do you prepare a plan?
- How should we communicate about approving that plan and then checking on its performance going forward?
- How are you going to charge me for your services?
- Would you be taking over my investment portfolio in any way, and how will we execute the purchase or sale of any of those items in the portfolio?

TIP: HOW TO CHECK THE DISCIPLINARY RECORD OF A PLANNER

Depending on the full extent of your planner's services (some may sell stock or mutual funds; others may sell insurance), you might want to inventory those services and then contact the appropriate regulatory agencies to see if their name has come up in any disciplinary proceedings:

Certified Financial Planner Board of Standards, Inc.: 888.237.6275 **(www.CFP.net/search)**
North American Securities Administrators Association: 202.737.0900 **(www.nasaa.org)**
National Association of Insurance Commissioners: 816.842.3600 **(www.naic.org)**
National Association of Securities Dealers Regulation: 800.289.9999 **(www.nasdr.com)**
Securities and Exchange Commission: 202.942.7040 **(www.sec.gov)**

Overall, do your homework. Check the ADV form given you when you first contact your planner for disciplinary histories. Check your local courthouse to see if any lawsuits have been filed against them; and if they sell insurance or any other investment product, check with your state's relevant agencies to see if there is any disciplinary history there. ☒

- Are there any potential business relationships you already have that might present a conflict with mine?
- If we agree to work together and there is ever a dispute we need to settle, how do we handle that? Does your particular licensing stipulate any specific procedures for dispute resolution?

ANOTHER POINT ABOUT LICENSING

Investment advisers are in the business of giving advice about securities to clients. Typically, they give advice to a specific person on investing in stocks, bonds, or mutual funds and they manage portfolios of securities for that person.

A financial planner can be an investment adviser if they are so licensed, but most have a broader purpose. Their goal is to advise a client on every aspect of their financial life—saving, investments, insurance, taxes, retirement, and estate planning and creating a strategy to meet those goals.

It is very important that you understand what the person calling himself or herself a financial planner is licensed to do and sell to you. It is also very important to know whether the planner will make a recommendation outside what he or she has to sell if it makes sense for your plan.

This is a critical point to address before you agree to work together.

WHAT THE PLANNER NEEDS TO KNOW ABOUT YOU

During an initial phone call, you probably won't exchange a lot of detailed personal or financial information, nor should you. But if you do agree to meet, a planner will probably ask you to answer some basic questions that he or she will probably want to file away to record the meeting and as a basis in case you agree to create a relationship:

- Why are you coming to see me?
- What are the general financial details surrounding the issue or problem you want to work on? Do be prepared to answer some detailed financial questions— bring a copy of a pay statement, current investment statements, or financial tracking records from your computer.
- Are you working with any other advisers (lawyers, accountants, tax advisers, brokers) on matters that could intersect with your financial planning issues?

The planner may also ask you to fill out a detailed questionnaire that not only outlines your current assets and liabilities, but tries to determine your risk tolerance.

In Chapter 4, we'll talk about how a long-term relationship with a planner should operate.

PLANNING TIPS: 8 MYTHS ABOUT "REAL" FINANCIAL PLANNERS

While American consumers generally hold financial planning and financial planners in high esteem, they also hold many myths about financial planners that can make them hesitant to employ the services of a qualified financial planner. Here are eight truths behind the myths about "real" financial planners

Myth #1: Financial planners are the same as stockbrokers or other financial salespeople. The primary function of a stockbroker, insurance agent, or other financial salesperson is sell financial products. The main purpose of a financial planner is to help clients crystallize their goals and effectively manage their personal finances in order to achieve their goals and financial independence. This may or may not involve the purchase of securities, insurance, or other financial products. While many financial planners are licensed to sell certain financial products, true financial planners put the interests of the client first, not the sale of products.

Myth #2: Financial planners are primarily investment advisers. Financial planners counsel clients in many aspects of their financial lives: determining goals, cash flow, taxes, retirement, college, business planning, estate planning, and insurance, among others. Investing can certainly be an important part of these areas, but it is not the only part and it usually is not the primary focus of a planner. Think of the financial planner as a football coach designing a financial game plan and seeing that it is executed in the best interests of the client, often with the help of outside specialists such as attorneys, stockbrokers, insurance agents, and CPAs.

Myth #3: Financial planners only do "big plans." Financial planners frequently assist consumers with a single issue, such as saving for college, developing a realistic budget, rolling over a retirement account, or helping them through the financial aftermath of the death of a spouse. Yet good planners provide this focused advice in the context of a person's overall financial goals, needs, and situation, so that recommended actions don't undermine other aspects of their financial life.

Myth #4: Financial planners serve only the affluent. While some financial planners work exclusively with affluent clients, many work with modest-income clients.

Myth #5: Financial planners aren't worth the "expense." Naturally, financial planners

Continued on page 38

PLANNING TIPS | Continued from page 37

charge for their services just as attorneys, doctors, or any other professionals do. But you might think of it as an investment rather than an expense. That's because any good financial planner should save and earn you far more money than what you pay the planner in fees or commissions. This "investment" might be accomplished by improving cash flow through better budgeting, reducing your tax liabilities, boosting investment returns, or even preventing a costly financial catastrophe through the application of insurance or other defensive measures. This is to say nothing of the intangible benefits such as peace of mind, time saved, and a better focus on one's financial life.

Myth #6: Legitimate financial planners charge only fees. Financial planners charge in a variety of ways, including hourly fees, fees based on clients' invested assets, annual retainers, and commissions from the sale of financial products. Some planners offer a choice of compensation, depending on the services. Each type of arrangement has its advantages and disadvantages. The key is that the planner fully discloses how he or she charges, you understand the pros and cons of each form of compensation, and the arrangement best fits your needs.

Myth #7: Most people don't need financial planners. During the heyday of the bull market of the 1990s, the prevailing attitude among consumers was to "do it yourself." As many have painfully learned in recent years, the expert advice and objectivity of a planner is to keep them financially diversified, flexible, and focused on their long-term goals during a soft economy, growing unemployment, and bad markets. A financial planner is someone to "lean on" in this complicated financial world and during troubled personal financial times.

Myth #8: All financial planners are CERTIFIED FINANCIAL PLANNER™ professionals. Many people who call themselves financial planners are not CFP® professionals. Planners who earn the CFP® certificate must meet certain work and education criteria, pass a rigorous exam, and meet continuing education and ethical requirements in order to attain and maintain their certificate. ☒

4 | *Signing On for the Long Haul*

You've decided on your financial planner and are looking forward to a long and fruitful relationship. But exactly how is that relationship supposed to go?

To a great extent, the rules of the game are hopefully set at the moment you agree to work together. Obviously, the issue of compensation and how you'll work together are closely linked. Fees, commissions and other compensation structures differ from planner to planner, so you should check out in detail what kind of working relationship you'll be getting for your money. (Go back to Chapter 2 to review the basics of fee structures that planners use.)

HOW OFTEN SHOULD YOU MEET WITH YOUR FINANCIAL PLANNER?

Most planners support long-term investments and financial strategy that doesn't involve a lot of sudden moves. Therefore, it makes sense that you shouldn't have to meet with your planner any more than what makes sense for you. Some people might require a sit-down meeting every year or two years; others may require more frequent meetings based on their needs. What happens if you suffer a major life change? You should follow the communication procedure you set at the time you sign on with the planner.

The bottom line: no two planners handle communication the same way. Ultimately, it is up to you and your planner to decide how you will deal with each other based on a variety of scenarios, and those should be discussed before you sign on.

Again, be extremely clear with the planner what you want your communication structure to be and what that will cost. Remember, you are paying for time, expertise, and what will be necessary for you to understand what you're doing.

THE FIRST MEETING—WHAT SHOULD YOU BRING?

The simple answer is ask the planner first. If you are someone who keeps financial records in a shoebox, it might be okay to bring the shoebox to your first meeting. If you are a computer person who has your financial information online, the planner might welcome a compatible disk with that information and paper documents for your major accounts and investments, representing what you own and owe.

What qualifies as a financial record? Let's go down the list:

- Bank statements
- Pay stubs
- Check registers
- Credit card balances
- Mortgage or loan payment books
- List of assets
- List of liabilities
- Completed expense worksheet
- Any wills, trusts, health-care powers of attorney, health-care proxy, or other powers of attorney
- Business agreements
- Titles for homes, cars, real estate, etc.
- Retirement account statements
- Social Security statements
- Pension benefit statement and booklet

- Investment statements
- Listing of available investment options in investment and retirement accounts
- Stock options
- Homeowner and automobile declaration pages
- Life, disability, or long-term care insurance policies
- Business liability, director, and officer insurance policies
- Tax return
- Tax estimate for next return (for example, deductions, credits, etc.)
- List of employee benefits
- Credit report

As far as what you'll talk about, the planner is not only trying to figure out what shape you're in, they're trying to find out where you want to be by the time you retire. They're going to do this even if you have no clue where you want to be—that's part of their job. They may ask a lot of nonfinancial questions to help you get there, and they should get you thinking about all the factors that enter into your money picture—your career, your family, even the hobbies and activities you like to do.

At its best, financial planning is a process that helps you find clues to why you do both good and bad things with your money. Sometimes that means analyzing your life in a way where you change behaviors you never expected to change.

INTEGRATING YOUR FINANCIAL TEAM

Depending on your career and financial circumstance—such as whether you're a business owner or an individual working for a traditional employer—you may have other experts in your life who have a perspective on your finances. Lawyers, accountants, and business consultants are among them.

Your financial planner should ask whether these experts exist in your life, what they do, and what you pay them to do what they do. In a perfect world, your planner, your estate attorney, and your accountant should know the others exist as well as contact information in case there's a burning question or emergency.

Again, your needs will determine the level of connection these experts should have. For example, if a client is dealing with a serious illness, there might be a physician or a geriatric care manager drawn into the mix. A planner should be able to advise and coordinate interaction between these key players.

HOW DO YOU SETTLE DISPUTES WITH A PLANNER?

Again, you hope a new relationship won't turn into trouble, but the time to discuss what may happen in a dispute should come at the beginning of a relationship, not when things go wrong.

Many financial fields that have direct contact with individuals have moved toward arbitration and mediation to settle disputes. You need to ask a planner whether they have been through this process before, and for that matter, whether they have ever had to settle disputes in court. You may find out some information you hadn't counted on, and that's important to know at the beginning. The American Arbitration Association (www.adr.org) has more information.

SIGNS THAT YOUR RELATIONSHIP WITH YOUR PLANNER MIGHT BE GOING SOUR

Clients and most financial professionals tend to disagree most often on transaction issues, so if you have a relationship with a planner who handles investment transactions for you, it's very important to discuss the terms and situations under which those decisions will be made.

Overall, here are trouble signs you might look for:

1. You find your account records show unusually high trading activity that your planner cannot explain to your satisfaction.
2. No matter what the issue, you have trouble getting in touch with your planner.
3. You start finding fees on service statements and other documents that you don't understand and can't get adequate explanation for.

4. Your statements are chronically late.
5. You start hearing about all sorts of new investing opportunities in a tough market—and they're not bargains.
6. You feel your entire planning philosophy has shifted without any discussion or rational explanation.
7. You're not getting positive financial results from your relationship…period.

BREAKING UP—THE AMICABLE WAY

It might not be a bad idea to find a new financial planner before you make this transition so they can look over your plan and make appropriate suggestions. You'll also need to check the portability requirements on the investments you might have bought through the planner and any other possible restrictions on moving accounts.

The best time to discuss the process for ending a client/planner relationship is before both sides agree to work together. Both the planner and the prospective client should approach "what if" in a friendly way. Consider this a version of a prenuptual agreement (which we'll discuss in later chapters). Talking about what could be a deal-breaker on both sides of the relationship can be eye-opening and can accomplish one of two things—a more efficient, honest way of working together, or an indication that you shouldn't be working together at all.

Some questions you should discuss:

• If you will be recommending investments and I'm not satisfied with their performance, what then?
• How often do you think we should talk?
• If we don't meet in person, what kind of communication is best—phone, e-mail, regular mail?
• How often should we meet?
• What kind of written communication should we have?
• If we decide not to work together anymore, how will I regain control of my investments and will there be any fees or delays in doing so?

It's important to realize that there is not one standard right answer to any of these questions due to the issues you will bring to your planner and the ways he or she will approach them. The bottom line is to address every aspect of the relationship, including its end.

In Part 2, we'll look at one of the biggest challenges in financial planning—dealing with problem debt.

Part II

Dealing With Problem Debt

What a Planner Can Do for Someone in Debt Trouble

Clark Randall, CFP®

"Understand that the credit card preys on human behavior. Those card companies understand us very, very well," explains Clark Randall, a Dallas-based CERTIFIED FINANCIAL PLANNER™ professional. "They reinforce bad behavior. Planners are there to help reinforce good behavior."

Randall believes that chronically indebted individuals face economic pressures, but they tend to stay where they are because they're no longer able to envision a life without debt.

"Debt in itself isn't bad when it's managed. But an overwhelmingly large area of mistakes in debt happen when people place short-term gratification ahead of long-term consequences."

Randall believes that behavior modification may require temporary solutions that break the rules a bit. "We've always been taught that you pay off the highest-rate balances first, and that's solid advice in the vast majority of cases. But from time to time, I have had clients take a lower-rate credit card balance and pay it off first just so they have a sense of accomplishment that they've extinguished all the debt on a particular account. Then they can go back to paying off the highest-rate balances. People need to know they can do this."

Randall also believes that lenders' own technology can be used more effectively to keep their customers out of debt trouble. "Who says you have to use electronic bill payment only once a month? I advise my clients to set up automatic bill payment and pay down a little each week. They save a stamp, the amount is smaller than the big hit at the end of the month, and they lower their balance faster—progressively, the interest charges fall too."

5 | *Good Debt vs. Bad Debt*

You know, there was once a time when the picture was a little clearer on this point.

About ten years ago, experts would tell you that all home-related debt was "good" debt, meaning that the near-guaranteed appreciation of property values and the tax deductibility of interest on loans to buy those properties invariably made borrowing a good deal for the consumer.

All other debt? Bad or worse.

But today, you have an interesting situation— people increasingly using the equity in their homes and other real estate properties as personal piggy banks for everything from new kitchens to fancy vacations. There are now gradations of "good" debt within the real estate arena thanks to the home equity issue.

So as you apply the lessons here to your own situation, you really have to think about the old perceptions of debt and how they've changed in today's marketplace.

DEBT LEVELS OVER THE PAST 20 YEARS

Figure 5.1 is simple, elegant and tells the tale—consumer debt is now a staple of American life. What happened? Was it the temptation of credit cards? The move toward more personal management of our assets that we thought gave us permission to take on more risk? Was it the record-breaking appreciation in real estate properties over the past decade that convinced us it was okay to harvest our home equity to pay for the stuff we need—including the bills on other outstanding debt?

It was all this and more. We can talk all day about what created the borrowing addiction that exists in this country, but before individuals can successfully address their debt issues, it makes sense to look at facts about debt and how they can reverse their borrowing practices.

Here are some interesting—and perhaps frightening—facts about personal debt in this country.

- As tougher bankruptcy legislation went into effect late in the year, one in every 60 U.S. households filed for bankruptcy protection in 2005, bringing total filings for the year to more than two million, a new record, according to the American Bankruptcy Institute.
- According to 2006 statistics from the Federal Reserve, 46.3 percent of all families now carry a credit card balance.
- Household mortgage debt recorded by the Fed increased by 14.1 percent in 2005; it rose 13.4 percent in 2004, 14.3 percent in 2003 and 11.9 percent in 2002.

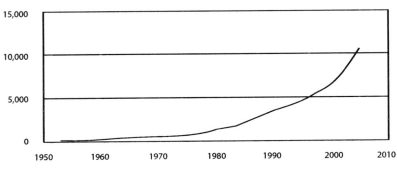

Figure 5.1: Household Sector: Liabilities: Household Credit Market Debt Outstanding (billions of dollars)

2005 Federal Reserve Bank of St. Louis
research.stlouisfed.org

Source: Board of Governors of the Federal Reserve System.

- The average American household has an average credit card balance of $8,900.
- According to the Bureau of Economic Analysis, the savings of U.S. households in 2005 totaled a negative $34 billion, or -0.4 percent of total disposable personal income for the year. Although the personal savings rate has trended consistently lower over the last 20 years, 2005 marks the first year since the Great Depression for which the ratio fell below zero.

WHEN "GOOD" MORTGAGE DEBT GOES BAD

In 2006, the real estate market was slowing, interest rates were rising and many consumers were stuck with dangerous adjustable-rate debt. In fact, one statistic—by LoanPerformance, a San Francisco-based mortgage loan research firm—showed that one out of every four new mortgages at the time was an interest-only loan—a loan that delays principal payments for three years or more to guarantee a borrower a lower monthly payment.

Skyrocketing real estate values drove supply and demand for loans that allow lower monthly payments in exchange for slower or, in some cases, negative buildup of equity. It wasn't a complete surprise. In July 2005, Federal Reserve Chairman Alan Greenspan told the House Financial Services Committee, "There's potential for individual disaster here."

Yet no matter what the rate environment or economic situation, individuals have to keep in mind that they have choices, and some of the seemingly risky ones might be the right choices given their financial situation and how they use the loan product. In any event, it's best to get some advice before you respond to these offers. Your tax adviser or financial planner not only can help you understand these options, but he or she can assess your overall financial picture to see what's right for you in the first place.

Whether they come from your current lender or a late-night infomercial, here's an overview of several nontraditional loan options on the market and their potential risks and rewards.

Interest-only loans. This immensely popular loan option allows a borrower to pay only the interest on the mortgage in monthly payments for a fixed term. After the end of that term, usually five to seven years, the borrower can refinance, pay the balance in a lump sum, or start paying off the principal, in which case the payments can rise. They do work for some people—for instance, those who expect their income to jump considerably in the next few years. Some types of interest-only mortgages have been around for decades and were used by wealthy borrowers who were sophisticated and disciplined enough to find profitable uses for money saved on monthly payments. But today's loan products are increasingly marketed to ordinary homebuyers and, in many cases, to "sub-prime" borrowers who could not have qualified for standard loans in the past. That's where the risk comes in.

Zero-down mortgages. An increasingly common option for borrowers with less-than-perfect credit, these loans allow borrowers to buy with no money down. It gets a borrower into a home, but any chances of acquiring equity in a home will have to come from rising market values, and that's not something every borrower can count on. It might be better to ask for a low-down payment alternative—such as FHA financing—that allows a borrower to have some small amount of equity at the start.

Piggyback loans. Some borrowers who can't make a 20 percent down payment may consider an end-run around private mortgage insurance by taking out a first and second mortgage concurrently. Typically, a piggy-back loan works as follows: the most common type is an 80/10/10 where a first mortgage is taken out for 80 percent of the home's value, a down payment of 10 percent is made and another 10 percent is financed in a second trust at possibly a higher interest rate. Some lenders may allow a piggyback loan for less than a 10 percent down payment.

100-plus loans. Also known as loan-to-value (LTV) mortgages, lenders promote these mortgage loans of 100 percent or more of appraised market value as a way to draw in customers who can't make a down payment. An overly high appraisal value in a sliding market, a loss of home value, or even worse, a loss of a job can lead very quickly to rising debt and the possible loss of the home.

Negative amortization loans. Negative amortization means that a loan balance is increasing instead of decreasing. With a negative amortization loan, if a payment isn't enough to cover the interest and principal payment, the shortage is added to the loan balance, which means you never really start paying off the loan. Again, this may work for people in short-term housing situations in markets with rising rates, but those conditions are never guaranteed.

SMART WAYS TO HANDLE CREDIT CARD DEBT

It's a fact—you have credit card debt. So often, we tell ourselves it's okay to use a credit card because we'll be earning miles or some other incentive. Stop doing that now.

Here are some good ways to get rid of it.

Go debit. Your bank probably issues debit cards that carry a Visa or MasterCard label, and we say get one, but only because some necessary merchants don't allow you to use a plain-vanilla ATM card for transactions. But *do not* start using a branded debit card without making sure you ask your bank to tie your usage strictly to your checking account, and use that card only for debit transactions that require a PIN (your secret access code). And yes, make sure you write *every* transaction in your checkbook, if you don't already do so with your ATM card.

As for your real credit cards? Keep one nearby only for emergencies and cut up or lock up the rest.

Make a weekly electronic bill payment on your credit card balance. You've probably noticed that your credit card company allows you to pay by phone or through the Internet. It's intended to be an option for people who can't pay until moments before their bill is due. But why not make that option work in your favor? For instance, sign up for the service, and then every Friday or Monday, set aside a specific amount in your checking account that will go toward your monthly balance—pay it ahead of time and you won't incur interest charges or waste so much as a minute or a stamp.

High balances first. This is not 100 percent true for everyone, but generally, you want to eliminate high-rate debt first and then pay down lower-rate balances as you go. As long as your payments are steady, this is

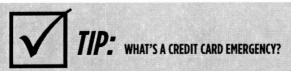

TIP: WHAT'S A CREDIT CARD EMERGENCY?

A credit card emergency is not an emergency latte fix. Redefine your definition of a financial emergency. It might also help to start thinking again like a kid who might get in trouble for using your parent's credit card for anything but an emergency—if you ever had to do that. Here's your new checklist of when it's okay to use a credit card:

1. Car breakdowns, not scheduled repairs
2. Hotel and rental car payments on trips
3. Out-of-town emergency medical bills (See Chapter 46, "Preventing the Vacation from Hell")
4. The occasional mistake when you don't bring enough cash to pay for a special dinner out (Note to self: Stop eating out so much)

The exception to all the above? If you can fully pay your credit card balance every month. The key is learning to live within your means, not using your credit cards as a constant bridge loan. ☒

generally the better approach. Also, talk with an adviser first, but you may want to consider rolling higher-interest debt into a lower-rate card (make sure the higher balance won't raise your rate on that lower-rate card) so you pay less in interest and more in principal.

Watch that HELOC. Many people are tempted to pay off their consumer debt through home equity lines of credit (known as HELOCs). True, in many cases, you'll be able to write off the interest on your taxes. But if you have a financial calamity, home debt is secured debt, which means a lender could take your house if you start missing payments. Credit card debt doesn't leave you nearly as vulnerable. Talk to a financial adviser first about the best way to go on this.

Start tracking every penny. You won't get out of debt until you fix the leaks in your wallet. We'll talk about budgeting several times in this book, but dealing with debt is a good place to start the discussion. If you are not presently tracking where your spending is going, then start either by hand or with the help of a computer program like Quicken or Microsoft Money that forces you to plug every dime into a category. The results will surprise you, and it'll make your tax filings easier too. (You might even save money with deductions you didn't know about.)

CHECKING YOUR CREDIT REPORT AND LEARNING YOUR CREDIT SCORE

There are three companies that create credit reports—Equifax (www.equifax.com), TransUnion (www.transunion.com), and Experian (www.experian.com). These reports are purchased by lenders, employers, landlords, and other service providers that use this information to help them decide whether to approve your application for a loan, credit card, job, or housing, or to offer you a product or service at a particular rate.

Credit reports have produced a particular form of shorthand—the credit score, which we'll get to below. But you need to monitor your credit report for accuracy since it basically determines so many critical things in your life. It includes when those accounts were opened, and closed or inactive accounts stay in your file for seven to ten years. It also reports which organizations have requested to view your credit reports.

Credit reports also may record public records such as liens, bankruptcies, and overdue child support, felonies, student loans, overdue taxes, overdue parking tickets, overdue library books (and the list keeps growing)—and that's information that also stays on a credit report for seven years.

A credit report actually doesn't include information about checking or savings accounts, bankruptcies that are more than ten years old, charged-off or debts placed for collection that are more than seven years old. It also doesn't identify you by gender, ethnicity, religion, political affiliation, medical history, or criminal records.

Your credit score is a three-digit number that represents your creditworthiness to the individuals and organizations mentioned above.

Credit scores determine far more about our lives than we realize. Not only do these computerized three-digit measurements of creditworthiness influence how much we'll pay for a credit card or a house or car loan, plenty of nonlenders—such as future employers—like to check that information as well. (The average credit score nationwide is 677, while generally, a credit score above 720 is considered attractive to most lenders.)

You need to check your credit report every year at staggered dates that are consistent year-to-year. Doing it more often or at different times actually serves to lower your credit score. You can do it for free at a Web site sponsored by all three credit bureaus: www.annualcreditreport.com. When you receive the report, look it over carefully to check every detail from addresses and employment information to the information on each account listed. Make sure everything is correct, and if it isn't, follow each credit bureau's exact instructions for how to put your appeal in writing.

In the next chapter, we'll discuss how young people can get control of credit temptations.

6 | *Getting Control of Debt in Your Teens and 20s*

The move to put credit in the hands of teenagers began in earnest about 25 years ago when solicitations to college freshmen became the norm. Today, credit issuers are marketing low-limit cards ($300 to $1,000) to parents for kids as young as 15.

HOW EASY CREDIT CAN BECOME PROBLEM CREDIT

According to Consolidated Credit Counseling Services, 78 percent of college students had at least one credit card. Nearly 40 percent of freshman students sign up for credit cards and almost 20 percent get them in high school.

Of the 78 percent who have credit cards:

- 32 percent have four or more cards
- Average number of cards = three
- Average credit card debt = $2,748
- 13 percent have credit debt between $3,000–$7,000
- 9 percent have credit card debt greater than $7,000

And maybe the most sobering fact of all—8.7 percent of bankruptcies are from people under 25 years of age.

SNAPSHOT

In 2005, a *Time* magazine survey showed that more than half of American students owed money when they finished college. Of that number, two-thirds said they owed over $10,000, a quarter said they owed over $30,000, and 5 percent owed over $100,000.

The magazine pointed to "the new demographic of Twisters—young adults who live off their parents, bounce from job to job and hop from mate to mate. The years from 18 until 25 and even beyond have become a distinct and separate life stage."

Over a third reported that they were just getting started on finding the job or career they want.

According to Nellie Mae, a student lender, undergraduate students' use of credit is at an all-time high. The agency's most recent analysis of student credit card debt showed that for students who applied for credit-based loans with Nellie Mae in the calendar year 2001, 83 percent of undergraduate students attending four-year institutions (aged 18–24) had at least one credit card. This was is up from 67 percent of undergraduates holding a card in 1998, and 78 percent in 2000. Furthermore, 47 percent of students with credit cards had four or more cards, up from 27 percent in 1998 and 32 percent in 2000.

Credit cards are intended to be used by people with income, and most working students don't make the kind of income to support credit card use.

The best way to deal with the dangers of credit is to teach them about the basics of money early on—well before their teens.

CREDIT SCORES AND YOUR CAREER

As we noted in Chapter 5, credit scores aren't merely for people over 30. As credit begins going into the hands of younger people, borrowers are going to be ranked earlier than ever. That means a high school student needs to assume that they are building a credit history the moment they borrow their first dollar.

PLANNING TIPS: IS YOUR COLLEGE STUDENT READY FOR A CREDIT CARD?

The credit card companies know what they're doing. Roughly three in four students keep the first credit card they receive for 15 years or longer.

Credit cards can have their place in a college student's life. They can be useful for emergencies, help the student learn about the proper use of credit, and establish a credit history (if the card is in their name). To help your child make the most appropriate use of credit cards during their school years—and later—here are some tips.

Educate them about credit cards. According to CCCS, only 44 percent of students understand the word "budget," only 34 percent understand the concept of buying on credit, and a meager 8 percent understand compound interest. And like many adults, they don't grasp the often-expensive issues of grace periods, late payments, finance charges, and minimum payments. Students also need to learn about the importance of building and keeping a good credit history— it affects their ability to get future loans and even their ability to get a job.

Have a spending plan. Keeping a budget for the school year can help your student think more carefully before spending, and better understand how a credit card fits in the picture.

Keep only one card. Even if the credit limit for a card newly issued to a student is relatively small, a student with a handful of cards can run up a lot of debt in a hurry. Credit limits tend to climb depending on age and the student's credit history, so the student might be smart to ask for a low credit limit initially and keep it there.

Watch the teaser rates. Select a card based on its full rate, not a teaser rate. Some recent cards for college students offered rates at around 8 percent, but jumped to 16 to 17 percent within a few months. Also look for cards with low or no annual fees, and reasonable late payment, grace period, and billing policies.

Practice. Consider having your child start out using your credit card so you can keep tabs on the charges and discuss inappropriate charges. Only after they show responsibility should they get their own card. Another way is to start them out with a debit card, which deducts charges from their checking account, or a secured card, which allows them only to charge up to what they have deposited in the card's account.

Don't co-sign their card. When it's time for your student to get a card on their own, don't co-sign the card. As the primary borrower, they can run up charges without you being

Continued on page 60

PLANNING TIPS | Continued from page 59

able to control their use of the card, and you'll be legally responsible to pay for the debt, late fees, and so on if they get in over their heads. In short, you could harm your own credit rating.

Keep it paid off or pay more than the minimum. This is good advice for any credit card user, but especially for low-income students who can ill afford to get behind. If they keep their purchases small or only for emergencies, they'll probably be okay. Also be sure they understand the high cost of paying only the minimum payment, which runs up interest charges over time.

Make them read all correspondence. Those occasional envelopes containing the sheets of paper with really small type contain news about fees, shorter grace periods, and other moves that cost cardholders money. Students need to understand when their costs are going up like anyone else.

Average college debt—and how to begin paying it off

On average, students owe more than $20,000 at graduation, and those numbers are so staggering that it may seem they'll never be paid off. Yet there should be a game plan for paying it off.

- **Start with highest-rate debt first.** That typically means credit cards. Students shouldn't ignore their student loans, but they should pay the minimum on low-rate debt first and concentrate on getting the expensive loans out of the way first.
- **Pay a little extra on other loans if you can.** Some car loans charge a prepayment penalty (do what you can to avoid prepayment penalties). If you're paying for depreciating assets, just get the loans extinguished as quickly as possible.
- **Start an emergency fund.** Last hired, first fired. Graduates should try to sock away at least three months of expenses in a savings or money market account in case they lose their jobs.
- **Start saving for retirement.** If college graduates have access to matching 401(k)s, then it makes sense to start putting away 10 percent of their incomes for retirement. It's a good habit to get into.
- **Attack the student loans.** See if you can pay off a little more than the minimum each month. Lenders are fairly understanding when you ask for lower-rate or consolidation solutions. ☒

Always assume that someone—a future employer, your first home lender, your first landlord—is going to be watching the way you spend money.

Spend like you're being watched. Refer to Chapter 5 for ideas about how to clean up your credit and save money.

In Chapter 7, we'll be discussing how people over age 50 are still wrestling the debt monster.

7 | *Debt over Age 50*

There was once a time when nearing the age of 50 meant that your house was just about paid off, your college fund actually covered the kids' education and everyone lived close enough to take care of the folks.

That's not the world of today.

The Sandwich Generation—individuals with kids still in the house and elderly parents who need care—are particularly susceptible to debt trouble. Consider what they face:

- Kids headed into college—or kids who have graduated college and want to come home to live for cheap
- Inadequate retirement savings
- Parents with health issues who either don't want to move into a nursing homes or simply don't have the means to do so

It's estimated that more than 25 percent of American families are involved in some way with elder or parent care. For many, the responsibility of caring for aging parents hits at a time when they also are raising children and anticipating sending them to college.

These people have come to be known as the Sandwich Generation because they find themselves "sandwiched" between two generations of family members that simultaneously need their attention and care.

THE SANDWICH GENERATION AND DEBT

In 2002, the American Association for Retired Persons (AARP) reported that during the 1990s, the median amount of money owed by Americans over 50 nearly doubled in virtually every income bracket. Mortgage debt rose from about one-third to over one-half of total elder debt.

The AARP study blames the debt troubles of older Americans on a variety of factors—job loss, medical expenses, rising health premium costs at employers, and postretirement, rising cost of prescription drugs, death of a spouse, divorce, financial support for children or grandchildren, and generally less retirement income due to the post-9/11 economic slowdown.

Credit cards were also a factor, particularly during the latest boom times of low inflation and double-digit market gains.

WHAT DEBT DOES TO RETIREMENT...AND WAYS TO DOWNSIZE

Consider what it's like to live in a world where your income is going to be fixed...where CDs are paying less than 5 percent and stocks are growing at less than 10 percent a year. Then consider what it's like to pay down debt at rates of 15 percent or more.

That's the reality many over-50 individuals face. Even if you're still working, it makes sense to start thinking like a retiree of the old school:

- **Develop a permanent plan to get out of debt.** Talk to a trusted financial adviser about your debt situation and develop a game plan for attacking it. Learn to live without credit cards except in emergencies and put a stop to any borrowing you're doing against home equity unless your situation is dire. Think of this as the last debt rescue you'll be able to do for yourself—no further bailouts with convenience checks, home equity borrowing, or more credit cards.

- **Plan now what your health care will cost in the years before and after Medicare.** Don't put off thinking about what your health-care premiums will cost you after you retire. Sit down with a financial adviser and an insurance professional and talk about your health insurance options as if you had to carry them out-of-pocket before your Medicare coverage kicks in. Why? Because that very well may be the case. Individuals can no longer count on the government or former employers to shoulder the burden of adequate health-care insurance. Plan a worst-case scenario, and don't forget about the cost of prescription drugs.

- **Consider joining AARP early.** Did you know you could join the American Association of Retired Persons at any age? You won't get access to full discounts and benefits, but you will receive important publications and policy updates that will make you a better-informed future retiree. AARP and other organizations won't take the place of a good financial adviser, but a little knowledge does indeed go a long way.

- **Plan for long-term care.** You may not want to or be able to count on your children to take care of you. At the same time, your future health situation may require trained medical care far beyond what your children can provide. Talk to an adviser about long-term care insurance options with a focus toward staying in your home. One of the key questions here is buying the right insurance at the right time—early LTC purchasers have been disappointed at the cost of their plans and what they will provide later. Keep in mind that these plans are evolving as the years go on, so get all the help you can in assessing them.

- **Get in shape.** You've heard the sayings. It's easier to lose weight at 30 than 40. Now that you're 50, it's not going to be a piece of cake, but getting your health in better shape is not only going to keep you out of the hospital, it will lower your cost of health insurance. Also, if you do face considerable work caring for older relatives, that's stressful activity, and it will require you to be in good health to deal with it properly.

PLANNING TIPS: REVERSE MORTGAGES

If you're at least 62 years old and the owner of a home that has significant equity, you have an opportunity to turn that equity into tax-free cash without having to move or make a monthly payment. It's called a reverse mortgage and can be a great financial tool—if you make sure it's truly right for you.

There are plenty of pros and cons involved, and it really makes sense to discuss it with an expert.

A reverse mortgage gets the name because it is essentially the reverse of a traditional mortgage. Instead of the borrower making payments to the lender, the lender makes payments to the borrower, building the owner's debt level in the property as time goes on. The borrower gets to stay in the house and doesn't have to pay back the money as long as he or she continues to live in the home. When the owner dies or moves away, then the house is sold, the loan is paid off, and any leftover money goes to the living owner or the designated heirs.

There are three basic types of reverse mortgages. The first are single-purpose reverse mortgages, which are offered by some state and local government agencies and nonprofit organizations; federally insured reverse mortgages, which are known as Home Equity Conversion Mortgages (HECMs), and are backed by the U.S. Department of Housing and Urban Development (HUD); and proprietary reverse mortgages, which are private loans that are issued by the companies that develop them.

Borrowers may receive the money from a reverse mortgage in three ways:

- A lump sum cash payment
- A monthly cash payment
- A line of credit
- Some combination of the above

Reverse mortgages have traditionally been chosen by older Americans who can't cover a major medical bill or who otherwise have a need for cash for such things as long-term care premiums, home health-care services, or domestic help. More recently, though, they've gotten popular with

Continued on page 67

PLANNING TIPS | Continued from page 66

individuals who see them as a better alternative to home equity lines for a variety of purposes from funding travel to financing second homes.

It's a good idea to consult with your financial adviser, such as a Certified Financial Planner™ professional, before you make this decision. These loans can be very complex. You may be required to meet with a counselor before you can apply, and this may delay closing on this type of financial arrangement for two to three months.

There are several potential drawbacks to reverse mortgages that need to be considered:

If the housing bubble *really* pops. For individuals who take out significantly large amounts from reverse mortgages, a significant drop in housing value could lead to real liability if you decided to sell the house or ceased to live there.

They're expensive. Reverse mortgages are generally more expensive than traditional mortgages in terms of origination fees, closing costs, and other charges. For instance, a $200,000 reverse mortgage may cost as much as $10,000 in various fees. Private lenders are generally the most expensive, and some may charge ongoing fees for the life of the mortgage. You'll need to shop several lenders to compare, and focus on total annual loan cost.

You'll still need to watch interest rates. Reverse mortgages may have fixed or variable rates, and they're typically higher than those charged on conventional mortgages. Interest is charged on the outstanding balance and added to the amount you owe each month. Again, check the total annual loan cost.

You'll need to make sure you're not endangering your Medicaid eligibility. If the proceeds you withdraw from your home exceed allowable limits under federal guidelines, you might endanger your benefits. Make sure the monthly amount of your cash advance doesn't leave you with too much cash after your bills are paid.

Your mortgage can be called. If you fail to pay your property taxes, fail to adequately maintain your home or pay your insurance premiums, the lender can declare the mortgage due or reduce the amount of monthly cash advances to pay those overdue amounts.

You may not leave much to the kids. If your house is your major asset, getting involved in a reverse mortgage may not leave much to the next generation—if it appreciates, there may be some difference that the kids can have. That's why, in addition to discussing a reverse mortgage with a financial adviser, senior citizens really need to talk about it with their families. ☒

- **Think about safety nets.** The Depression-era generation learned to live on very little. Most of us have never had to think in these terms. Learn how to maximize your assets in case you have to draw upon them. Pay down your mortgage if you have the opportunity to do so. Learn about prescription drug plans that fit your health situation.

THE NEED TO TALK TO PARENTS

It's extremely unwise to wait until catastrophe strikes to discuss money issues with older relatives—relatives you may have to help financially.

Talking about a parent's finances needs to happen long before the elder is ill or incapacitated. In fact, the best situation is when the older relative raises the conversation first.

In Hurricane Katrina's aftermath, we should all be aware that planning makes serious emergencies more manageable. Nevertheless, many families don't discuss finances until a crisis occurs. An older relative may be unable to understand questions or express their wishes in detail. If there is no plan, family members grasp at responsibilities—or shirk them—without any idea of what the older relative would prefer.

What's critical to understand is that such talks go far beyond money. They are discussions about independence and basic preferences for the way an individual wants to live or die. And demographers believe that with the rising number of single Americans—those divorced or never married—these conversations will become increasingly complicated as they fall to nieces and nephews, younger friends or designated representatives.

If you are a younger relative wondering how to manage the conversation and get control of the situation, here are some suggestions:

Decide what's important to talk about first. Maybe this conversation isn't just about where the will or health-care power of attorney is. Maybe this conversation is about you noticing that a parent or loved one is moving slower, is more forgetful, is clearly looking like their health has taken a turn for the worse—and maybe that's why you want to know where the will is. Jumping into money issues first is usually a mistake. Deal with immediate health and lifestyle issues first.

Explain why you want to talk about finances. In some families, having a successful financial discussion means several attempts and some frustration. Don't let yourself become angry or frustrated—just keep starting the conversation until it catches on. It might make sense to say something like, "You've always been so independent, Mom. I just want you to give us the right instructions so we do exactly what you want."

Write down questions. When a parent or relative is unconscious or unresponsive, the younger relative is immediately in the driver's seat. That's why it's critical to make a list of questions for the elderly relative to answer in detail. The basics: where important papers are, how household expenses are paid, who doctors and specialists are, what medicines are being taken and whether there's a will, an advanced directive, and a funeral plan (and money or insurance proceeds to pay for it). There may be dozens more questions beyond these based on your family's personal circumstances. But in creating this list, ask yourself: "What do I need to know if this person suddenly becomes sick or dies?"

Offer to get some advice. If you don't fully understand your relative's financial affairs, it might make sense for you both to talk to an attorney or a tax or financial adviser, including a CERTIFIED FINANCIAL PLANNER™ professional. A qualified adviser can offer specific suggestions on critical legal documents you should have in place and ways to make sure accounts to pay medical and household bills are accessible to the older person and the designated friend or relative who will hold power of attorney.

Plan a caregiving strategy. You should discuss the relative's preferences and trigger points for various stages of heath care. An individual always wants to stay in his or her home, but you should have an honest discussion about how much you can do at home as a caregiver and whether various services (home health aide, geriatric care manager, assisted living) should be introduced at various stages. Talking through what a parent will be able to live with at various health stages—and putting that information in writing—will save plenty of doubt and bitterness later.

Discuss liquidating the home. If an elderly relative becomes sick and irreversibly incapacitated, the equity in his or her home may come under consideration as a resource to pay uncovered medical or household maintenance. Since the home is both a major asset and an emotional focal point, it's best to get good advice and spell out specifically what the elderly relative wants done with his property and under what conditions.

Make sure everyone knows the plan. Once you settle on a strategy, make sure all family and friends understand the plan and their assignments.

THE NEED TO TALK TO KIDS

If parents need to step in with an aging relative, particularly with a financial contribution, that's a family matter worthy of discussion. In some cases, such a financial contribution may limit the amount of help a parent can give a child with their college education.

These are issues for discussion with the college-bound child in a household where college savings are not secure. Some suggestions:

1. Talking to minor children about the caregiving situation is crucial. Parents and kids need to discuss fully what it means for the family emotionally, operationally, and financially. Caring for an older relative—particularly if it's going on in a multigenerational family home—always entails big changes.
2. If this is going to endanger or reset college plans, discuss it right away. Kids aren't going to be happy that they have less money to work with, but that has to be laid on the table immediately.
3. Adult children need to avoid dipping into retirement savings to pay for their parents' care or for their child's education. The child and the ailing relative need to understand this.
4. The family needs to have an open dialogue as the situation continues so no one in the equation feels neglected.

Also, during recent tough economic times, we've seen a significant uptrend in adult children moving back to the nest—some call them "boomerang kids." Parents may be delighted to see their kids come home, but an extended free ride is dangerous to the financial futures of over-50 parents.

The decision to accept an adult child back in the home may be a happy one, but it has a better chance of staying happy if parents and children set rules and timetables together. Some suggestions:

1. **Parents should set house rules.** If you don't want your adult child bringing home friends at all hours or staying out all night without some form of contact, it should be discussed, agreed upon, and formalized in some way. Write it down if necessary.

2. **Agree on a financial or in-kind contribution.** It costs money to live anywhere. Even if the parent is helping a child dig out of debt from a lost job, divorce, or other life change, the child owes the parent something for the safety net. Payments or chores need to be agreed upon before the moving van arrives. Rent is great, but even if the payment is made in yardwork, housecleaning, or cooking, something needs to be exchanged in kind.

3. **Help the child restructure debt.** Parents help their kids with money problems all the time, but this also requires an agreement for dual participation, not a bailout. If a parent makes a contribution to debt payments, they are owed full disclosure from the adult child that the child is changing his or her money habits for the better. That may mean a monthly financial review of what the child is spending and review of all credit card and bank statements.

4. **Create an endgame.** A three-month stay shouldn't turn into a three-year stay unless there's an agreement for that to happen. Otherwise, the risk of bitterness and rancor is high.

5. **Don't take on debt to support the child.** No parent should have to take on additional debt, drain their savings, or otherwise risk his or her financial future to accommodate a child. Parents have to make a serious review of their finances and circumstances before they say yes.

In Chapter 8, we'll discuss personal bankruptcy and what it means to any individual's financial future.

8 | *What Bankruptcy Really Means*

At this writing, America has undergone one of the most sweeping changes in bankruptcy law in its history. The Bankruptcy Abuse Prevention and Consumer Protection Act of 2005 was intended to cut the pace of personal bankruptcies by increasing filing costs, using income means testing in regards to liquidation and repayment, and requiring credit counseling.

The rush to file under the old law created the heaviest pace in personal bankruptcies in the country at more than two million petitions. And for a while, it seemed the chill would stick. But as 2006 progressed, the American Bankruptcy Institute noted that bankruptcy filings were starting to rise again.

Apparently, a nation that can't seem to wean itself from credit can't quite seem to wean itself from a court-assisted clean slate either.

BANKRUPTCY STATISTICS

The following two charts from the American Bankruptcy Institute are eye-opening just to see how prevalent bankruptcy has become in society during this new century.

The first shows how rising debt payments as a

percentage of personal income have compared with bankruptcy filings nationwide. Yet the second chart, which shows the number of households per consumer filing in each state is even more of a shocker—to realize that one in every 34 households in the state of Indiana has filed for bankruptcy in 2005? Even though a significant portion of Indiana is rural, you could say that's one household every four or five blocks in an average neighborhood.

On a national level, there was one personal bankruptcy for every 60 U.S. households, a 23 percent increase from calendar year 2004.

SIX THINGS THAT TIP PEOPLE INTO BANKRUPTCY

A 2005 study by the University of Nevada at Las Vegas pointed out that hurricanes were actually a major force in bankruptcy filings, pointing out that filings in affected states increase by 11 percent in the 12 months

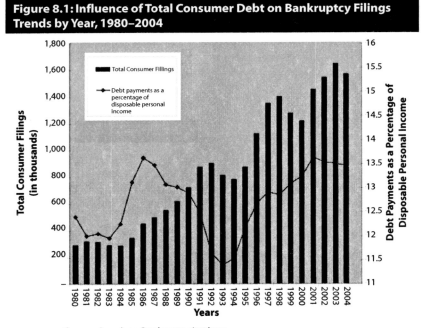

Figure 8.1: Influence of Total Consumer Debt on Bankruptcy Filings Trends by Year, 1980–2004

Source: American Bankruptcy Institute

States	Household per Consumer Filing	Rank
Figure 8.2: Households Per Consumer Filing, Rank During the 12-Month Period Ending December 31, 2005		
United States	60.16	
Indiana	34.41	1
Ohio	37.19	2
Utah	39.52	3
Tennessee	39.70	4
Oklahoma	40.86	5
Arkansas	40.91	6
Nevada	41.63	7
Alabama	43.33	8
Kentucky	46.23	9
Georgia	46.33	10
Colorado	47.68	11
Illinois	48.07	12
Oregon	48.70	13
Idaho	48.94	14
Missouri	49.26	15
West Virginia	49.61	16
Michigan	50.15	17
Mississippi	52.01	18
Kansas	52.96	19
Louisiana	53.29	20
Washington	56.49	21
Arizona	61.94	22
Nebraska	64.12	23
Maryland	65.07	24
Wisconsin	65.84	25
Pennsylvania	69.42	26
Virginia	69.85	27
New Jersey	69.93	28
Iowa	70.83	29
New Mexico	71.22	30
New York	72.75	31
Wyoming	73.09	32
Montana	73.36	33
Texas	75.22	34
Florida	75.38	35
Rhode Island	78.26	36
California	78.78	37
South Dakota	86.19	38
North Dakota	87.34	39
Delaware	88.54	40
North Carolina	91.04	41
Minnesota	91.94	42
Connecticut	93.57	43
Massachusetts	101.57	44
New Hampshire	104.46	45

Source: *American Bankruptcy Institute.*

after a major hurricane, up to 30 percent two years afterward, and up 46 percent three years afterward. It will be a valid issue to watch in the aftermath of Hurricane Katrina.

Obviously, not everyone lives in a major storm zone, but unexpected personal disasters are a primary culprit, and they take many forms:

Divorce. Today's divorce rate is lower than it was in the 1980s, but it is still a major driver of financial disaster. Two people who once paid a monthly housing bill now need to pay two, on top of legal bills, new child care costs, and the possibility of alimony or child support payments that may put a strain on one or both spouses. Add that to the debt the combined household was already wrestling with, and the pressure for many quickly reaches the breaking point.

Serious illness. Nearly 40 million Americans have no health insurance of any kind, and while at other points in our history the numbers have been greater, the sheer cost of care tips many into bankruptcy. Various surveys report that more than 20 percent of all bankruptcy filers mention medical debt as the major contributor to their late payments.

Sudden unemployment. So many people live paycheck-to-paycheck. The simple interruption of that income, even for a few weeks, could bring their debt and other expenses to a crisis.

Overuse of credit cards. Individuals with high revolving debt—sometimes at rates as high as 20 percent—are ripe for financial failure as soon as they lose a job or another major source of income. Simply, the rates for this type of borrowing are too high to be practical for most people.

Gambling. This is a controversial explanation, because most people who gamble do so responsibly. But some researchers believe there is a higher correlation between residents who live in casino states and those who don't. Temptation to gamble irresponsibly, like the temptation to overuse credit cards, may occur where the best opportunities are to do so.

Getting the wrong advice. If you watch TV, you'll see any number of ads on consumer credit counseling. There are reputable credit counselors—agencies that help you renegotiate debt payments and then ride herd to make sure you do it—but many more disreputable ones. Some

PLANNING TIPS: THE BIGGEST FINANCIAL MISTAKES PEOPLE MAKE IN DIVORCE— AND HOW TO AVOID THEM

At best, divorce is a time of distraction in one's life, when emotional and family concerns take center stage and financial issues often take a back seat. Yet divorce is one of the biggest triggers of bankruptcy in a world where bankruptcy has gotten a lot tougher to file. That means that financial planning is crucial when a marriage breaks up.

Anyone filing for divorce should seek the help of financial and tax advisers as well as attorneys skilled in divorce, experts say, because the financial issues that get pushed to the background eventually can take a surprising and disastrous toll on the newly single ex-spouse and his or her children.

Here are some ways to avoid a money debacle on the other end of divorce.

Start with a budget. No matter how sophisticated you think you are about your finances, don't pass up the opportunity to set a basic financial budget for your new life. A CERTIFIED FINANCIAL PLANNER™ professional can help you ask the important questions that will assist you in understanding what life will be like when you are living with a single job income stream or a temporary income stream provided by an ex-spouse. It's always an eye-opener. The Lilac Tree (www.thelilactree.org), an Evanston, Illinois-based not-for-profit organization for divorcing women, routinely stresses that the budgeting process is crucial, since women now outnumber men in filing for bankruptcy and their long-term earnings prospects are generally dimmer.

Find experienced divorce advisers. A good divorce attorney isn't necessarily a shark. The choice of attorneys—for men as well as women—should fit the challenges being faced on both sides. Good divorce attorneys definitely cost money, but they pay for themselves when talking with financial advisers in advocating for their clients. Some CFP professionals are also certified in divorce planning and can help your team with financial discovery, analysis, and long-term projections. Among other financial issues, they should understand qualified domestic relations orders—known as QDROs (pronounced "quad-rows")—to ensure that pension assets will be shared fairly.

Properly value your assets. If you're getting the house, does it have a 20-year-old furnace and a roof that's about to cave in? A thorough inspection by a licensed inspector

Continued on page 78

PLANNING TIPS | Continued from page 77

could help. If you're getting the family car, is it past warranty with a funny sound coming from under the hood? If your spouse runs a lucrative business that you've worked for or invested in, how do you know you're getting the right share? Hiring a valuation expert may be necessary. Divorcing spouses need to make sure they have enough money to finance repairs and replacement of assets that they'll be paying for as a single person.

Remember—kids have rights. In many states, college-age children have the right to demand financial support or college funding at the state level so their education isn't interrupted. While both parents should advocate in their kids' best interest, this isn't always the case. Be aware of your state's divorce laws with respect to secondary child support.

File taxes wisely. There are always special situations in a divorce that will determine whether a couple will need to file jointly or separately during the last year that the marriage exists. This is definitely worth discussion since tax fraud can be a liability issue for the spouse who had no involvement or awareness that the fraud was taking place.

Get help documenting child support. Child support guidelines vary from state to state. But generally, the criteria for establishing child support amounts is typical throughout the United States and these guidelines are established by each state's legislature. If your state has a special program that allows a spouse to pay into a special account so child support is recorded every month, consider it. It provides a paper trail and enforcement system for ensuring that kids get the money they need. Federal law requires all child support payments be made by wage assignment and health insurance by health insurance orders. Child support collection statistics reflect that only 20 percent of noncustodial parents pay their court-ordered child support monthly. That's why so many laws have been established to force compliance. Make sure you know them.

Once the divorce is over—watch the spending. Budgeting early in the process may cut down on the risk of overspending, but divorced spouses setting up new homes may not be able to resist. For some, spending makes them feel better, and this is one of the biggest reasons ex-spouses face financial disaster after divorce. ⊠

disreputable agencies can delay or fail to pay your bills altogether. It is best to go into bankruptcy with qualified financial and tax advice than picking an 800-number off of late night TV. It is also better if you get some guidance to renegotiate your debt payments yourself. In most cases, lenders are willing to negotiate debt payments as long as individuals are proactive in making those discussions happen.

HOW BANKRUPTCY HAS CHANGED

As mentioned at the start of this chapter, the difficult decision to file bankruptcy became more stressful for individuals on October 17, 2005, when the Bankruptcy Abuse Prevention and Consumer Protection Act went into effect.

The most highly publicized aspect of the new law involved tough new restrictions on who may qualify for Chapter 7 bankruptcy, the most common form of individual filing that allows consumers to erase their debts.

Yet advisers say it's important to understand one important fact— *your own state laws might override certain parts of the new federal restrictions*, making the payment and asset-retention outlook for debtors better or worse than they would be strictly under the letter of the federal law. That's why it's critical that potential filers get the advice of a qualified local bankruptcy attorney, a CERTIFIED FINANCIAL PLANNER™, or a tax professional—sometimes all three.

Here are some basic questions to ask about filing for bankruptcy and how the new law may affect the assets you have under your control:

What are the most important changes involving Chapter 7? New federal requirements for the most popular category of individual bankruptcy—Chapter 7—now impose an income test (also known as a "means test") that includes the following:

- If the debtor's average monthly net income for 60 months is greater than $10,000, they won't be able to file under Chapter 7
- If the debtor's average monthly net income for 60 months is less than $6,000, then filing will likely be permitted

- Between $6,000 and $10,000, the debtor can file under Chapter 7 only if net monthly income is less than 25 percent of all nonpriority unsecured debts

Also, filers now have to supply proof that they've completed six months of credit counseling, preferably with a payment plan. These detailed reporting requirements will show if you were running up your credit cards before filing or acting irresponsibly in other ways.

Will documentation change? Tremendously. Under Chapter 7 requirements at the time this book was published, filers needed to file a relatively basic list of current assets and debts, a list of current income and expenses, and an overall statement of financial affairs. This has made things complicated. The courts want to see tax returns and detailed projections of earnings. They'll want to see assets in retirement accounts and even educational accounts such as 529 college savings plans (see below).

What about home-ownership issues? If you want to use a new state as your domicile, you have to live there for 730 days. However, regardless of what state laws apply, the new bankruptcy act states that you must live in a home for 1215 days (40 months) to receive your state's homestead exemption. Otherwise, protection for the home is capped at $125,000. Also, there's a ten-year review period to determine if the debtor attempted to transfer money or equity into a homestead with the intent to hinder, delay, or defraud a creditor.

What about retirement assets? For filings under the new law, retirement funds that are exempt from taxation (including qualified plans, qualified annuities, IRAs, Roth IRAs, or deferred compensation plans) will likely stay exempt in bankruptcy. However, funds in a traditional or Roth IRA (but not SEP plans or SIMPLE IRAs) are exempt only up to $1 million. Again, check state law.

What about education savings? All money held in a Coverdell education savings account or a section 529 college savings plan for *more than two years* is protected from payment of bankruptcy debts as long as the account beneficiary is a child, a stepchild, grandchild, or step-grandchild.

Where can a consumer find advisers? One resource for bankruptcy attorneys is the American Board of Certification (www.abcworld.org), which provides a state-by-state listing of attorneys certified in bankruptcy law. The National Foundation for Credit Counseling (www.nfcc.org) lists nonprofit consumer credit counseling agencies nationwide. Advisers can also be located through the Financial Planning Association® (www.plannersearch.org). All references should be checked locally.

In Chapter 9, we'll focus on the moves necessary to create a new financial life.

9 | *Building a New Financial Life*

You don't have to go through a bankruptcy to make a positive change in your relationship with money. It's something you can do the minute you wake up tomorrow—resolve to make a fresh start in your financial life.

The first thing you should do—particularly if you've never done it before—is create a household and personal budget.

WHAT'S A BUDGET?

A budget is a written document that lays out your necessities, goals, and wishes, and details how much you spend on them based on the money you have coming in. As months go by, you see how far apart your income and spending figures are, and you tweak them into alignment. That's called meeting a budget.

It's a simple idea, so why do so few people do it? Because it involves something very few people really like to do, and that's face facts.

It doesn't matter whether you create a budget on paper, on the computer, or even on the Internet, as long as you attempt to create one. Figure 9.1 outlines the basic elements of an average person's budget; you might choose to tailor it more precisely to your individual spending and income needs, but most budgets use similar headings and categories.

A budget isn't something that's automatically set in an afternoon's work, though it would be nice if that were the case. You have to build up several months of behavior on paper first to get an idea where you can cut and add. In previous chapters, we talked about the need to start tracking your spending—you'll need that data to create an effective budget.

We should note that a budget shouldn't force you to cut out all the fun in your life, but it should get you thinking about what is critically important. You might need to forego a little fun to get your finances in better shape in the short-term, but you'll learn that fun is something you can also save and plan for. Once you get in the habit of setting aside money for gratification, there's less worry and uncertaintly attached to it.

THE ANNUAL CREDIT CHECKUP

As you start your new financial life, it makes sense not only to check your credit report and credit score, but also to understand the proper things to do to maintain the best numbers possible. Some new resolutions for your credit rating:

Get all three credit reports and scores at the same time. You'll have to spend around $5 to access your credit score, but you can get your credit reports for free at a Web site called www.annualcreditreport.com. This particular site accesses all three credit bureaus, Experian (www. experian.com), Equifax (www.equifax.com), and TransUnion (www. transunion.com). Stagger your requests (you'll spot trouble more easily if you check each credit report at a different time each year). You can respond quickly to inaccuracies in writing either by mail or online, and make sure you do this at the same time every year.

Resolve to pay on time. Yes, it's obvious, but with such busy schedules, many people fail to remember the day to put the checks in the mail so they'll clear on time. Do any of the following. First, get a calendar, and when bills come in, mark payment days five to seven days ahead of due dates so the U.S. Mail gets your payment in on time. Second, check out

FIGURE 9.1 Category	Monthly Budget Amount	Monthly Actual Amount	Difference
Income:			
Wages & Bonuses			
Interest Income			
Investment Income			
Miscellaneous Income			
Income Taxes Withheld:			
Federal Income Tax			
State and Local Income Tax			
Social Security/Medicare Tax			
Income Taxes Subtotal:			
Expenses:			
Home:			
Mortgage/Rent			
Homeowners/Renters Insurance			
Property Taxes			
Home Repairs/Maintenance/Assessments			
Home Improvements			
Utilities:			
Electricity			
Water and Sewer			
Natural Gas or Oil			
Telephone			
Food:			
Groceries			
Eating Out, Lunches, Snacks			
Family Obligations:			
Child Support			
Alimony			
Day Care, Babysitting			

FIGURE 9.1 *(continued)* Category	Monthly Budget Amount	Monthly Actual Amount	Difference
Health and Medical:			
Health Insurance			
Unreimbursed Medical Expenses			
Fitness (Gym Expense)			
Transportation:			
Car Payments			
Gasoline/Oil			
Auto Repairs/Maintenance/Fees			
Auto Insurance			
Public Transportation/Cabs			
Debt Payments:			
Credit Cards			
Student Loans			
Other Loans			
Entertainment/Recreation:			
Cable TV/Videos/Movies			
Internet/Computer expense			
Hobbies			
Magazine Subscriptions			
Club Dues			
Vacations			
Pets:			
Food			
Grooming/Boarding			
Vet			
Clothing:			
Investments and Savings:			
401(k) or IRA			
Stocks, Bonds, Mutual Funds			

FIGURE 9.1 *(continued)* Category	Monthly Budget Amount	Monthly Actual Amount	Difference
College Fund			
Savings			
Emergency Fund			
Miscellaneous:			
Toiletries, Household Products			
Gifts/Donations			
Grooming (Hair, Makeup, Other)			
Miscellaneous Expense			
TOTAL INVESTMENTS AND EXPENSES			
SURPLUS MINUS SHORTAGE **(Total spendable income minus expenses** **and investments)**			

the electronic bill payment service at your bank, and program in payment reminders so you never forget to push that button. You can also use your creditor's electronic payment option, but pay a few days ahead at the start so you can see how quickly your payments are recorded (some electronic payment systems still delay recording payment by a day or two even if the debtor pays on the due date).

Get current. If you have missed payments on an account, do whatever it takes to get current and then never let yourself fall behind again. According to www.myfico.com, the longer you pay bills on time, the better your credit score. Placing your bill payment schedule on a calendar will help.

Understand the problems with your credit. It takes seven years to remove a collection account from your credit record, even if you've paid it off. Write down the exact month when that mark on your report will be removed, and make sure it happens.

Get rid of balances in sequence. Come up with a plan to pay off credit card balances in a sensible order. There's a temptation to move around outstanding balances if you get a good offer. Sometimes it still makes legitimate sense to do this if it cuts your borrowing cost, but make sure you don't shift balances too often—focus on paying balances off, the highest-rate ones first.

Limit your credit inquiries. You might get sexy credit card offers and refinancing notices at a rate of five a week, 52 weeks a year, but that doesn't mean you need to check all of them out. In fact, an excess number of credit inquiries can lower your credit score. When you do investigate credit, do so within a focused period of time, optimally two weeks, and then stop. Lenders watch very closely how many credit card and loan opportunities you check, even if you don't end up taking the offer. They see you investigating credit opportunities as a first step to you getting in trouble.

If you do borrow, ask lenders which bureau they use. If you are making an effort to keep your credit in check and your reports accurate, this won't make a lot of difference, but it always pays to ask a potential lender—particularly a mortgage lender—if there is one brand of credit report they favor over others. It's important because you may have a significantly higher or lower score on one report compared to the next one.

Cut up the card—don't close the account. Closing accounts—even those that have had zero balances for years—can be a lousy idea. Lenders want to see a long record of credit management, and longtime accounts that you haven't touched in years may actually help your score because it shows you have some restraint.

Get some perspective before you make these moves. Borrowing may seem like a process for the masses, but in reality, borrowing effectively means understanding your specific needs and circumstances. Someone like a CERTIFIED FINANCIAL PLANNER™ professional can help you look at your credit issues from all appropriate angles.

LOOKING AHEAD

In this chapter, you've identified the basic building blocks of getting a handle on your finances—identifying sources of income, expenses, and most importantly, debt. The next section of the book will explain how to set up your financial strategy for the long term.

Part III

Setting Up Your Financial Strategy

How a Financial Planner Can Help You Organize Your Financial Life

Roy Diliberto, CFP®

Roy Diliberto, a CERTIFIED FINANCIAL PLANNER™ professional from Bonita Springs, Florida, realizes that financial organization doesn't mean sorting paper and receipts.

"That's not even the first step," he stresses. "The first step in financial organization is figuring out what people really want to accomplish in their lives, what's really important. Then the next step is to build a structure that will deliver those goals."

Not that paperwork isn't important. Diliberto does try to get clients to do a better job of record-keeping and evaluating goals. "Most people who are consulting a planner for the first time have never attempted to compute the basis on their mutual funds or stocks, and that's necessary. How many people think at midyear about harvesting tax losses? A planner can keep you up to date and help you track complicated issues."

There's another good reason to keep your financial life up to date with a planner. If you die, suffer a health emergency that leaves you incapacitated or a natural disaster that wipes out your home and records, a planner would have an updated copy of your financial details on a CD-ROM. A good planner makes sure that he or she has all the information necessary to play air traffic controller—they have all your contacts on file to make sure they know they have necessary information, including the executor of your will.

"Keep in mind that since 9/11 we all have a greater appreciation for offsite maintenance of records," explains Diliberto. "Your planner can be an important part of that."

10 | *What Financial Expertise Do You Need?*

There are many people who run their financial lives solo and do a great job. But for most of us, we don't have the time to get our knowledge and skills up to the professional level required as our financial, career and personal lives get more complex.

To do these things, and more important, to keep abreast of the latest information out there, we often pay experts to handle our financial planning, tax strategy, and investments. That doesn't mean we are required to do these things. But let's start by assessing our skills. Do you have the ability *right now* to do the following:

1. **Set specific goals?** Goals define what financial independence will look like for each of us. Equally important, goals—particularly specific goals written out with timetables—can motivate us to initiate and stick with the other keys to financial independence.
2. **Consistently spend less than you earn?** Yes, your mother probably taught you this when you were receiving an allowance as a youngster, but so many of us forget. Unless you spend less than you earn, it's impossible to become financially independent, short

of winning that lottery. Consistent saving is even more important than what investment rate you might earn with that savings. Aim for saving 10 percent or even more of your pre-tax income, but even a smaller percentage helps, especially if you start saving while you're younger and can let the power of compounding work for you.

3. **Create a spending plan?** The key to spending less than you earn is to create and follow a spending plan: earnings minus expenses equals savings. Better yet, treat savings as an expense item and put it at the top of your budget—have the money taken out at work and put into your savings and investments so you won't miss it and won't spend it. You can help your efforts to spend less than you earn by eliminating frivolous expenses, buying smart, and cutting taxes.

4. **Invest?** To build financial independence, you'll need to earn a reasonable return on your savings. A savings account alone won't cut it. That means investing in stocks, bonds, perhaps real estate, and other assets that involve an acceptable level of risk. Yes, there's the risk of some loss of principal, as the 2000–2002 stock market demonstrated. But understand that investing is for long-term goals (at least five and preferably more years away). When goals get closer, shift the invested funds into those lower-earning but less risky savings accounts and money markets.

5. **Stay invested?** One of the big mistakes many investors make is waiting until the market is really hot to invest and then bailing out when it sinks—in short, they buy high, sell low. Get in and stay in, making adjustments if necessary. Keep in mind that the bulk of the returns of a bull market tend to come early in the upswing, and people often miss out on them because they're waiting for the market to turn "hot."

6. **Diversify?** As the recent markets have also shown, it's key to diversify your assets. Overloading on company stock, on stock in the industry in which you work, or on other higher-risk investments is an open invitation to trouble. By spreading your investment money among several asset categories, you minimize the impact of the downturns of a particular segment.

7. **Use tax-favored accounts?** A significant number of individuals with access to 401(k)s, IRAs, and other tax-deferred retirement accounts don't bother to sign up. Yet these plans are among the most efficient ways to build toward financial independence because you get more bang for each invested buck, especially if your employer matches your contributions.

8. **Bulletproof your independence?** As you accumulate money for financial independence, you need to protect it. The primary way is insurance—not just life, health, auto, and homeowner's insurance, but often overlooked disability and liability coverage. Disability insurance helps offset the loss of income if you can no longer work due to a disability, and liability coverage is a cushion against lawsuits. Another form of insurance is a cash-reserve emergency fund where dollars are kept in a savings or money market account to see you through emergencies such as major car repairs or a stretch of unemployment, so you don't have to dip into retirement accounts or other investments.

If you're not able to do this yourself, it may be time to get some help.

Most people have a team approach to their financial well-being. They're in the loop, but they work with a professional tax preparer every year (depending on the complexity of their finances, they may need a certified public accountant or a tax attorney), an investment adviser on a quarterly or annual basis, and a financial planner who pulls everything into shape every two or three years, or when a life change (see Part 1) warrants review of the overall strategy.

LOCATING A FINANCIAL PLANNER

Go back to Chapter 3 for a review of all the steps to consider and questions to ask about finding a financial planner, but remember that the best ways to locate a financial planner include the following:

- Speak with friends and colleagues you trust who have obviously been successful working with a planner.
- Check lists of planners with advanced certification such as CERTIFIED

FINANCIAL PLANNER™ practitioners. To find CFP in your area, go to www.fpanet.org.
- Make sure you check disciplinary and court records on all planners you consider.

Just remember, planners do not necessarily handle the functions of tax preparers or investment advisers (see below). You need to thoroughly research a planner's training and areas of expertise.

LOCATING A TAX PROFESSIONAL

For the preparation of a simple individual return, you don't need a pricey CPA. However, you should consider going to a tax preparer if you've sold a home in the last year, bought and sold investment assets, started or sold a business, or experienced a divorce or the death of a spouse. If you receive much of your income from sources other than a salary, such as investments, self-employment, or rental income, a tax preparer may help you sort out the complex forms and reduce your tax liability.

To find the preparer that's right for you, start with your CERTIFIED FINANCIAL PLANNER™ practitioner if you use one. More and more planners are doing tax preparation work themselves. The advantage to their clients is that the person preparing their taxes is the same person providing them with tax planning advice and who knows their financial situation.

If your planner doesn't prepare taxes, however, he or she will likely be able to recommend a CPA, enrolled agent, or other tax-preparation expert. Be sure the preparer is someone available year-round. The planner also may recommend a tax attorney for specialized tax problems when such a need arises. Visit two or three of the referrals and pick the preparer that fits you. Some preparers are conservative in their interpretation of the tax code, while others aggressively seek write-offs that may be questioned by the Internal Revenue Service.

If the services of a tax preparer are appropriate, you can use the preparer most efficiently by keeping good tax records throughout the year. Routinely file all investment transactions, home improvement expenses, tax-deductible donations, previous tax returns, and other records that will affect your tax return. The more orderly and complete your records, the lower your preparation fees and the less likely that errors will occur.

If information is missing, such as what you paid for a particular investment, obtain the information yourself instead of paying the preparer to track it down. Answer all the preparer's questions as fully as possible.

Finally, remember that not all tax preparers are qualified as tax planners who can provide long-term tax advice. Many financial decisions, from buying a home to getting married, have tax implications, and tax strategies can have important (and sometimes conflicting) consequences on other financial goals. Consult with your financial planner before making any significant financial decisions that may have tax implications.

LOCATING AN INVESTMENT ADVISER

If you gathered five people in a room and asked them what the term "investment adviser" meant, you might get five different answers, and there's a reasonably good chance they'd all be right.

Some people think that an investment adviser is someone who sits around all day and buys stock for their portfolio. Well, depending on how much money and other assets you have, that definition might fit. It might also fit a broker.

Others just want someone to tell them what to buy so they can go out and buy it themselves through an online broker. That can easily be done by a financial planner who can give overall suggestions on types of investments that would work well for a particular person's investments and goals.

One more might want to get a suggestion on what to buy and for the professional to execute the trade. That professional could be a broker.

Here's the point. Before hiring someone to handle your investments, you need to take at least ten steps back from that question. Start by figuring out what your goals are, what you have to invest, and how you want to do it. In truth, if you have several thousand dollars or even several hundred thousand dollars, there are people out there to help you. But you really need to make sure you need them.

Here are some general questions you should prepare to ask anyone who offers to advise you on investments or to invest your money for you:

1. Are you registered with the Securities and Exchange Commission, your state securities regulator, or NASD (the National Association of Securities Dealers)—or some combination of those three? What do those certifications allow you to do? (Check his or her answer at the various Web sites for those agencies, and make sure they are listed.)
2. What professional credentials do you have—CFP (Certified Financial Planner), CFA (Chartered Financial Analyst), ChFC (Chartered Financial Consultant), or another? This question is all about the initial and continuing education this professional has received.
3. How much experience have you had working with individual investors like me, and what are the average-size portfolios you work with?
4. What kinds of service or recommendations will you offer me, and how will decisions to go ahead with those recommendations be handled? Do I execute trades, or do you?
5. Do you earn commissions or fees on what you buy for me beyond what I'm paying you? In other words, are certain investment firms giving you an incentive to sell me their products over other competitive ones?
6. Can you show me an example of the advice you've given another investor similar to me?
7. Can I have references?
8. Have you been sued, censured, or otherwise had complaints filed against you in court or with any other public or private governing body?
9. How do we evaluate the job you're doing?
10. How often should we meet?

HOW OFTEN SHOULD YOU MEET WITH YOUR EXPERTS?

Nothing is set in stone on this point, but this is where references help, as does cross-checking one expert's answers against the other. Obviously, if you have a dramatic lifestyle or legal change, you will need to see your planner to see if you need to reset your goals. Most qualified planners don't recommend frequent changes, so you may be meeting with them once every two to three years. When you're working with a tax professional, plan to meet annually, with quarterly meetings required only for major changes in a complex financial picture. Investment advisers can hold your hand as much as you'd like—but remember that the meter could be running unless you have another type of compensation agreement in place.

Indeed, compensation is a key point here. Experts never work for free, and you shouldn't expect them to, if they have talent. Ask polite but pointed questions about what that compensation buys you in terms of advice and its frequency.

No matter what expertise you choose, you're going to have to acquire a new dedication to researching investments (even if someone is finding them for you) and organizing all your financial data. We'll cover some of those ideas in the next chapter.

11 | *How to Get Organized*

Whether you work with experts or not, getting your finances under control means taking actual steps to do so. And again, whether you are working independently or with an expert, you need to be able to research various investment and tax choices and catalog that information before you make the choices you need to make.

START BY BEING SKEPTICAL ABOUT INVESTMENT RESEARCH

When talking about investment research, trust no one—at least initially. When the markets climbed in the 1990s, so did the number of sources of investment information—cable TV, dozens of publications both new and old, and last but not least, the Internet. After the fall, there are plenty of resources out there, but here's how to check them out.

Pay attention to the source. Since the stock market fell during 2000–2002, there's been a wakeup call on investment stories and who the sources are behind them. More often these days, you will hear business reporters ask on TV and in print whether investment managers, analysts, and any number of financial players have an interest in the investment they're talking about.

That didn't happen much before the value of the NASDAQ was cut in half during the worst of the downturn.

Much of the investment research easily available to us is on the Internet, particularly in weblogs, or blogs. Blogs—online diaries that specialize in virtually any topic—have exploded in the last five years. On the Internet, on newsstands, on the air, financial advice is everywhere. An August 2005 report in the *Wall Street Journal* estimated that there were are about 5,000 personal finance blogs, up 40 percent from the previous six months.

The primary attraction of blogs is their immediacy. Also, they offer a sense of community around a singular personal finance topic or a broad range of financial topics.

The best blogs are useful when they are run by a good editor (the blogger)—someone who provides a depth of factual information in digestible form. But look before you blog. Here are some guidelines:

Check the rankings. Major business publications regularly publish lists of blogs they believe have quality content. These listings are not in themselves endorsements or guarantees that the content within will make you money or at the very least be accurate. But check those listings to get a feel for what the experts believe are the best blogs and why.

Check out the blogger. Many noted authors and experts create and run their own blogs. Make the effort to check the person out as you would any guru—run an Internet search on their careers, their accomplishments, their publications, and especially any evidence of criminal record or fines for disseminating questionable information. Take some time to visit the Federal Trade Commission (www.ftc.gov) and the Securities and Exchange Commission's Web sites (www.sec.gov) to see if your blogger could be under potential investigation for statements made on their blog. Be persistent and make the time to check out anyone on the site you're e-mailing thoroughly.

Watch the message boards. Believing everything you read on any kind of message board is usually a mistake. A blog may have a very talented group of regular participants who share incredibly useful information.

But remember one key fact—in the majority of cases, you will have absolutely no idea who these people are, and there will be no way to check. Make every attempt to corroborate blog information with tested, reliable sources. And don't hesitate to call your financial adviser before you invest in anything.

Be wary of privacy issues. To enter many blogs, particularly to participate on their message boards, you have to register by name and possibly by e-mail or home address. Be particularly wary of what you are asked to tell anyone. Unscrupulous bloggers might be asking for demographic or personal information that no one should share, particularly in an unsecured environment. Other blogs might install cookies—little electronic tracking devices that are installed on a user's computer after they visit a Web site. Cookies not only make it easier for a reader to find things the next time they return, they may also enable the blogger to keep track of your behavior online. Ask yourself the true price of participating.

Watch what you write. While the courts to date have largely protected bloggers and posters from liability from outside content posted on various blogs, negative comments about companies or institutions are starting to draw legal fire. There have been court cases calling blog postings into question for alleged false and defamatory statements. In most cases, the blogger gets sued, but if you are a participant in that blog, you could potentially be liable. At the very least, use a pseudonym and don't write anything that identifies you.

Consult an expert before you invest. If an investor finds himself or herself moving toward a purchase, sale, or financial decision based on something found on a blog, there is one simple course of action—consult an expert. Much like investment message boards on Internet service providers or other Web sites, the Internet shouldn't spark life-altering financial decisions. Research and debunking all bad information should.

GETTING ORGANIZED ON PAPER

Many people are migrating all their financial tracking and planning to their home computers, and it's a time-saver. Yet there are key questions that should start the process of getting all the intelligence and numbers down in the same place:

Start tracking all spending. If you haven't purchased financial accounting software or set up a reliable accounting method of your own, this is the year to do it. Expense tracking is the first critical step to getting personal finances in order.

Write down your goals. Have you ever written down the big things you want in life? Granted, all great dreams don't cost money, but many of them do. Money buys freedom—to travel, to retire early, to start a business, to change careers. Putting goals in writing gives them a formality and a starting point for the planning you must do.

Start gathering all the records you need. Start with a good documents checklist—you can find them online, in office supply stores, magazine articles, or your CERTIFIED FINANCIAL PLANNER™ practitioner might supply a complimentary organizer. During the review, you may realize that you don't have everything you should, such as a durable power of attorney, or that documents, such as a will or life insurance policy (coverage and beneficiary designation, for example) aren't up to date. One record that's often neglected is an inventory of all your property. This is invaluable if your home is destroyed.

WHAT RECORDS SHOULD YOU KEEP AND FOR HOW LONG?

Here are some of the most critical ones.

- Obvious ones to keep indefinitely include wills and related estate planning documents such as living wills and trust documents, Social Security cards, birth certificates and adoption papers, military records, marriage certificates and divorce decrees, driver's license numbers, and passports.
- Financial and tax records get a little more complicated. You generally

should keep mortgage records (and home improvement receipts) indefinitely, even if you've bought and sold several homes. But you probably won't need to keep car titles or most other property documents once the item has been disposed of. Keep indefinitely all records documenting retirement plans and individual retirement accounts.

- Tax records make many people nervous, so they tend to hang on to everything. Certainly keep your filed tax returns indefinitely if that makes you feel more comfortable, but you generally don't need to keep supporting documentation beyond three to six years. Regular audits must be done within three years and the IRS has six years to challenge if there's reason to believe you underreported by at least 25 percent. However, it has no time limit if it believes you didn't file or filed fraudulently.

- Investment records can pile up quickly, but they're even more important than before because your estate executor will need them to establish the basis for assets you hold at your death. Keep the year-end statements from mutual funds for as long as you own the funds, plus three to six years for tax purposes. Pitch the monthly statements at year's end. The same goes for other investment records. Leave stock and bond certificates with your broker.

- Dump canceled checks (except those for tax purposes) and ATM receipts once you've confirmed the transactions are cleared. You can throw out credit card slips once they're accounted for, except for those related to tax records or warranties. You don't need to keep the monthly statements forever, either. You can get copies from the company if you need them.

HOW TO ORGANIZE RECORDS

Here's where you can do yourself and your loved ones the most good, even if you hang on to records unnecessarily. A filing cabinet with clearly marked files is a good start. Some experts suggest making copies of critical documents and putting them in accordion files or a box that can be easily taken out of the home in an emergency. Software is another good way to store financial records. It can be updated and backed up easily.

For the most important paper documents, consider a fireproof safe. And given all the attention we've given to natural disasters, edit down what you consider "critical" documents so you can easily grab the safe and throw it in the car or outside the house if you have to leave.

But the most helpful is to keep a master list of where all the financial records are located, along with insurance policy numbers, bank account numbers, and phone numbers of financial professionals. Make sure key family members know where the list is kept—your financial planner will probably instruct you to create your filing system and this master index, which he or she will keep a copy of. Keep one copy at home, one with your tax or planning professional, and if you're close to your executor, make sure they have a copy as well.

ORGANIZING FOR YOUR PROFESSIONALS

Unless you are working for the rare professional who wants to see paper, start leaning toward computer software. Ask your planner or tax preparer if they prefer that you work with a preferred list of financial categories to make your and their work easier.

In Chapter 12, we're going to discuss another key aspect of organizing your finances—a disaster plan.

12 | *Planning for Disaster*

Disaster can't be predicted, but it can be blunted by preparation. In the wake of 9/11, businesses with the most sophisticated offsite technology backup were able to get back on track. After Hurricane Katrina, the individuals and families who had an escape plan had the best chance of survival.

What's happened since the turn of the century has given us many examples of how to ensure our *physical* survival. So why do so few people have a *financial* survival plan?

Here are key steps toward making such a plan.

STEP #1: THE EMERGENCY FUND

Again, think Katrina. If you suddenly lost your home, your job, or were disabled with limited health or disability benefits, how would you afford a hotel, transportation or medical bills? How would you pay for all that? Credit cards? Okay, but how would you pay off those cards?

An emergency fund needs to be three to six months' worth of cash kept in an easily accessible place—not as accessible as a mattress, but not in a stock fund or some other investment that might fluctuate in value and then be tough to access for a week or more. You need to treat that cash as money that isn't there unless a disaster occurs. And try to open it with a high enough balance so you'll keep it from being eaten away by any account maintenance fees.

Do yourself a favor. Write down a list of things that are potential disasters—and sign it as a personal contract with yourself. That agreement should state that you will not touch the funds except in case of:

- Loss of employment
- Medical bills that exceed your insurance payments (if you have insurance)
- Emergency home or car repairs in excess of insurance that are required to make the home livable or the car drivable

STEP #2: PAY DOWN YOUR DEBT

A financial emergency can put unprepared individuals at risk of late or missed payments of credit card, auto, and home debt. The emergency fund will help you deal with these issues on a temporary basis, but the better approach might be to minimize debt as much as possible while your financial situation is relatively healthy.

Need some convincing? Do a mental trick. Pretend you've lost your job and you won't find another one for six months. Then ask yourself how you'll make those payments on your credit card, auto loan, student loans, and mortgage if you have one.

If you fully consider those consequences, you'll be that much closer to putting yourself on a disciplined budget (See Chapter 9) to minimize your problems in good times and bad.

STEP #3: INSURE YOURSELF PROPERLY

Insurance exists to prevent financial devastation. You owe it to yourself to buy whatever coverage you can afford for risks that affect you directly. Not everyone needs life insurance or particular forms of liability insurance, for example. But most of us need help knowing what coverage to buy, and that's where the help of a financial adviser might come in handy—there is no one-size-fits-all insurance solution.

We'll go over insurance needs in more detail in Chapter 13, but generally, individuals need to check out the best options available in the following relevant categories:

- Health insurance
- Life insurance
- Home or rental insurance
- Disability insurance
- Auto insurance
- Liability insurance related to a particular business or work activity

As we've mentioned, more than 40 million Americans are currently without health insurance, and many more will face reductions in overall insurance benefits from their employers in the future. Depending on the state and city you live in, there may be options to buy coverage—not particularly affordable and well beneath the benefit levels enjoyed by most CEOs, but basic health coverage is necessary. You can't afford not to look for it.

STEP #4: WHAT IS THE WORST POSSIBLE SCENARIO YOU MIGHT FACE?

You need to sit down and think about a variety of events that may pose the worst financial risks to you and then consider how you'd pay for them if they actually happened. We're not asking about the probability of a telecommunications satellite crashing on top of your house—we're merely suggesting that you consider risk factors that have a realistic chance of affecting your financial life, and not just health risk. Some examples:

- If there was hereditary evidence of cancer or heart disease among your closest relatives, how would you pay for treatment if you were stricken?
- If you live in a flood plain, do you have adequate flood insurance?

- If your company has been losing money for the last year, how likely is it you might be laid off?
- Will you need additional training or education to stay in your job going forward?
- If you were disabled, how would you make up your lost salary?

The questions you might ask are as individual as you are. With the help of a financial adviser like a CERTIFIED FINANCIAL PLANNER™ practitioner, you can play devil's advocate on a variety of scenarios. And once you've planned for them, you don't have to spend another minute worrying about them.

STEP #5: MAKING AN ESCAPE KIT

We're not talking about anything illegal here. Ask yourself the question—if a natural disaster, fire, or any other devastating threat befell your home, what could you grab within five minutes?

If you're like most of us, you have a sudden picture of you running from room to room in a panic grabbing insurance policies, picture albums, and beloved keepsakes that really have nothing to do with your survival. With every step, you're hoping you haven't forgotten anything major. You can prevent this anxiety by staging this scene in your head and planning for it.

Start by consolidating critical financial documents in one place. These documents can be stored digitally, easily carried or placed in fire-proof and waterproof containers that have a reasonably good chance of surviving a physical disaster in your home.

Your kit will be as unique as your circumstances, but consider this as you formulate it. What would you pack if you had only five minutes to run? How about 30 minutes? How about one hour? How about one day? And how would you move all this stuff?

Your list will get longer—and probably more emotional—as you go through these time frames, but here's a list of essentials to keep at the center of each scenario. Once you prepare a list that fits you, give a copy to a trusted friend or relative or a financial adviser in case you die or are incapacitated—such a list will work in that event as well.

1. Birth, death, marriage certificates (and make a note to the person you trust with this information to immediately make at least ten copies of each of these in case they are executor or are asked to help an executor)
2. Divorce decrees with all relevant settlement information
3. Location of wills, trusts, and any legal or health-care power-of-attorney information
4. Advanced health-care directives
5. Adoption papers, if applicable
6. Key identification numbers, including driver's license, passport, and employee identification data
7. Recent bank and brokerage statements
8. Detailed funeral and burial wishes
9. Location of cash that may be used to handle emergency expenses
10. Recent medical records that may be good to have on hand if the individual is incapacitated
11. Copies of residential deeds and mortgage data
12. Car title, lease, loan information, and license plate data
13. All insurance policy (health, disability, and life) and agent contact information
14. Photocopies of credit and debit cards, front and back (displaying the individual's signature)
15. A current copy of the individual's home financial software program reflecting up-to-date financial data
16. All password information necessary to get inside any computers the individual owns
17. The locations for all critical paper documents and stocks and bonds
18. Where safe-deposit, lockbox, and filing cabinet keys are
19. The name and number of the individual's human resources department at work

20. Location of tax returns for the last three years
21. All relevant contact numbers for executors, financial advisers, trustees, guardians, attorneys, and any other individuals who will need to step in if the person is dead or incapacitated
22. All user IDs and passwords for online accounts
23. Guidelines on what to do about orphaned pets, including set plans for who will adopt them and pay for their care
24. A general statement of family origins, values, parental guidance, and expectations for the family

In organizing all this information, it makes sense for you to put yourself in the shoes of the people you selected to handle things in a crisis. Since these individuals may be capable but still frazzled or upset, it's essential this information be updated as often as possible and simple to navigate. Some guidelines in organizing the documents:

- **Start with a simply written table of contents.** When someone dies or is incapacitated, loved ones are understandably distracted. They may forget details they've been told. That's why a detailed index of this data (with page numbers or folder labels) is so critical. Many people think that putting together a comprehensive binder or box of information is all they need to do, but a simple one- to three-page summary is particularly appreciated at stressful times.
- **Set a time each year to review and revise this information.** Some experts advise individuals to update their will and other estate preparations every five years, or as often as change takes place. This crisis information should be updated more often—optimally, every year. A person's address, relationship, job status, and financial details can certainly change within a given year—that's why record keeping needs to keep pace with this information.
- **Keep the team informed.** It's never easy to talk about death or illness with loved ones, but individuals need to make time to show their chosen family members and professionals this crisis kit, preferably where all

this information is kept. If family members or advisers have questions or suggestions on how to better present this data, those ideas should be incorporated as time goes on.

STEP #6: MAKING SURE YOUR PORTFOLIO CAN WEATHER A MAJOR DOWNTURN

There is no such thing as a completely bulletproof portfolio, but if the market downturn of 2000–2002 was any indication, planning investments for good times as well as bad is part of any solid disaster plan.

Creating a truly diversified portfolio was something no one thought they had to think about in 1998, but the impact of the crash on individual investors still lingers today.

While the market is still relatively healthy, it makes sense to ask yourself the following:

- **Have you invested with a plan?** Much of the riskiest investing, overbuying, and panic selling during the late 1990s and early 2000s would have been avoided if individual investors had created their own investment plan for achieving *long-term* specific goals such as retirement or a college education. For example, someone who can reach an investment goal by earning a modest average annual return is less apt to jump into higher-risk investments than someone with no plan except to always "go for the highest return."

  Smart investors draw up an investment policy statement (IPS) that specifically outlines realistic return goals, what types of investments they will and won't invest in, what mix of investments, and so on. This IPS serves as a reminder of their goals and strategies, guides them through market declines, and restrains them during boom times.

- **Are you prepared to stay invested?** At the worst of the last market downturn, investors bailed out of the stock market or drastically cut back, only to get back in after they were "convinced" that the market was rebounding. Yet, missing out on the stock market gains during the early stages of recovery can dramatically reduce returns, and the longer you wait, the more you miss out.

  According to a study by SEI Investments of 12 bear markets since

World War II, investors who either stayed in the market through its bottom, or were fortunate to enter at the bottom, saw the S&P 500 gain an average of 32.5 percent (minus dividends) during the first year of recovery. Investors who waited at least three months before returning to the market gained only 14.8 percent.

- **Are you diversified?** Investors chased hot tech stocks in the late 1990s and got badly burned come 2000 and 2001. The NASDAQ lost 39 percent of its value just in 2001, and another 21 percent in 2002. Investors also overloaded on company stock, frequently with poor results.

  Meanwhile, real estate investment trusts, which performed poorly in 1998 and 1999 when stocks were booming, had banner years in 2000 and 2001, performed so-so in 2002, and had an excellent 2003. Bonds also returned well during the bear market. By adhering to your investment policy statement and spreading out your investment portfolio, you usually can reduce risk, minimize losses, and take advantage of the next "surprise" winners.

- **Are you realistic about returns?** As investors painfully learned, those high double-digit annual returns of the late 1990s—one year the NASDAQ jumped 85 percent—aren't *average*. Average annual returns for the past 75 years have been around 11 percent for large-cap stocks and 12 percent for small-cap stocks, and many observers believe stocks will average 3 to 4 percent below those averages during the coming decade.

In the next part of the book, we'll examine how financial planning and career planning go hand-in-hand from your first job to your last.

Part IV

Financial Planning and Career Planning Go Hand-in-Hand

Creating a Lifetime Career/Money Strategy

Elizabeth Jetton
CFP®

At one time, Americans could count on the three-legged stool of traditional pension, adequate savings, and Social Security. No more. Atlanta planner Elizabeth Jetton knows that personal saving and investing and making the most out of employer benefits is more important than before.

But a financial planner adds value to the process in other ways too. "A planner should be asking you if you're happy with your choices. And if you're not happy with your choices, you need to be able to make a change. And you do have to plan for change."

Many times, Jetton has welcomed new clients into her office who arrived with the goal of redoing their 401(k), and, "Sometime later in the conversation I'll hear, 'But I really want to quit,'" she explains.

The earlier she can get clients, the better. "We deal with two types of capital: financial capital and human capital. With financial capital, we start off young people with the bucket system—creating separate buckets for basic expenses, emergency fund, retirement and home savings, and fun. We also do a dream bucket—if the person's goal is to take time off from work in five years or to return to school, you can make a plan for that."

Human capital means a person's ability to earn money, Jetton explains. From a planner's perspective, it means taking a close look at what an employer is offering the worker right now—and whether the job is worth keeping based on that and other factors. "Benefits are hugely important at every stage of your career. If your current employer seems to focus more on child care benefits than educational benefits and you're not planning to have kids for a decade, you either need to find a new job with benefits that suit you or if you really want to stay, you need to plan for that educational choice on your own."

Jetton believes in long-term financial planning, but believes that in the future, more people will want to plan their life in "blocks."

"The younger we are, the more we discount it, but I have to remind people that they are going to live a very long time. You'll spend a portion of your life working, and then you may cut back on working so you can get some education. You may want to explore a creative outlet so you won't be earning as much. Planning allows you to say yes to all those choices."

13 | *Your First Job*

It's the first day of your career. You're excited, a little scared and probably more than a little focused on that first paycheck and what you're going to do with it.

Consider for a moment what that first paycheck really means. Is it sponsorship money for a celebratory beer bash with your friends (which may not be a bad idea) or is it the first installment of a secure financial future?

The answer is that it can be both. With that first paycheck, you now have the two critical tools to build a solid financial future—money and time. Money is always great, but as you get older, you will realize how valuable time really is to the value of money.

Visualize that first paycheck being torn into pieces—a piece goes to everyday expenses, a piece goes to savings, a piece goes to investing, and a piece goes to fun. This chapter is all about allocating that first paycheck.

THE EMERGENCY FUND AND WHY WE KEEP TALKING ABOUT IT

Yes, you might have student debt, a need to set up your first apartment, and if you conform to current statistics, some credit card debt. It's going to be tough to handle all of that without thinking about putting aside three to six months of your income.

But you really need to do it.

First of all, the concept of "last hired, first fired" is still very common in today's workplace, and it happens even in relatively good economic times. Perhaps today's younger generation understands this better than anyone. The Bureau of Labor Statistics reports that the average American will change his or her career five times in a lifetime, with at least 10–12 employers.

All the more reason to set money aside in case some of those job changes are unexpected.

MAKING THE MOST OF YOUR 401(K) OPTIONS

If your employer has a 401(k) plan, we have the following advice—the minute you can get into the plan, max out.

Young people who aren't married and have no dependents may already have a number of financial responsibilities, but they're really in the best position to develop savings habits that will last a lifetime. Getting money taken out of your paycheck for retirement savings is a good habit to get into early. Money taken out of your check is out of sight, out of mind.

When it comes to 401(k)s, try to avoid the following mistakes:

Failing to participate. According to the Profit Sharing/401(k) Council of America, 20 to 25 percent of eligible workers don't participate in available 401(k) plans. This means they are missing out on one of the most tax-effective ways to save for retirement, and could end up depending mostly on Social Security benefits when they retire. Failing to participate is especially costly because over seven in ten employers match up to a certain amount of each employee's contribution, according to the Council. Consequently, failing to join essentially means passing up free money.

Failing to save while waiting. The majority of 401(k) plans don't allow you to join the plan until you've worked for the employer for a year, and many require you to be at least age 21. If that's your situation, set aside money each month in a savings account. Then when you join the plan, you can use this extra savings to supplement your cash flow so that you can maximize your regular 401(k) contribution over the next year.

Failing to contribute the maximum possible. Not every employee can afford to contribute the maximum allowed by the plan, but many employees don't contribute the maximum they can afford to contribute. The average 401(k) participant contributes less than 7 percent of pre-tax salary, according to the Employee Benefit Research Institute, though plans usually allow higher limits of, say, 15 or 20 percent of gross pay (not to exceed $11,000 in 2002). At the very least, contribute enough to maximize the employer's matching contributions, but put in more if you can.

Not adjusting automatic enrollment. An increasing number of 401(k) plans automatically enroll workers, unless they opt out. This increases the participation rate, which is good. However, participants often fail to adjust the enrollment's initial default choices. Consequently, they probably aren't contributing as much as they can afford to, and the investment defaults are likely too conservative. Take the time to study what you have and make adjustments as needed. For guidance on this, you may want to bring a financial adviser into the mix.

Poor diversification. In 2005, human resources consultant Hewitt Associates reported that employer stock was the number one holding in company 401(k) plans, with large U.S. equity funds second, and guaranteed investment contract (GIC)/stable value funds coming in third. (A GIC fund invests only in guaranteed investment contracts issued by insurance companies and sold only to pension plans and certain other types of retirement funds.) What's wrong with this picture? First, an overinvestment in company stock opens employees up to incredible risk if their employer's fortunes go south. An investment in only large U.S. company stock doesn't typically offer much opportunity for growth as smaller-capitalization companies would. And investment in GICs—while perceived as a stable investment—totally ignores an employee's potential need for investment growth.[1]

Failing to balance asset allocation with outside investments. Your 401(k) or similar employer-sponsored retirement account is the main investment for most workers (outside of their home). However, you may have other significant investments, such as your spouse's retirement account, individual retirement accounts, real estate, college savings, and so on. So when choosing retirement plan investments, make investment choices that take into account the outside investments as well. It's your overall portfolio that needs to be properly balanced for risk and return.

Overinvesting in company stock. After all the publicity about Enron and Global Crossing, this seems like obvious advice. Yet many workers have been quoted as saying they will continue to load up heavily with their particular employer's stock because they're confident *their* employer's stock will continue to do well. CERTIFIED FINANCIAL PLANNER™ professionals generally recommend that workers keep no more than 20 percent of company stock in their retirement account.

Borrowing from the plan. It may be financially attractive to borrow from your 401(k), but avoid it unless absolutely necessary. You're taking money out of the account that otherwise would grow tax-deferred, and if you fail to pay back the money, you could face income taxes and penalties. Instead, build an outside emergency fund you can draw on.

Cashing out plan account. A majority of workers under age 35 cash out their 401(k) accounts' accumulated value when they switch jobs, according to the 401(k) Association. That money not only can no longer grow tax-deferred, but the withdrawal faces taxes and usually a 10 percent early withdrawal penalty. Avoid this at all costs.

INSURANCE FOR YOUNG ADULTS

You've recently graduated from high school or college, or just finished a brief stint in the military. For the first time, you're truly on your own. Having adequate insurance coverage is probably not uppermost on your mind.

Being independent, however, means you are no longer covered by your parents' insurance. Many young adults, feeling invincible, go without insurance, but that's not a wise decision, caution financial planners. A serious or prolonged illness, auto accident, or an apartment fire could set you back financially for years. Here are several insurance coverages that young adults should consider.

Health. Most health coverage occurs through employment, but even that's not a given. According to the National Coalition on Health Care, young adults (18 to 24 years old) remained the least likely of any age group to have health insurance in 2004—31.4 percent of this group did not have health insurance. If you're between jobs, and you were covered under the previous employer's plan, you probably can continue that group coverage for up to another 18 months through the federal program COBRA. But you're responsible for 100 percent of the costs, so compare premiums against similar-quality individual coverage.

Another option for workers without employer coverage are health savings accounts. This involves buying a qualifying medical policy with a high deductible ($1,650 to $2,500 for individuals, according to the law). The advantage is that you can stash away tax-deductible money in an IRA-like account (also tax-free) to pay for deductibles and other out-of-pocket medical expenses. These policies are especially attractive to younger, healthier people who are more likely to face minimal medical expenses, yet still need protection in the event of a medical catastrophe.

Disability. Your working income is likely your most precious financial resource. Thus, a long-term illness or injury could prove financially devastating. And your odds of being disabled at least 90 days or longer before age 65 are significantly higher than the odds of dying, according to the Insurance Information Institute. Disability insurance, sometimes called income-replacement insurance, pays a portion (around 60–80 percent) of lost wages if you're unable to continue working due to an accident or illness.

Employers typically provide some short-term disability coverage, but usually not long term, and what they provide may be insufficient for your wages. State-sponsored workers' compensation programs may provide income, but normally only if you're injured on the job (a few states provide for short-term, non-work-related disabilities). Social Security may provide benefits, but only if you're unable to work at virtually any job.

If your employer's coverage doesn't pay at least 60 percent of wages and doesn't last to age 65, you'll likely want to supplement it with private coverage. Buy it while you're young—it'll cost less.

Renter's. Your personal assets are probably modest at this point in your life, but nonetheless, it could cost you thousands or tens of thousands of dollars to replace clothes, electronic equipment, and other property if stolen or destroyed.

Many renters mistakenly believe that their landlord's insurance would cover their lost or destroyed personal property. Not true. Fortunately, personal renter's insurance is usually quite affordable— $150 to $300 a year will probably buy the coverage you need. You may need additional coverage for specific high-valued property or if you're in a flood or earthquake zone. Be sure the policy includes liability coverage in the event you are sued for injuries suffered at your residence. You often can save premium dollars by buying renter's insurance through the company that insures your car.

Automobile. You may still be able to continue under your parents' policy if you're under age 25, unmarried, and the car remains in their name. If you have to buy for yourself, get multiple quotes.

Life. Assuming you are single and have no one financially dependent on you, you probably don't need life insurance. On the other hand, the longer you wait the more expensive it becomes and the greater the risk of becoming uninsurable.

FIGURING OUT TAXES

Young people tend to do one of two things when it comes to tax withholding. They either do too much or too little. You may want to consult a tax adviser to discuss how your financial goals dovetail with your tax situation and calculate your withholding as part of that process. Generally, you don't want to overpay the government. Also, if you're working extra hours to help meet certain financial goals, you will probably be putting yourself in line for a greater tax liability. Just make sure you're setting aside the right amount.

We've talked about setting up your financial structure after you get your first job. In Chapter 14, we'll talk about setting up your first home.

ENDNOTES

1. www.hewittassociates.com/_MetaBasicCMAssetCache_/Assets/Articles/2005_benchmark highlights.pdf.

14 | *Living on Your Own for the First Time*

You're getting ready to move out of the dorm. You've given notice at Mom's crib. Maybe you're leaving a relationship you were in since you were very young. Whether you're 22 or 60, the experience of living completely on your own for the first time is exciting, daunting, and filled with potential financial pitfalls.

DO YOU KNOW YOUR LOCAL COST OF LIVING?

For many of us, living on our own for the first time means we might be doing so in a city or town we've never lived in before. Do you know what it costs there to rent an apartment, operate a car, or buy a bagel? (In the nation's largest cities, new workers might pay more than 30–50 percent of their gross earnings on rent alone.) Do you know what it will cost you to buy a house or condo later on? Before you fire up the U-Haul, do a little research.

A lot of this you can do anecdotally, and it makes sense to do it well in advance. If you're moving to a new city to work for a company, ask your future boss about what it costs to live there, or make full use of your future employer's human resource department to see what they know and to make sure that there's no money-saving option unturned. After bugging them, go to some official resources:

- **Call the Chamber of Commerce.** Yes, it immediately conjures up images of cigar-smoking guys who are darn glad to meet you, but most chambers are one-stop shops for key living and business information on a community. Give them a call and press them to answer your questions. Take notes. They'll probably also send you a packet with maps and other useful stuff that will come in handy later.
- **Bookmark the local newspaper's Web site.** Unless you're in a fairly small town, many newspapers now feature property transfers (that's the public record of what homes sell for) online. They might also do apartment listings online. Get a feel for neighborhoods and prices. Also, get to know the local news and business section—that's where you'll find out about employment, jobs, crime, real estate, state and local tax issues, and other important pocketbook information.
- **Check the local public transportation system's Web site.** See what public transportation options you'll have if you don't have a car or if your car fails. You might want to build your neighborhood search around public transportation. Also bookmark the city's transportation department site to see if you're going to need to buy expensive city stickers and other licenses that will make it more costly to drive a car. Generally, larger cities tend to be more expensive to drive in, so it's important to check fees for parking, licensing, and public transit alternatives.
- **Check local entertainment Web sites.** Find places where you can have fun on a budget.
- **Buy a good, old-fashioned budget travel guide to the city.** There's no better way to get to know individual neighborhoods while finding out cheap alternatives for entertainment, culture and food. Touristas do it, why shouldn't you?
- **Get a subscription to that city's local magazine or newspaper.** If you have more than a few months to think about where you're going, see if your chosen city has a monthly magazine. Particularly in larger

cities, local city magazines give you an in-depth impression of what it's really like to live there. If you get the newspaper, check which day the food section runs. That's when you'll get an idea of grocery, drug, and retail store prices in your chosen city.

- **Go to the local city library's Web site.** So many municipal libraries in cities large and small are now online. Even if it's a little tough to find resources in the card catalog, you can usually e-mail a librarian, and with a kind note, you'll probably find all sorts of unexpected resources for newcomers. Also, it's a good way to save money by borrowing CDs, DVDs, new best-sellers, and other resources that take cash out of your pocket.

BUILDING THAT FIRST BUDGET

This is the second time we've covered budgets in this book (the first was in Chapter 9), but it's worth a second treatment here. Living alone for the first time, when it comes to money, is full of experimentation, trial and error. You'll find that your wallet is empty more times than you'd like.

That's why it's so important to track what you're spending and then develop a spending structure with limits and allowances for the long term.

That's what a budget is.

You can definitely tell yourself on the first day you move in how much you're going to spend for lunch, furniture, gas, movies, and other things you will spend money on. It's good to get in the habit of doing that right at the start. But the second important part of budgeting involves tracking— not only to find out where your wallet is leaking, but also to prepare for future spending and savings you might accomplish with a few tweaks.

For a sample budget you can use to build your own budget, go to Chapter 9.

MANAGING COLLEGE DEBT

The average undergraduate student borrower graduates with nearly $19,000 of college debt, at least 50 percent more than a decade ago. If you attend graduate school, that level of debt can easily triple or quadruple.

There's an easy reason for this. The American Association of Colleges and Universities notes that over the last ten years, the average tuition at four-year public colleges has risen 51 percent, at private four-year schools 36 percent, and 26 percent at two-year schools. Wherever you went to school, you're probably facing some form of debt, either in student loans or credit cards.

That's why one of the kindest things you can do for yourself after graduation (heck, maybe ask your parents to give this to you as a graduation present!) is a first-time visit to a financial planner and tax adviser. This way, you'll be forced to lay all your money issues on the table at one time. You'll also get another set of eyeballs on future expenses so you can budget properly.

Questions you might want to ask a financial expert, such as a CERTIFIED FINANCIAL PLANNER™ practitioner:

1. **Which debt should I tackle first based on my future income?** Student debt has certain tax advantages, so this actually may not be the first line of attack. Most advisers will tell you to wrestle down credit card debt first.
2. **How should I save for a car?** The first question is, do I really need a car? Wheels are great, but unless you can pay cash for a reliable used vehicle (something of an oxymoron in itself), you're just piling on more debt and expense.
3. **How much can I spend on an apartment?** Living alone may not be an option. Part of the reason so many young people return home to live is that they can keep their living expenses at a cut-rate level. If this is a good option for you and your parents are agreeable, consider it for a fixed period of time and put every dime you save in the bank.
4. **What's the best way to sock away an emergency fund?** If you give up three lattes a week, that's $7 bucks. Even if you have a change jar on your bureau that you empty and take to the bank each month for deposit, that's better than doing nothing. Tell yourself that every penny saved —thanks to compounding—will be

much more significant later. And don't listen to anyone who tells you socking away small amounts is silly.

5. **How do I save for retirement and pay off my debt?** You might as well learn this balancing act now because you'll be living it all your life. The point is that you have to start doing both from the start, even if it means putting the absolute minimum away for retirement in an IRA or 401(k). Again, even a pittance saved in retirement at 22 has the chance of growing exponentially for 40 years without any attention to it at all. Again, this is why it's wise to get help with this process, because you might find sources of money to save and pay off debt that you never knew you had.

CLEANING UP YOUR CREDIT

If you were careless with credit cards, car loans, or any other debt in your life up until now, you are going to feel the burden of late payments or overly high balances the moment you strike out on your own. Credit scores and credit reports are pored over by employers, landlords, car dealerships, banks, and even adoption agencies. Since you've dedicated yourself to saving and investing, you're going to have to dedicate yourself to cleaning up your credit as well.

Here are some steps:

Take responsibility and fix it yourself with the right advice. So-called credit-repair scams and companies are everywhere. Even consumer credit counseling can occasionally pay your bills late, and you don't want that. You see them advertised on late-night TV all the time—they pay for those commercials with the money they're making off of you. The smart thing to do is to talk to a trained, licensed financial adviser— such as a CFP® professional—about the best way to tackle your total debt—credit cards, auto loans, student loans, and other liens—so you have a strategic plan of attack. There is nothing more paralyzing than looking at a single huge debt figure with no idea of what to tackle first. Get help first, set a plan, and then write the checks yourself. Don't let anyone do it for you. This, actually, is a critical part of your recovery.

Do an annual credit check. We've mentioned this earlier, but you have the right to get each of your credit reports (TransUnion, Experian, and Equifax) for free once a year. Get in the habit of scheduling receipt of those reports at staggered times (example: TransUnion in January, Experian in May, Equifax in June) so you can see whether all your credit information is correct and it hasn't picked up any inaccuracies during the year. Make this a lifetime habit, even when your credit rating is recovered.

The three companies have set up a central Web site, a toll-free telephone number, and a mailing address through which you can order your free annual report. To order, go to www.annualcreditreport.com, call 1-877-322-8228, or complete the Annual Credit Report Request Form and mail it to: Annual Credit Report Request Service, P.O. Box 105281, Atlanta, GA 30348-5281. You can print the form from www.ftc.gov/credit. Do not contact the three nationwide credit reporting companies individually; just go to www.annualcreditreport.com or the number above. Again, don't order all three at the same time—do it in staggered form.

Go debit and save one real, lower-limit credit card for emergencies. Emergencies, as a refresher, are sudden car breakdowns in strange towns and last-minute plane tickets so you can visit a sick relative. They are not concert tickets, dinners out, or double-shot lattes. To enforce the reality that you are spending real money whenever you open your wallet, ask your bank for a debit card with a Visa or MasterCard link and tell the bank to limit the funds available on that card only to what you have in your checking account. Otherwise, those branded debit cards will act like regular, high-interest credit cards and you'll be back in trouble again. Why a branded card? Some retailers won't accept your plain-vanilla ATM card for purchases.

Set up an electronic payment link for your credit cards—and pay it every week. If you're constantly chipping away at a credit card balance instead of doing it only once a month, you're lowering the amount of the balance the credit card company uses to compute the interest they're charging you. Good for you, bad for them, which is fine. If you send them a payment every week electronically, you're saving a stamp and interest too.

If you need to renegotiate payment schedules, do it yourself. And by all means, take notes. Most creditors aren't super friendly when they hear you want to stretch out or lower your debt payments, but it's a lot cheaper for them to work with you than to have to chase after you later. Suck up whatever fear you have about doing this. Negotiate in a friendly and firm way, and don't hesitate to call a financial adviser before you do this. Be sure to ask them to put any new payment terms in writing and mail them to you on their stationery just in case someone messes up and doesn't record your new terms properly.

SHOULD YOU BUY OR LEASE A CAR?

Again, if you *really* need a car, you need to fully understand your options.

Leasing is attractive because down payments are low and monthly payments are significantly lower than outright purchase. But there are upfront costs such as acquisition charges, security deposits, and so on, and there may be potential back-end charges such as an early termination fee or "excessive wear and tear," the determination of which is up to the dealer and with which you may not agree.

And there's always that excess mileage charge waiting in the wings. You may feel confident that you won't exceed the mileage limit, but circumstances may change—and excess miles are very expensive.

Owning has its pros and cons too. Owning the car longer than the loan payments is usually a good financial—and psychological—deal. You also can put any resale profits toward buying a new car—with leasing, you're always making car payments, yet you never end up owning it.

On the other hand, the car you buy may depreciate in value far more than you anticipate, whereas the amount of depreciation is locked into a lease deal—the dealer takes the risk. You may end up owning the vehicle beyond the warranty, which could mean costly repairs you pay for— something you're not likely to do when leasing.

If you decide to buy instead of lease, you have another key decision to make: should you buy a new car or a used one? Many experts say the best deal is to buy a car that's one or two years old. A brand-new car usually loses the largest percentage of its value in the first two years. Right now, the used-car market is overstocked, which means better deals. A trade-off, of course, is that the first years of the warranty are already gone when you buy used.

Whether new or used, should you pay cash or finance? Few people can afford to buy a brand new car with cash. But often, the more cash you can put down, the better. An all-cash deal, for example, may allow you to negotiate a better price, and a larger down payment means you end up paying less in finance charges. On the other hand, with interest rates so low—some deals offer 0 percent financing—it might pay to finance if you can invest the cash you don't pay toward the car payments at a higher-earning return than what you're paying in finance charges.

Clearly, the decision whether to buy or lease a particular vehicle can mean hundreds and often thousands of dollars in potential savings if you take the time to run the numbers before jumping into your dream car.

DON'T IGNORE YOUR FIRST EMPLOYER'S RETIREMENT OPTIONS

We've already talked about the importance of starting saving early, even if it's only a few bucks a week. But your retirement options are maximized by finding an employer willing to match your retirement savings. Obviously, go where your dream job is, but don't forget to check whether your future employer provides a good range of retirement choices in their 401(k) plans and matching and if they have any other savings or stock options that you can take advantage of. Jobs are not just about doing what you want to do—the best employers provide the best for their employees.

One more thing—you may be tempted to drain your retirement savings to purchase a house at some point, but remember, you're going to have to pay it back, and you'll lose the tax-free appreciation of those dollars while you're doing so. If you can, find another way to take care of that down payment.

LONGER-RANGE PLANNING FOR SINGLES

Yes, even with all your new money pressures, you still have to plan for the unexpected financial considerations if you get sick or die.

Depressing, yes, but necessary. Ask yourself the question—do you really want to saddle your relatives with excess medical debt or caregiving if something happens to you? It's a tough reality to accept when you're 22, but it happens. Some ideas:

Write a will, living will, and health directive. Maybe all you own is a futon and a stereo right now, but down the line, you might have real assets that should go to people you care about if you die—not to the state. Even if it's done on a reputable software program, you need a simple will that tells people where you want your money and stuff to go. Put it in a safe place and make sure one trusted individual knows where it is.

What's a living will and how does it differ from a health directive? A living will is a document that says you want certain things to happen if you are incapacitated by an irreversible health condition. You might back it up with a videotape of yourself reading it, which makes it tough to dispute in a court of law. Do you want to be kept on life support if doctors decide you're never really going to get better? This is the stuff you need to decide and write down, no matter how old you are. A health directive is a supplement to a living will that gives detailed instructions for a family member you've given health-care power of attorney to carry out specific medical instructions if you're incapacitated but not in an irreversible condition.

Insurance choices. If you don't have dependents, you probably don't need life insurance. If you want to leave assets to someone, focus on retirement savings instead, and make sure you have beneficiaries listed correctly on every investment you have. If you're worried about family members paying for your burial, put money in a cash account your executor can get to easily. If you are planning to become a parent later, go for term insurance which buys more than a whole or variable life policy and you can lock in your rates for decades if you're under 40. We'll go into more detail on all insurance issues in Part 9.

If you do become a single parent. Set up appropriate financial vehicles—such as particular trusts—to direct and safeguard your assets if you die before your kids reach adulthood. If you have a lot of assets, it makes sense to talk to a CFP practitioner and a tax adviser to make sure the solution you choose works smoothly and doesn't eat up your estate in excess taxes and penalties. You will also need to designate a legal guardian for your children if you die suddenly. We'll go into this more in Chapter 24.

Don't forget your pets. If you adore your dog, cat, or ferret, you need to think about them if you die or become incapacitated. You need to make legal arrangements for them too—some people make provisions for their financial and living support in their living trust. If you don't want to be that formal, put your exact wishes in writing and keep it with your will so nobody can fight over your pet later.

Business power of attorney. If you're a business owner, you may want to set out steps for the continued operation of the business if you are incapacitated or die. The person you designate business power of attorney will have the legal authority only over your business and its operation, not your personal assets or other financial issues outside the business.

Long-term care insurance. This is an important issue only if you're in your mid-50s or older, and we'll discuss it in more detail in Chapter 35.

Critical illness insurance. Sometimes, people choose this insurance over a traditional life policy, but definitely get some advice here. Critical illness insurance pays a lump sum in cash if the holder survives more than 30 days after the diagnosis of specific illnesses, and the amount is paid to you or your trustee in tax-free cash that can be spent for any purpose. It's no substitute for health insurance and it is more expensive than traditional life policies.

Most individuals will change jobs and employers a number of times before they retire. Chapter 15 focuses on moving from job to job and how best to handle your retirement assets when you do.

15 | *Moving from Job to Job*

A quarter century ago, very few people left the companies they started with, and nobody needed to discuss the "portability" of their pension assets. Companies were paternal, and attractive insurance benefits were an unshakable part of the corporate landscape.

At that time, pensions were known as defined benefit plans, corporate-funded accounts that determined a total benefit for an employee based on pay, years of employment, age at retirement, and other factors. Today, pressured by costs and shareholder demands on financial performance, many corporations have dropped such traditional plans in favor of so-called cash-balance plans that combine elements of traditional pensions and 401(k)s.

The responsibility for retirement now rests on the shoulders of employees who must actively decide how much to contribute into the new breed of defined contribution plans—primarily 401(k) plans at private employers and 403(b) plans offered within government. As things have turned out, most of us aren't equipped to do it.

MOST AMERICANS NEED HELP MANAGING THEIR RETIREMENT

An April 2006 survey by the Employee Benefit Research

Institute said that more than two-thirds of Americans say that they and their spouses have accumulated less than $50,000 in retirement savings. This modest level of saving is more prevalent among younger workers: 88 percent of workers ages 25–35 have less than $50,000 saved for retirement, compared with 52 percent of workers ages 55 and older. But it's still significant that half of workers over age 55 are similarly unprepared.

This movement toward more personal responsibility for our retirement savings has ironically made us less responsible about our retirement.

Asset allocation is critical if we expect to retire successfully, but few individuals understand asset allocation, much less practice it. For more information about asset allocation and how to practice it, see Chapter 41. And as employees move from job to job while investing in IRAs and other investments, it's not unusual for a person's finances to become unfocused and disorganized very quickly.

Workers need help organizing the mess. That's why so many workers could benefit with the aid of a financial analyst such as a CERTIFIED FINANCIAL PLANNER™ professional. What follows are retirement planning issues you'll face throughout your working life.

SHOULD YOU STAY IN YOUR OLD 401(K)?

Every year millions of workers who are either retiring or changing jobs struggle with a difficult decision regarding their old employer's defined-contribution (or 401(k)) retirement plan.

They know they don't want to cash in their account because of the income taxes, potential penalties, and loss of tax-deferred growth. Yet they're unsure whether to leave their money in the old plan, roll it into a new employer's defined-contribution plan if available, or roll it over into an individual retirement account. Each option has its benefits and disadvantages, depending on personal circumstances.

ADVANTAGES OF STAYING WITH AN OLD EMPLOYER'S PLAN

Roughly one in three workers leave their money behind in old employers' 401(k) plans, according to the Employee Benefit Research Institute.

Often it is because they don't want to fuss with the rollover paperwork or they're afraid of making a costly mistake.

Staying put in the old employer's plan or rolling it into a new employer's plan does offer some advantages. One is creditor protection. Federal law prohibits creditors from invading 401(k) accounts. The law does not protect IRAs, though some states shield IRAs from creditors. Up to $1 million in IRAs is protected under the new bankruptcy laws. This limit does not apply to money rolled over into the IRA from 401(k) or other retirement plans.

If you leave work due to termination or retirement, you usually can begin withdrawing from a 401(k) as early as age 55 without the 10 percent early withdrawal penalty. With rare exceptions, you have to wait to age 59½ for penalty-free withdrawals from an IRA.

Two-thirds of 401(k) plans offer stable-value mutual funds, which are less commonly offered in IRAs. These funds appeal to conservative investors because they tend to offer healthier yields than money markets but with the same stable principal.

Investment choices are more limited in a 401(k). Why might this be an advantage? Some studies show that investors who trade a lot hurt their personal returns more than those who don't trade as much. IRAs typically offer a much bigger universe of investment choices than 401(k) plans. Thus, investors tempted to trade or who are so overwhelmed by too many investment choices they do nothing, may actually be better off sticking with their 401(k). But the option to stay will depend in part on the quality of the investment options your particular 401(k) offers compared with an IRA.

You can borrow from a 401(k) if you're working for that employer, but you can't from an IRA. Financial planners generally discourage borrowing from a 401(k)—the borrowed money no longer grows tax-deferred, and there's a risk you won't be able to repay it in time, resulting in heavy taxes and penalties. Still, it is an option that often beats borrowing from a credit card.

If you want to leave your money in the 401(k) when you leave the company, make sure it stays there. For accounts valued from $1,000 to $5,000, the employer must automatically roll the money into a default IRA unless the employee wants the cash or requests a rollover.

ADVANTAGES OF ROLLING INTO AN IRA

For prudent investors, one of the biggest attractions of IRAs is their wider universe of investment choices, particularly if the choices are superior to those available in their old or new employer's plan. And you don't have to worry about future investment options changing, as they often do in employers' plans.

Workers who change jobs frequently may find themselves accumulating a lot of employer retirement accounts and may risk losing track of some accounts. It's easier to manage a single IRA than multiple employer plan accounts. Or you might consolidate into your current employer's plan, if you're allowed.

Another major benefit for the IRA option is the potential for significant tax savings. With an IRA, you can designate a younger nonspousal beneficiary and "stretch out" the minimum withdrawals over that person's lifetime. A 401(k) plan probably will insist that the account be immediately cashed out if the heir is not a spouse, resulting in a much larger tax bite and loss of further tax deferral. With a rollover IRA, you may also be in a position to convert to a Roth IRA if that conversion makes financial sense for you.

In Part 5, we'll examine leaving the workplace altogether and starting a business of your own.

Part V

Planning a
Small Business

How a Planner Can Help You Start a Business

Scott Kahan, CFP®

Many of us fantasize about telling The Man what he can do with his job. But making fantasies come true takes careful planning, particularly when you're thinking about becoming self-employed.

"There are too many people who don't get past the fantasy stage when they think about quitting their jobs to go into business for themselves," notes Scott Kahan, a New York-based CERTIFIED FINANCIAL PLANNER™ professional. "The fact is that when you go into business for yourself, your entire financial life changes."

How so? Kahan points out that personal cash flow—the availability of money to pay living expenses while the business is getting on its feet—is the first rude awakening most new business owners have. "The weekly paycheck isn't weekly anymore," says Kahan. "Depending on the type of business you're in, you need a cash reserve fund of three months to a full year of personal expenses. That's separate of any funding you need to operate the business."

A trip to a financial planner can help you address both personal and business issues before you leap. "A planner is a good sounding board for your concept and how much planning you've actually done to support yourself and the business." Kahan notes. Figuring out how your lifestyle will change is crucial, he explains.

"Retirement goals sometimes change when people start a business. If they're finally doing what they want to do, they may want to delay a traditional retirement, but they have to keep saving for it. Also, prospective business owners need to deal with the prospective expense of health and disability insurance before they start, and they also have to know that lenders tend to take a tougher line with self-employed people for personal as well as business loans," he notes.

"Starting a business means that you're going to need to constantly seek out information for your business and personal finances on a regular basis," says Kahan. "Most business owners don't have time to do it by themselves."

16 | *Making the Transition from Employee to Employer*

Many of us dream of quitting our jobs and starting a company that will make us happier and hopefully more money than we ever dreamed of. Most business owners don't become millionaires, but if they succeed, they're usually more satisfied with their work.

According to the National Federation of Independent Business, small business creates 80 percent of all new jobs in America. Making a new company a success requires preparation.

The first decision of creating a business pertains directly to your character. Do you have the right material to start and sustain a company? Take a minute to complete the following worksheet.

PICKING A BUSINESS STRUCTURE
Small-business owners have more factors and choices to consider than they once did when choosing the best

WORKSHEET: Are You Ready to be in Business?

Here's a questionnaire to determine whether you've got the right stuff for the job of being a business operator:

Question	Yes	No
1. Are you an organizer? A self-starter?	___	___
2. Can you tolerate a variety of personalities?	___	___
3. Can you make important decisions quickly?	___	___
4. Is your health in good shape?	___	___
5. Do you understand business finance?	___	___
6. Can you work 10–12 hour days with no weekends (Particularly in the start-up phase, many business owners seldom see a traditional eight-hour day. Some business owners regularly work 60–80 hour weeks.)	___	___
7. Have you talked with your family?	___	___
8. Do you have a business plan?	___	___
9. Will you have to borrow money?	___	___
10. Do you really believe in your ideas?	___	___
11. Have you ever hired anyone before?	___	___
12. Have you ever talked to anyone in this industry before?	___	___
13. Have you thought about where you'll locate the business?	___	___

If you've determined you're right for the job, the next step is to pick a business structure.

business structure for their company. Yet many owners casually pick off the shelf "what everybody else is doing" instead of what's best for them.

That's why a trip to a financial adviser—such as a CERTIFIED FINANCIAL PLANNER™ professional—might be a good second step in your fact-finding process. A trip to your tax adviser is definitely worthwhile too, not only for your personal finances, but to help you formulate the financial aspects of your business plan (see below).

Before choosing a business structure, such as a sole proprietorship, S or C corporation, partnership, LLP, or LLC, owners should reflect on their business in the context of their overall financial life and ask themselves a series of questions:

- Is the business going to be your primary source of personal wealth and daily cash flow, or is it a side business?
- Do you expect the business to pay for your retirement?
- Do you want it to provide other financial benefits?
- Do you want to pass it on to family members or sell it to existing employees or outside buyers?

The answers to these questions figure importantly into the decision of business entity, along with other key factors such as what type of business it is, current tax laws, and regulations such as workers compensation. Here are four major issues to consider when choosing a business entity:

Asset protection. Buying liability insurance remains critical in providing asset protection for a business, but choosing the right business structure is becoming increasingly important as the chances for lawsuits increase and the cost of liability insurance climbs. It's also important if you're starting a business that could amass substantial debt.

If the risk of lawsuits and creditors is a major concern for you, you'll likely want to incorporate using a business entity such as a C or S corporation, or form a limited liability partnership or limited liability company. These structures generally shield your personal assets from business creditors, unlike a sole proprietorship or general partnership (where even your personal assets are vulnerable to claims against your partner). Or vice versa: depending on state law, some business entities may shield your business assets from claims by your personal creditors.

LLCs have become especially popular in recent years because they protect personal assets from business creditors. But some planners caution that LLCs may not shield the personal property of a single LLC owner. In fact, some states don't allow single-member LLCs. In such cases, an S corporation might be a better choice.

Income taxes. From a federal income-tax perspective, sole proprietorships, partnerships, and LLCs are about the same—all are "pass-through" entities in which all taxable income is passed directly through to the owner(s) and taxed on their individual tax returns.

An S corporation is also a pass-through entity, but the owner can set a relatively low salary (how low is a "gray area") and take out the rest of the profits as distributions. There is no FICA tax on these distributions, though they are taxed at the owner's ordinary tax rates. Minimizing salary in favor of distributions often works best, however, if the owner invests what he or she would have paid in FICA taxes. On the other hand, maximizing distributions may reduce what you are allowed to contribute to a retirement plan.

A C corporation is taxed on the corporate level first, and issued dividends are taxed at the shareholder's level, though generally at a maximum of 15 percent. Despite the double taxation, planners say a C corporation can still be a good tax choice particularly where profits are less than $75,000. That's because they are taxed at rates lower than the top individual rates. But to work most effectively, the business needs to have some discretionary cash flow, say planners.

And don't overlook the potential impact of state taxes on your entity choice. The impact can be different from that of federal taxes.

Fringe benefits. Recent tax laws have reduced the advantages of incorporating and taking tax deductions for fringe benefits and charitable giving. In particular, the 100 percent deduction for health insurance premiums now allowed to LLCs and S corporations has undermined the fringe-benefit role of C corporations. Still, fringe benefits remain a factor to consider when choosing a structure, especially if you want a cafeteria plan.

Estate planning. Certain business structures are more ideal than others for owners wanting to pass the business on to heirs. A C corporation, for example, can pass on shares of stock with preferential treatment, whereas an S corporation can't. LLCs and limited partnerships also have estate planning advantages.

WHY A BUSINESS PLAN IS NECESSARY

A business plan is a road map not only for you, but also for potential lenders who won't give you the time of day otherwise. Very few business owners can finance a business start-up completely out of their pockets.

A business plan may seem like a lot of bother when you are absolutely, positively sure that your business concept will work. But producing one will allow you to really think through the idea, structure, and money resources for what you plan to do.

Putting everything on paper eliminates the dream aspect of going into business—you are putting your dreams in black and white.

A business plan should cover the following:

Executive summary. This kicks off the plan, but you should write it after you've had the chance to create the rest of the document (see below). An executive summary should be no longer than one page and capsulize the business, its products and services, risks, opportunities, target strategies, competition, finances, and finally, your projected return on investment.

Mission statement. A one- or two-sentence statement that describes the culture of your business and its goals.

Business concept. Explains the business that you want to finance and the technology, concept, or strategy on which it is based.

The team. Lists CEO and key management by name, experience, and very important, past successes.

Industry analysis. This section gives an informed overview of market share, leadership, players, market shifts, costs, pricing, and competition. The company wants to deliver the message that it has the leadership and ideas to overcome the obstacles.

Competition. Outlines the competitive challenges faced and how you plan to defeat them.

Goals and objectives. Essentially a three- to five-year plan. This section requires you to outline measurable objectives for market share, revenues, and profitability.

Day-to-day operations. Describes staffing plans, training, and other personnel-related issues. How will you use people? This section also talks about business support activities such as advertising and marketing.

Financing. This is the detailed section that explains what you have to invest and what you'll need from lenders. Most important, explain how long you expect to pay it back.

Appendix. Lenders want to see tax returns and any other third-party information that will help the lender know about the business.

WHAT TO DO WITH YOUR RETIREMENT FUNDS AT YOUR SOON-TO-BE-FORMER EMPLOYER

The time to start thinking about what you'll do with your retirement funds as well as your benefits (see Chapter 17) is before you leave your current employer. You don't have to advertise you'll be leaving the company, but you should really do your homework on the transferability of what you've earned and get some solid financial advice on what you'll do with the money once it's in your control. For more information about this, refer to Chapter 15.

WHAT IS COBRA?

We're not talking about a snake. COBRA is the Consolidated Omnibus Budget Reconciliation Act, a federal law passed in 1986 that amended the Employee Retirement Income Security Act (ERISA), the Internal Revenue Code, and the Public Health Service Act to provide continuation of group health coverage that otherwise would be terminated.

You might want to consider COBRA coverage on a temporary basis—

SPOTLIGHT

KEEPING RECORDS: Developing and maintaining business records is essential for new business owners. As entrepreneurs, they typically throw their heart and soul into marketing their products or services and running the business day-to-day. As for record-keeping, they sometimes put that at the end.

Little do they realize that keeping accurate business records can affect the company's profitability, its attractiveness to lenders, and in many cases, can be the difference between success and failure. Here are key steps to putting your records in order:

- **Buy financial tracking software.** Today, software manufacturers such as Quicken design financial tracking and tax software for the smallest of businesses. Even if you get help, make sure all your accounts, income, and daily expenditures are posted on the computer—it makes it easier to track what you're doing and categorize various transactions for tax time. **If you're a paper person...** At least separate accounts between business and personal. Not doing so makes it a nightmare to separate records at tax time.

- **Ask a tax professional to help you set up your record-keeping system.** If you are planning to work with a tax professional annually—and if you're in business, it's generally a good idea—take the time to set up your record-keeping for tax purposes correctly as you start the business. You won't develop as many bad habits that need to be corrected later.

- **Do a P&L.** A profit-and-loss statement should be done at least every quarter, and even monthly if you own a cyclical business such as a restaurant. Keeping a close eye on the numbers can help you spot problems before they loom so large as to endanger the business.

- **Track meetings and registrations.** New businesses typically require a host of documentation, including registering the business, applying for appropriate identification numbers, tax records, and so on. Incorporated businesses need

Continued on page 152

SPOTLIGHT **Continued from page 151**

organizational meeting records, articles of incorporation, annual shareholder meeting records, board of director minutes, and dozens of other records. Failure to meet necessary requirements can result in fines or other liabilities. For instance, if an Internal Revenue Service (IRS) field auditor finds a lack of documentation for actions taken by the corporate officers, the IRS may challenge certain business deductions.

Keeping all these records can be a headache for companies, but the headache is minor compared with the pain of a business that performs poorly or even goes bankrupt. Talk with your CERTIFIED FINANCIAL PLANNER™ professional about establishing a good record-keeping system. Some planners even provide corporate record services including generating records, minutes, and notes.

---

it tends to be very expensive—when you start your business. But you might be better off immediately checking independent insurance options. Consult a financial planner for these and other benefit details, which we'll cover in more detail in the next chapter.

GET DISABILITY COVERAGE BEFORE YOU LEAVE YOUR EMPLOYER

This is a really crucial step because disability coverage you buy is based on a percentage of current income. In the first few years of a business, you might not match your current salary, so you wouldn't be able to buy as much coverage as an independent. Get that coverage in place now.

You should be able to specify the level of benefits you receive, up to 60 percent or 80 percent of your income from work. (Insurers won't cover 100 percent of income, because they want you to be motivated to return to work after a disability.) Generally, the higher your benefit level, the greater your premiums.

KEEPING YOUR RETIREMENT PICTURE ON TRACK WHEN OTHER NEEDS ARISE

This might be one of the most important resolutions you'll make when going into business, and it will also be one of the toughest to keep. Talk to your tax and financial adviser(s) about retirement issues before you quit. You will be very tempted to use money you would otherwise place in your retirement accounts to fund your business.

Don't do it.

Make an annual promise to fund your retirement and do it with the best advice you have available.

In the next chapter, we'll go into more detail about buying insurance and planning your retirement strategy as part of your business.

17 | *Buying Insurance and Planning for Retirement on Your Own*

It's tough enough starting a business without having to be your own benefits counselor. You don't have to do it alone. Before you start a company, it's best to meet with a financial and tax adviser to set up your own benefits plan and a retirement strategy you won't be tempted to abandon if times get tough.

If there is any consolation about buying your own benefits, it's probably that the benefits you left behind at your previous employer were costing you more each year. Even though your coverage will likely be 100 percent deductible come tax time, the sticker shock of insuring yourself is a constant in business.

As we mentioned in Chapter 16, the best time to go shopping for benefits is before you leave your current employer. Why? You can get a great deal of detail on your current coverage, match it to current needs, and set a baseline for what you'll need to buy.

DO AN OVERALL INSURANCE CHECKUP BEFORE YOU START YOUR BUSINESS

Take a holistic approach to your benefits picture—you're not just insuring your business-related needs. You need to take a new approach to insuring your life. In the 21st century, Americans have learned that the world is a riskier place and self-employed individuals need to make sure they have the right health, property, disability and life insurance.

Here are points to consider in that process:

Medical deductibles and limits. Property can be replaced. Lives can't. In a health emergency, you or your family might need to go to an emergency room. Does your current coverage provide for such out-of-network care? If not, how will you pay for it? You might want to consider a health savings account (HSA)-linked insurance policy that will keep premiums relatively low for catastrophic coverage while allowing you to save money tax-free to cover the high deductible that typically accompanies that coverage.

Prescription coverage. See what options your health coverage provides you for prescription discounts and prescription-by-mail availability so you can have uninterrupted access to important medications wherever you are.

Homeowner's inventory. If you've been routinely paying your annual premiums without checking coverage for collectibles, home office equipment, or additional furniture or assets when you've renovated your home, start making a list of those changes and review them with your agent. Also, take up-to-date photographs of all major belongings in your home and keep those photos in a safe place.

Home replacement coverage. Go to several providers to estimate how much you would get for maximum replacement coverage in your area. With so many homeowners so heavily mortgaged, this coverage is critical.

Water damage and earthquake insurance options. If you live in a flood plain or an earthquake zone, chances are you probably already know you do, since that disclosure may be a legal requirement. But review the need for this coverage with your agent. Particularly after Hurricane Katrina and the damage it did in the Gulf states, many insurers started cutting back on the benefits for particular risks.

Disability coverage. Disability insurance takes care of lost income if you are sick or injured. This is nonnegotiable—if you're self-employed, you need it. And as we've mentioned, you need to buy that coverage while you are still employed at your current salary to maximize the amount of coverage you can buy. You'll almost certainly qualify for less coverage in the first years of your business unless your documented salary is much higher once you're working for yourself.

Hurricane and windstorm coverage. This coverage varies by state and sometimes by individual county. States including Alabama, Florida, Louisiana, Mississippi, North Carolina, South Carolina, and Texas offer windstorm coverage pools for people who can't get private insurance through their agents. Residents of some coastal counties in Georgia and New York can get wind and hail coverage through FAIR (Fair Access to Insurance Requirement) plans, which are high-risk pools run by insurance companies. Your insurance agent or state insurance department will have more details. Even if you work in a spare bedroom, your home is your office, and you need to make sure it is insured properly for the area it's in.

Auto insurance. If you are using your personal vehicle to serve your business, it is worth going back to your agent to discuss whether your coverage is adequate. A truck that got you to your old job needs a particular type of insurance; a truck that now carries merchandise or tools may need a review for theft, liability coverage, and other issues to protect both you and your business. Also, while it's not precisely an insurance issue, start keeping good mileage and expense records for that vehicle to properly track its operation for tax purposes.

Business interruption insurance. A good business interruption policy can cover costs up to 12 months, as long as there is proper documentation. If you don't have this coverage, think about whether it might be right for you in a crisis. Structure your policy for the best coverage possible, and have all pertinent income documents (including your most recent IRS filing) in a file you've created with all your emergency documents.

Property coverage for the business. Home-based businesses that require little more than a computer to run may be adequately insured on the business owner's homeowner's policy. Check the policy limits with your agent; many policies do not cover software and may exclude computers used for business purposes. But if you are running a legal business on your property that involves construction, manufacturing, or some other mechanical support, you definitely need to call your agent to make sure you're properly insured for that. Obviously, if you are working at an offsite business address, you need to check with a professional to make sure you have the right coverage as well.

Life coverage. Talk to a number of agents about life insurance coverage that will protect your spouse and children with enough money to help them continue their lifestyle and their educational goals. That includes money for ongoing expenses, mortgage payments, and tuition. Your spouse should also consider similar coverage, particularly if he or she is working. Even if he or she is not working, you may want to consider coverage. A recent poll (in FPA's *Journal of Financial Planning*, May 2005) estimates that replacing the services of a stay-at-home child-care provider can cost up to $137,000 annually. You might consider life insurance for the children, if only for burial coverage.

Create a disaster book. Create a disaster section in your binder or folder of information your loved ones would need in case of your death. The tragedy in New Orleans makes a single go-to guide a sensible item so family members can access insurance, home, and estate information in a crisis.

EIGHT THINGS TO KNOW ABOUT BUYING HEALTH COVERAGE

A Harvard Medical School study in 2005 pointed out that nearly half of all bankruptcies, involving 700,000 American households and more than 2 million people annually, are attributable to illness or medical debt.

In June 2005, the Commonwealth Fund, a nonprofit health-policy research group in New York, reported that people with high-cost, high-deductible health insurance are catching up to the uninsured when it comes to medical debt. That means that rising uninsured medical costs are not just for low-income Americans anymore. They attack so-called "insured" Americans.

As the population ages and there is no move toward a lower-cost national health insurance solution, consumers and business owners need to be aware of ways to control medical costs—preferably before they get sick. Smart consumers understand they will have to become the purchasing agent for their own health-care.

Here are some ideas on how to mitigate your insurance costs and what you'll pay out of pocket as time goes on:

- **Deal with your weight.** While dealing first with the numbers on your bathroom scale will have immediate health benefits, it will also make your health insurance options and potential out-of-pocket costs more affordable over time. A recent Stanford University and Rand Corporation study reported that lifetime medical costs related to diabetes, heart disease, high cholesterol, hypertension, and stroke among the obese are $10,000 higher than among the nonobese. It added that lifetime medical costs could be reduced by $2,200 to $5,300 following a 10 percent reduction in body weight.

- **Grill your agent or HR person while you have the chance.** Whether you buy health insurance through an agent or your employer, insist that they explain exactly what you're getting for your premium, and where deductibles do and don't apply. That way, you'll have a baseline when you buy your own coverage. If you're purchasing your own insurance policy, compare the premium savings from a higher-deductible plan with your usage pattern of health services. What you save can often cover your high deductible.

- **Always discuss the potential cost of a diagnosis.** If your physician diagnoses a particular illness that requires tests, prescription drugs, a hospital stay, or ongoing therapy, be very blunt about what you'll be charged, from the doctor's bills to ongoing ancillary costs associated with treatment. Ask the doctor or his office manager to possibly negotiate a discounted fee for service. It's possible to get discounts through cash payments as well.

- **Ask for generics and samples.** Many physicians are willing to recommend a generic substitute or at least supply you with a few samples of the drug they're already prescribing. While doctors can't get away with passing sample drugs to all their patients, always ask. As long as they are prescribing the medication, samples with the proper dosage can provide cost savings to patients.

- **Politely question all physician recommendations.** If, in your research, you find that more than one drug or course of treatment may be effective in your situation, always ask the physician why they made their particular choice. Physicians, hospitals, and other players in the health-care system face pressure from suppliers to pick their product or brand, so if you're paying for the most expensive form of treatment, you need to know why it's the best choice.

- **Check local pricing resources.** In nonemergency situations, you should always compare prices on treatments. Check with local medical boards and state health officials to see if they have online databases on costs for various medical procedures. Also, if there is a support group for your condition, talk to members about what they paid locally for care.

- **Talk to a financial adviser about planning for long-term care.** If you or a loved one are diagnosed with a chronic illness, that's a financial issue that requires a plan. As tough as it may be to focus on money issues at a stressful time, make an appointment with a tax professional or a CERTIFIED FINANCIAL PLANNER™ professional to discuss affordability options that will safeguard your assets, including Medical Spending Accounts that can backstop out-of-pocket costs on high-deductible policies.

- **Begin negotiations before there's a problem.** The best time to speak with hospital bean counters isn't when you're behind on your payments. Once a diagnosis is made, either you or someone you designate as your agent needs to contact the hospital business office to check on payment schedules and possible discount plans if you are uninsured or fear your insurance may not cover a significant portion of costs. Any creditor appreciates a customer who's willing to come to the table first.

PLANNING FOR RETIREMENT

Many self-employed small-business owners with either a few employees and perhaps a partner, or no employees other than themselves, don't have a company retirement plan. They complain that the choices are too confusing, the plans too costly to set up and maintain, and too expensive to include employees.

But small-business owners have better options than they may realize, say financial planners, and the reality is that many cannot afford *not to* set up a retirement plan. While many assume they'll simply sell their business when it's time to retire and live off the proceeds, it's risky to project whether what they receive for the business will be sufficient. A well-funded retirement plan adds security.

Exactly which plan to choose depends on many factors, including whether you have employees and whether you want to help them with retirement, how long you have before your own retirement, what you currently have saved for retirement, and how much money you'll need to pay for the retirement you envision.

Here are several retirement plan choices for small-business owners.

Self-employed 401(k)s. These plans are available to self-employed individuals or business owners with no employees other than a spouse. They are typically sole proprietors, partnerships, corporations, and S corporations.

Check out how much salary you can defer to these plans in the current year. For example, in 2006, taxpayers could make tax-deductible 401(k) salary deferrals to the plan of up to $15,000 for that year, with taxpayers age 50 or over allowed an additional catch-up salary deferral contribution of $5,000 for that particular year. The plan also lets business owners make tax-deductible profit- sharing contributions of up to 25 percent of compensation, up to the annual maximum of $44,000 for the 2006 plan year.

Simplified employee pension (SEP). SEPs are set up as individual retirement accounts for each employee but allow contributions far larger than standard IRAs, and are easy and inexpensive to establish and maintain. Contribution percentage can vary each year, from 0 percent–25 percent of compensation, up to $42,000 per participant for the 2005 plan year and $44,000 for the 2006 plan year.

The major drawback of SEPs for some owners is that they must fund contributions for eligible employees at the same rate they fund their own accounts. Moreover, employer contributions are immediately vested. Generally, owners must include employees if they are at least age 21, have worked three of the preceding five years for the owner, and have earned at least $450 for the year (employers can make eligibility less strict).

SIMPLE IRAs. The SIMPLE IRA plan was designed to make it easier for small businesses to offer a tax-advantaged, company-sponsored retirement plan. SIMPLE plans are intended for businesses with 100 or fewer employees. SIMPLE plans are funded by employer contributions and can be funded by elective employee salary deferrals.

Eligible employees can elect to contribute up to 100 percent of compensation up to a maximum of $10,000 for the 2006 plan year through salary reduction. (The amount elected by the employee may be expressed as a percentage of compensation or as a specific dollar amount.)

Participants age 50 and older in 2006 may be able to make an additional annual $2,500 catch-up elective deferral contribution to their SIMPLE IRA.

Other plans. Business owners have additional options, such as profit-sharing and Keogh plans. Another consideration is defined-benefit plans, which would allow an owner who's late to the game saving for retirement to quickly stash away large amounts of money. A defined benefit plan can be expensive to set up for small businesses and you're actuarially committed to setting aside a certain amount regardless of profits. But less expensive versions, even for the self-employed, are surfacing.

In the next chapter, we'll look at tax planning for the new business owner.

18 | *Tax Planning for the New Business Owner*

In Chapter 16, we covered tax issues in our section on business structure. Consider carefully your choice of business entity, and refer to that discussion to be sure you've made an informed choice.

THE TAXES YOU PAY

As a business owner and employer—you essentially act as your own employer even if you're a sole proprietor—you are required to collect various state and federal taxes and submit them to the appropriate agencies. It's best to work with a CPA or other tax professional in knowing what taxes to pay and when. Some of these taxes include:

Income tax withholding. These are "pay-as-you-go" tax that must be withheld from each employee's wages based on the exemptions claimed on the withholding exemption certificate (Form W-4), marital status, and length of the payroll period:

- **Social Security (FICA) tax.** The Federal Insurance Contributions Act, or FICA, provides for Social Security and Medicare, the federal system of old age, survivors, disability, and hospital insurance. The old age, survivors, and disability insurance part is financed by the Social Security tax. The hospital insurance part is financed by the Medicare tax.

Four different reports must be filed with the IRS regarding payroll taxes (both FICA and income taxes) that you withhold from your employees' wages:

1. Quarterly return of taxes withheld on wages (Form 941)
2. Annual statement of taxes withheld on wages (Form W-2)
3. Reconciliation of quarterly returns of taxes withheld with annual statement of taxes withheld (Form W-3)
4. Annual Federal Unemployment Tax return (Form 940)

Also, employers who pay compensation of $600 or more to independent contractors must report the payments to the IRS by filing Form 1099MISC for Miscellaneous Income.

- **State payroll taxes.** Almost all states have payroll taxes of some kind that you must collect and remit to the appropriate agency. Most states have an unemployment tax that's paid entirely by the employer. The tax is figured as a percentage of your total payroll (up to a specified limit of annual wage per employee) and remitted at the end of each quarter. The actual percentage varies from state to state and by employer.
- **Personal income tax.** Sole proprietors or partners don't get a salary like an employee, so there's no withholding. Instead, they are required to pay estimated taxes quarterly on Form 1040. At the end of the year, soloists must file an individual tax return and compute tax liability on profits; partners have to report their share of the profits on a Schedule K-1.
- **Corporate income tax.** If a business is organized as a C corporation—the basic designation for a corporation—owners get paid a salary like other employees. All profits accrue to the corporation, not to the owner. At the end of the year, the business has to file a corporate return on a calendar- or fiscal-year basis.

Reporting income on a fiscal-year cycle is more convenient for most businesses, because they can end their tax year in any month they choose. A corporation whose income is primarily derived from the personal services of its shareholders must use a calendar year-end for tax purposes. In addition, most Subchapter S corporations are required to use calendar year-end.

- **Sales taxes.** While most service businesses are completely exempt from sales taxes, you should check with your state revenue office to make sure you are paying these taxes correctly.

MONEY-SAVING TAX STRATEGIES

The best way to save on taxes is to consult a qualified tax expert familiar with business and personal taxation in the state where you're headquartered.

Optimally, it makes sense to get tax advice on running a business from a CPA or other tax expert before you launch your business. There are very few universal laws of tax savings—find the ones unique to your business.

KEEPING AN EYE ON THE END GAME

Individuals can't work forever, so a plan for ending a business can be as important as a plan for starting one. Ending a business is another tax issue since estate taxes can be a wild card.

There are many tax strategies available to business owners depending on what they want to do with the business—shut it down, sell it, or pass it to future generations.

Most experts will tell you to plan a business with an exit strategy in mind. If you want to build it to a size that will make it an attractive sale target, that's something you have to work toward from day one. Not every small business has a plan to go public or a chance of a huge profit at sale, so talk to your tax adviser to figure out the best way to turn out the lights for good.

KEEPING THE FAMILY BUSINESS IN THE FAMILY

Passing on the family business faces many hurdles, from tax issues and owner reluctance to family conflicts and greed that can rival a

Shakespearean play. It's not surprising that two of three businesses that are passed on to one generation never make it to the next generation.

The key to making a successful transition is early, comprehensive succession planning. That's often easier said than done, since business owners tend to be caught up in the day-to-day activities of running the business and don't take the critical time to plan for their succession. Perhaps the following questions will start you thinking about the process.

Should I pass on the business? Perhaps you've always assumed that you would keep the family business in the family. That may be the right choice. Then again, there often are valid reasons why a family business should be sold to someone outside the family. Perhaps the next generation is not up to the task, or no one may be very interested in running the business. Maybe the future of the business isn't all that promising.

Can I afford to pass on the business? You may be looking to the sale of your business to fund your retirement. Keeping it in the family may not provide enough income to reach that goal.

Am I willing to pass on the business? Business owners—especially those who created or significantly built the business—often find it difficult to let go. Many maintain tight control up until death, leaving family successors ill-prepared. Key employees, customers, and suppliers may disappear at the first signs of difficulty. Involve your designated successor in the business. Give them experience, let them make mistakes. It will improve the company's chances of succeeding down the road when you're no longer involved.

Who should I pass the business on to? Again, you may have made the assumption that it would simply pass to your children. However, most business succession experts concur that passing on a business equally to two or more children can create major problems. Let's say you have three children. Do you pass the business on in three equal shares? If so, who's going to actually run the business? Sharing command seldom works. Someone has to be in authority and this is an issue that should be settled before you die.

The key here is to be fair, not equal. Perhaps one of the three children isn't involved in the business, and doesn't want to be, but feels he or she should share in the profits. That child might be compensated by life insurance or other family property.

Choose a successor who's the best person for the job. This may not necessarily be your spouse, eldest child, or personal favorite. They might even be outside the immediate family, such as a son- or daughter-in-law.

Am I worried about a family feud? One reason owners sometimes put off succession planning is their fear that it will start a family feud over how everyone is going to get their share and who will run the business. If this is a concern—and it may be a concern you don't even realize—it's better to face it sooner rather than later. You don't want the family trying to resolve the issue after your death—perhaps in court.

Succession experts recommend discussing the issue openly with your family. Let them know whom you've picked to run the business and how you plan to treat everyone fairly. Listen to their concerns, and make appropriate adjustments in your plans.

What estate tax issues will I face? You'll want to bring in professionals here, such as an estate planning attorney and accountant. You'll probably need an expert to make an independent valuation of the business. And a financial planner can help coordinate the work of the other professionals and be a valuable ear for bouncing off some of the nontax issues.

In the next part of the book, we'll be dealing with financial planning for the full range of family issues.

Part VI

In a Family Way

Making Plans for Every Stage of Family Life

Peggy Houser, CFP®

Getting married, having kids, going through a divorce, or death of a spouse. Each stage of family life has its own expensive realities. It makes sense to plan for the best in life as well as the worst, says Peggy Houser, a Denver-based, fee-only CERTIFIED FINANCIAL PLANNER™ professional.

While no family situation is exactly alike and planners may take different approaches to sorting through problems, Houser believes there is one central issue to preventing financial crises and making tough transitions throughout a lifetime easier—debt management.

"Debt is the number one issue I see crippling families," says Houser. "I tell everyone that their first financial goal is to have no other debt than a mortgage, and that means a mortgage without a home equity line. That means holding on to a car for as long as it runs and buying a used car for cash. It means saying "no" to some things. If a parent loses a job or a spouse and the child is in college, not having any revolving debt may be the difference between a short-term cash crunch and bankruptcy."

Hers is definitely a tough-love approach, but Houser believes the healthiest family finances come from strict spending rules and high-quality investments with low fees. She also believes that families should look critically at even the most stylish investments of the day, particularly 529 college savings plans. "I believe that you should have free control of every dollar you invest. Your best fund values may not be in a 529 plan. Definitely save for college, but there are ways to pick tax-efficient funds that might serve you as well or better."

Houser also believes that family financial planning means involving the family. "I would like to have every child taught the basics of money. I like every member of the family to have an allowance and jobs they have to do. And when it comes to family vacations and other special expenses, it should be a family decision," she adds.

19 | *Planning for Marriage or Partnership*

If everyone who explored the institution of marriage explored their feelings about money first, the divorce rate in this country might not be so high.

There's a very understandable reason money is so tough to talk about—it's the touchiest of all subjects. The ability to deal effectively with money is a reflection of so many things—personal discipline and goals, family background, and past mistakes. It's often easier to discuss the unpleasant moments in one's relationship history than money issues. It is always wise to consult a financial adviser such as a CERTIFIED FINANCIAL PLANNER™ professional to help couples plan their financial future once they have made full disclosure of money issues.

DISCUSS YOUR MONEY "PERSONALITIES"
Does one of you love to spend money and the other hoard it? Does one like to trade stocks daily and the

other never venture beyond a passbook savings account? A clash of money personalities can produce far more strain on a marriage than a simple lack of money. Nothing says you and your future partner have to have identical money personalities, but it is important you go into the marriage with your money eyes open. You may need to plan around your differences or similarities (two spenders, for example, may quickly bankrupt a marriage).

DISCUSS YOUR GOALS AND DREAMS

Money is often about achieving goals and dreams: children, running your own business, traveling, buying a home, going to college. Talk about those goals and dreams before you marry. They will have a lot to do with how you earn, manage, and invest your money.

REVIEW YOUR INDIVIDUAL FINANCIAL SITUATIONS

This may not be easy at first. People don't like to talk about money. On the other hand, it can be unsettling, for example, to take your marriage vows and then learn that your partner is deeply in debt. You won't be responsible for his or her pre-marriage debts, but liabilities could certainly crimp future financial plans, such as buying a home.

Discuss current earnings, potential inheritances, or anything else financial that may suggest strengths, weaknesses, or potential disputes.

SHARING CREDIT REPORTS

It's not as romantic as the ring exchange, but couples need to have that uncomfortable but critically important kitchen table conversation where they lay their cards on the table about money.

And they need to do it before they move in together or wed.

This conversation should not only feature financial records showing assets and liabilities, but it makes sense to display each other's annual credit reports from all three agencies—TransUnion, Equifax, and Experian. These reports are available once a year for free at www.annual creditreport.com.

We'll feature many of the questions you should ask each other at the end of this chapter, but here are the high points that should be discussed:

1. The assets each person brings to the relationship and how they'll be held after the couple weds or moves in together
2. The debt each person is bringing into the relationship and how that will be dealt with
3. When or if you plan to make major real estate or car purchases and how you plan to do that
4. When or if you want kids and how you'll afford it
5. Whether you should both create and sign a prenuptial agreement

The sharing of credit reports has another important benefit. If you haven't checked your credit report in awhile, you'll definitely be able to spot errors and other problems you should correct before you walk down the aisle.

CONSIDER PRENUPTIALS OR SECOND MARRIAGE ISSUES

Prenuptial agreements, also called premarital agreements, are contracts between people who intend to marry. They spell out who gets what if the relationship breaks up.

Who needs them? Well, that's not always clear, but generally, couples in which one or both partners have significant assets or a business to protect like to have things in writing before they wed. Sometimes, they're also for average folks who aren't rich but who have married before and learned the hard way that divorces cost a lot more than they originally thought.

Second marriages raise a host of financial issues, not the least of which involve estate planning. Divorced people with minor or adult children need to address how wealth will be passed down in the event of their deaths. Will all wealth go to the second spouse before it passes down to the kids? It's not only a matter of planning and documentation, it's also a disclosure and discussion issue for the family. More than a few second marriages have ended in death and divorce with disputes over assets—settle these issues with the help of a financial planner, estate attorney, or tax expert before you tie the knot.

Everyone should at least consider the possibility that they might need an exit plan from a marriage. It's scary to think about when love has blossomed and everything seems rosy, but it's necessary. Prenuptial agreements should be drafted by an attorney in your state of residence. You would also be wise to consult with a CFP practitioner or other financial planning professional before you get to the point of drafting an agreement.

Consider the prenup the more formal, pricier equivalent of the kitchen table conversation. You'll be forced to face all your money issues in a more public setting, which may be good or bad.

WORK OUT MONEY MANAGEMENT

Today's newlyweds are, on average, older, with two incomes. Determining how you're going to combine those resources can be touchy. Financial planners often recommend that a couple have "his," "hers," and "theirs" checking accounts. The joint account covers household bills, while his and hers can be earmarked for personal use, vacation funds, investments, etc. It's also often recommended that each partner have separate credit card accounts so that each can establish credit in their own names in the event of a future divorce or death. However, partners should be sure not to run up large debts with the cards.

Both you and your future spouse should have a good overview of the other's finances. A large amount of financial secrecy in a marriage is a trouble sign. You should also assign financial responsibilities in the marriage. For instance, it's best to designate one to be in charge of paying the bills, balancing the checkbook, budgeting, investment oversight and so on (including tracking those credit card charges). That way, things are less likely to slip through the cracks.

TITLE ASSETS

In the flush of the honeymoon and getting settled into a new relationship, it's easy to forget the little things such as changing the beneficiaries of your life insurance policies, retirement plan, and so on. You probably don't want your parents or your ex-spouse receiving the benefits instead of your new spouse.

How you title property also can be critical. Joint ownership may not always be appropriate, particularly if this is a second marriage. Consult with your CERTIFIED FINANCIAL PLANNER™ practitioner and an estate planning attorney.

Update or draft wills to reflect your new marital circumstances, as well as put into place a durable power of attorney (to handle the financial consequences of incapacity) and living wills (to handle decisions regarding medical treatment).

REVIEW INSURANCE

New life insurance or a larger policy may be in order since marriage typically creates financial dependency.

All this may sound unromantic, but reviewing your finances before you marry could be the best gift you can give yourselves on your wedding day.

WHAT BANKRUPTCY CAN MEAN TO A MARRIAGE

Bankruptcy is a tremendous blow to a household, but timing does have some relevance (refer to Chapter 8 for more information on bankruptcy). Generally, if your future spouse faces a bankruptcy filing, it is best to insist he or she have their bankruptcy judgment finalized before you walk down the aisle. If nothing else, it will give the nonfiling spouse a better idea of the state of the couple's future finances in advance of the nuptials. It is also important to get the advice of a CFP practitioner before the marriage so both of you can fully understand the impact a pre-marriage bankruptcy will have to your postmarriage finances.

After marriage and even after divorce, bankruptcy can have a devastating effect on the financially healthier partner. A bankruptcy can have a negative effect on a couple's credit for a full decade after a filing, which means that if you're borrowing jointly for a house or other major purchase, you'll generally pay a higher rate than borrowers with squeaky-clean credit reports.

Couples who divorce can also feel a hangover from the other spouse's debt. Generally, when a divorced spouse defaults on an obligation made during the marriage, a creditor may turn to the other spouse to pay the debt. That means that a bankruptcy court can undo what a divorce decree supposedly set in stone.

That's why debt—any debt and any amount—has to be aired fully between two partners with an eye toward managing it effectively during the marriage.

THE PREMARRIAGE FINANCIAL QUIZ

Need a script for your kitchen table conversation? Here's what you and your partner or fiancé(e) should cover:

Is there debt? And if so, how much? The first money conversation should take place at a table with both sides showing their savings, investments, and debt figures—all of them. Both should start the process of talking about how that debt should be paid off—by the person who accrued it, or by both potential spouses. Couples also need to decide how they will handle debt going forward—jointly or separately.

Are there investments? If so, how will they be handled once the couple is married or living together for a length of time? Will they be held in joint tenancy, and what will the process be to effect that? From a tax perspective, does it make sense to do anything specific with those assets before the wedding? And after the wedding—assuming debt is being dealt with—how will you maximize those investments?

Where will we live? Many couples live together before marriage and stay right where they are. But the question of where you live shouldn't pertain only to right now—couples need to discuss where they want to live two to five years from now, particularly if they're going to have a family. And that means they'll have to understand how to afford it—total house payments, including taxes and insurance, shouldn't exceed 25 percent of any couple's take-home pay.

How will we handle the money? Couples need to understand how they'll share accounts and pay bills. The most common option is to create

SPOTLIGHT

UNMARRIED AND SAME-SEX COUPLES

Marriage isn't easy, but it definitely makes transfer of assets easier when one spouse is incapacitated or dies. Life is much more complicated for heterosexual and same-sex partners who aren't married. For you, it's not enough to write down on a sheet of paper who gets what and hope that your families honor it.

First, get some financial advice. Then get a lawyer.

You'd also be well-advised to craft an agreement on how assets should be shared while you're living together and dispersed should your relationship end. Not doing so could mean the partner with greater financial resources could command the upper hand once you separate.

The number of unmarried couples in the United States jumped 72 percent from 1990 to 2000, to about 5.5 million U.S. households, according to the Census Bureau. Roughly one of nine of these households were unmarried same-sex partners.

If one of you dies, and particularly if you have children, that legal documentation will be even more important. Some of the options you might consider:

- **Domestic partnership agreement.** This spells out how a couple should handle the assets each person brought into the relationship and those acquired afterward.
- **Financial power of attorney.** This designates your partner as the person who will manage money on your behalf in any number of circumstances.
- **Health-care power of attorney/medical directive.** Specific language that designates your partner in charge of all health decisions based on specific language you designate.
- **Wills.** Unmarried partners must have a will that designates a partner as the immediate beneficiary of all assets, executor of the estate, and most importantly, custody of the children in the relationship if one partner dies.
- **Beneficiary forms.** These provide more exact information on who will get specific assets not mentioned in the will.

one joint account. Others work with three accounts—one joint and then one for each individual.

What about insurance? Life, health, home, and disability—all insurance that couples have separately needs to be reviewed and consolidated to make sure they have enough coverage for their new life.

What about estate issues? Marriages require wills and exact directives on who will get what—particularly when children from previous marriages are involved. No matter how young the couple, there should be consideration of health directives as well.

Is there a budget? Budgeting is a good exercise before the wedding because it sets specific goals for the big things—a house, kids, education, and other big-ticket items. If the couple has to pay for their own wedding, a budget can determine whether a more modest ceremony might be appropriate.

What about retirement? Retirement discussions go beyond money. Couples should decide how they want to live in retirement, whether they'll continue to work, and what will happen if one or both get sick. This is where a financial planner can help the most—on such distant goals.

What about tax status? It makes sense for couples to consider their tax status before they marry—a tax expert is the best adviser to tell you how to file after reviewing your finances.

Does there need to be a prenuptial agreement? At the end of prenuptial planning is an important decision—should there be a prenuptial agreement? Some couples believe that a prenup indicates they don't have faith in their relationship, but if one spouse has more debt than the other or runs a business, such an agreement may make sense if only to limit the liability of the other spouse. These days, prenups aren't just for rich people. They can set the ground rules for a much healthier financial future.

In the next chapter, we'll look at one of the most important financial planning issues you'll ever face—starting a family.

20 | *Planning for Kids*

Kids are a wonderful, expensive proposition—your parents probably told you that more than a few times. But the reality is that child costs are daunting whenever and however you have them, and you'll need to plan.

Today, many people are waiting longer to have children due to later marriage, career issues, and a host of other reasons. While that works well for many people, aspiring parents can find a late decision to start a family may produce financial hardships down the line. At the very least, sending junior off to college at a time when you originally hoped to retire can make life very interesting. Yet today, couples and singles also have to plan financially for fertility treatments and adoption. Finally, financial planning for special-needs children provides its own daunting challenges.

WHAT WILL YOUR KID COST?

The U.S. Department of Agriculture compiles an annual survey on what it costs to raise a child from birth through age 17. In 2006, child-rearing expense estimates ranged between $10,220 and $11,290 per year for a child in a two-child, married-couple family in the middle-income group.

That means each child will cost a total of between $173,740 to $191,930 just to get them to senior year. We're not even talking about college yet. But since you asked…

The College Board estimated that in 2005–2006, annual average tuition and fees were $5,491 at four-year public colleges and $21,235 at four-year private colleges. And for room and board, the cost was $6,636 at four-year public colleges and $7,791 at four-year private colleges.

So for tuition, fees, room, and board, that means, at *current levels*, you would be paying an average of $48,508 for four years of public college, and $116,104 at a private school.

It gets better. Fast-forward to 2024, when the College Board estimates that four-year public school number will be $129,845 and private school will be $314,674. We'll deal with college affordability in greater detail in Part 7.

So with that knowledge, how prepared do you want to be?

PLANNING FOR KIDS…STARTING AT THE VERY BEGINNING

Throughout this chapter, you'll be reading about ways to afford kids if you're having trouble conceiving or if your child has special needs. But the first stop is how much it actually costs to bring kids into the world. (Hint: We're not just talking about what the health insurance doesn't pay.)

While so many individuals focus on the cost of college and day-to-day affordability of kids as they grow up, they forget to factor in the cost of lost income for one or both parents during childbirth and the immediate aftermath.

It's also important to consider the cost of child care for infants if you are planning to go back to work because it's generally more expensive to find the best child care for infants than it is for older children. Think of the following suggestions as a way to gather funds for immediate, first-year baby expenses, not an education fund—that's separate.

Setting up a delivery cost fund. First, figure out how much your health plan will pay for the baby's delivery and immediate aftercare. If you're in a non-HMO plan, you're typically going to have to pick up 20 percent of the total bill yourself. If the history of the pregnancy suggests a risk of complications during delivery, you might want to see if you can save more. A sensible way to set this money aside is in a flexible spending account (FSA) or a health savings account (HSA) if you have access to both options at your employer or within your small business. A FSA is an account that companies offer workers so the workers can deposit funds to pay their out-of-pocket health and dependent care costs on a pretax basis. However, you have to make a good estimate on the funds you will use over the year because any funds left over will be lost at year-end. A HSA is technically a trust that lets you save pretax dollars for health costs without losing it at year-end. HSAs are often paired with high-deductible health insurance.

Create a baby contingency fund. Kids always cost more than you think they're going to. Put money aside to cover contingency spending during the first year.

Check your short-term disability coverage. Women need to see if their pregnancy is covered under employers' short-term disability coverage or if a separate policy may provide that coverage. Keep in mind that if you plan to secure this coverage, you should do so well before you are pregnant.

Do some serious budgeting before the baby is born. Even if you've never done budgeting before, now's the time to get serious about it since you'll be budgeting until the day your kid gets out of college. (See Chapter 9 for more basic information on budgeting.)

Get used to bargain shopping. As you read up on the hundreds of things babies need, start clipping coupons, borrowing hand-me-downs, and cut spending wherever you can. Stockpile what you're comfortable with and plan how and where you'll shop so you'll save not only money once the baby's born, but time as well.

PLANNING FOR ADOPTION

Adoption is an extraordinary experience—sometimes lengthy, sometimes harrowing, and extremely rewarding. It can also be a shockingly expensive decision that will have a huge effect on your future finances.

In some situations, you'll be paying the price of a four-year public college degree just to complete the adoption process.

Let's start by looking at those figures. The least expensive form of adoption comes from your local foster care system. Your cost could conceivably be zero, since states often subsidize these programs to place these children. Meanwhile, agency and private domestic adoptions can range from $5,000 to $40,000 or more, depending on agency and attorney fees, travel expenses, birth mother health and living expenses, state requirements, and many other factors. International adoptions are typically the most expensive due to the cost of travel and the wide variety of fees and requirements imposed by the country handling the process.

All parenthood comes at a price. But with the help of a financial adviser such as a CERTIFIED FINANCIAL PLANNER™ professional, you can create not only a strategy to afford the adoption process, but a plan to save for the child's education and your retirement. Here's a way to start:

Create or review your financial plan. A financial plan is a written set of goals, strategies, and a timeline for accomplishing those goals. For many individuals, it may be the first time they seriously consider their financial future in such black-and-white terms. But it starts with the basics—determining how much you really have in savings, debt, insurance, and investments. Your adviser can also help you understand how much the additional costs of adopting and raising a child will affect all those numbers. A financial plan is a living, breathing thing. It should be reviewed once a year.

Get rid of your high-interest debt. A major decision like having a child is a good reason to take a "clean slate" approach to debt. Before you can build a reserve fund, it's wisest to pay off your credit cards first.

Make sure you have a will. If you die without a will, you won't have a clear path of guardianship for your child, nor will your assets be properly directed to support that child. Any good adoption attorney will insist that you develop and file a will as part of the adoption process.

Check your insurance options. In today's health insurance environment, the addition of a child to a policy can bring tremendous additional cost—sometimes without the guarantee of the best coverage. Before you start the adoption process, check with your employer or your independent insurance provider to make sure you have the best coverage for what you can afford. Also look into medical savings accounts with your adviser if you decide to take a high-deductible policy to keep premiums low.

Know your tax advantages. Families adopting overseas can get some tax relief. Parents were entitled to a one-time tax credit of $10,630 in 2005 for adoption expenses. Though the credit can't be reduced by the alternative minimum tax, qualifying expenses include paperwork costs, court costs, attorney fees, and all travel expenses, including meals and lodging. There are income limits—the credit disappears for individuals with modified adjusted gross incomes of $159,860 and for couples, $199,450.

Ask what your employer can do for you. If you're working at a family-friendly company, it's often considerably easier to apply for leaves of absence or work schedules that make more sense when you've got a young child at home. Some companies may offer to reimburse some portion of their workers' adoption expenses. If you know of a company in your field that provides these benefits, it might make sense to start looking for a job there well in advance of the start of the adoption process.

Build your reserve fund. When a baby, toddler, or older child comes into the house, money flies out the door at a velocity most childless people have never seen. Children always cost money and sometimes unpredictably so, but it pays to build your savings before they arrive so you won't overuse your credit cards. Also, it's possible that a birth mother's health may take a turn during the pregnancy, so that's an expense that needs to be anticipated.

THE COST OF INFERTILITY

As people wait longer to have children, more individuals and couples are fighting the fertility dilemma. According to the National Survey of Family Growth by the Centers for Disease Control, infertility affects about 6.1 million women and their partners in the United States.

Most infertility cases—85 to 90 percent—are treated with conventional medical therapies such as medication or surgery, according to the

American Society of Reproductive Medicine (ASRM). While we hear so much about in vitro fertilization (IVF) and similar treatments, they only account for 3 percent of infertility treatment.

But for those who opt for this minority treatment, costs are high, and often out-of-pocket. According to the ASRM, the average cost of an IVF cycle (one treatment, essentially) is $12,400. For some individuals, this process requires multiple treatments, so it's best to discuss cost issues with physicians before the process starts.

According to the organization, the degree of services covered depends on where you live and the type of insurance plan you have. In 2006, 14 states currently have laws that require insurers to either cover or offer to cover some form of infertility diagnosis and treatment— Arkansas, California, Connecticut, Hawaii, Illinois, Maryland, Massachusetts, Montana, New Jersey, New York, Ohio, Rhode Island, Texas, and West Virginia. However, the laws are very different in their scope and what types of treatment are covered.

FINANCIAL ISSUES FOR SPECIAL-NEEDS KIDS

Parents of special-needs children not only have to live with the day-to-day fears and concerns about their sick or disabled child, but they have to live with an even scarier prospect—that child outliving them.

According to a MetLife survey, 60 percent of parents don't expect their child with special needs to be financially independent. Yet, 68 percent of them also said they hadn't written a will and 29 percent report they haven't done anything to plan for the child's future.

Here are several financial planning issues you may need to consider.

Overall planning. Designing a viable budget is critical because of the often extraordinary medical expenses. It also is vital that you manage your money and create financial strategies that balance your own needs with those of your child's. Saving for your own retirement, for example, should not be ignored.

Medical coverage. Try to have your health plan cover the child for as long as possible. Eventually, usually when the child turns 18, federal supplemental security income and Medicaid may cover most—though not all—medical expenses.

Life insurance. You may want life insurance benefits to help support your child after your death. However, keep two issues in mind. First, large amounts of life insurance could make your estate vulnerable to estate taxes, so a life insurance trust might be appropriate. Second, you'll want to be careful about naming the child as beneficiary if the child needs government assistance to meet daily living needs. Insurance benefits would probably make the child ineligible.

Guardianship. All families should name a guardian for their minor children in the event the parents die prematurely. However, a child with a disability probably will need a guardian for life (including a successive guardian should the original guardian not be able to carry out his or her duties). Even if the child is institutionalized, it's generally advisable to have a relative or friend legally able to act on their behalf.

Letter of intent. This document details your child's medical history and your wishes and expectations for the child's future. Experts consider this to be invaluable for caregivers once the child's parents die.

Government assistance. The two most common programs for such assistance are Medicaid and supplemental security income. However, unless you have very low income, a disabled child living at home probably won't be eligible for these programs until he or she turns 18. At that point, only the child's assets and income are counted toward eligibility.

Special-needs trust. Also called a supplemental needs trust, this is a way to provide extra income to a child receiving government assistance without making the child ineligible for assistance. Money that's put into the trust by family or friends and relatives can only be used to pay for extras not covered by the government, such as a vacation, dental care, special equipment, education, or a CD player. It cannot be used to pay for basics such as food, clothing, and shelter, unless they are not adequately provided by government assistance. There is no dollar limit to the amount that can be contributed or earned by the trust. Parents can be trustees.

A variation of this strategy is for a charitable organization to set up a single trust for the benefit of several disabled children.

Irrevocable living trust. A living trust can be set up for children who aren't receiving government assistance. Parents fund the trust while they're alive to reduce the value of their estate and minimize estate taxes so more money can go to the care of their child. Financial institutions can serve as trustee, as well as friends or a financial planner or attorney, but you'll want successive trustees so you can be sure the child is cared for throughout his or her lifetime.

Estate planning. A will is essential, because if you die without one, you won't have a plan in place to support your disabled child. Also, a failure to plan might disqualify the child for government assistance at a time when it becomes necessary. Some parents leave all their assets to a sibling of the child, with the understanding the sibling will use the money to benefit the disabled child. However, you can't legally require the sibling to do that, and the assets will then become vulnerable to the sibling's creditors or the sibling's spouse. Generally, a trust is considered a more secure option. Also, plan for where any assets are to go once the child dies.

Because of the complicated nature of special needs trusts, government benefits, and estate planning, you'll want to work closely with a knowledgeable attorney and your CERTIFIED FINANCIAL PLANNER™ professional.

PLANNING FOR SINGLE PARENTHOOD

The critical issue for a single parent is what will happen if he or she dies. However, there are other critical issues:

1. **Finding secure, affordable housing.** When you're the adult doing everything, it's not important to have the fanciest house or apartment on the block. It's important to have a safe home in a safe neighborhood.
2. **Insure your income.** You'll need to carry life insurance equal to five or six times your salary. And if you can buy disability insurance privately as well as through your employer, max out as much as you

can. Employer-paid disability insurance typically replaces 60–70 percent of your income and you may be able to pick up an individual policy that replaces another 20 percent of income, tax-free.

3. **Budgeting is key—and make sure you involve the kids.** Single parents are typically not made of money, and that means you need to talk to your kids seriously about money. It's very likely, for example, that your kid will need to work for his or her spending money as they get older. Don't be afraid to talk to them about that. They might develop money skills earlier as a result.

4. **Plan.** No single parent's circumstance is exactly like another. You'll need a will, health directives, and possibly a trust or other financial structure to protect your child's education and future if something happens to you. Sit down with a planner before you become pregnant or adopt.

In the next chapter, we'll discuss teaching your kids about money.

21 | *Teaching Kids About Money*

Crippling consumer debt and bankruptcy are now common in America, and that makes it all the more surprising that children don't get structured money-management training in elementary and high school. That means that parents have to give their children the bulk of their money education, which is not always easy if the parents are fighting financial demons of their own.

Parents might do well to bring up the issue of their kids' money education with a trusted financial advisor such as a CERTIFIED FINANCIAL PLANNER™ professional while the child is very young. Family money issues cover a lot of territory, and every individual seeking out that advice should ask about how they should educate their children in the good habits they're trying to learn. It's one more valuable aspect of the planner relationship.

Money values—both good and bad—are among the most important lessons parents pass on to their kids. The best money values shouldn't stop at self-reliance. They should help a child form his ideas about rewards and gratification and hopefully, generosity to others less fortunate.

The right age to start. Maybe with the words "I

want!"—preschool is not too early. Children learn by observation and mimic the habits of their parents. For example, if your child is watching you get cash from an ATM, that might be a good moment to explain how that money got there and how you have only so much inside and you have to be careful not to overspend.

Watch your child's behavior—see what he or she wants to buy. Start asking them how they plan to pay for things. This is your window on whether your money messages are getting through. "I want" and "I need" are always opportunities for you to teach. Some pretty serious money issues can come out of the mouths of babes. Listen for them.

As children become teens, they want more autonomy with their spending. You need to match that trust with accountability. If you deposit money in an account for them to spend on essentials and treats, talk about what you are willing to pay for in addition, and make those agreements ironclad. Kids will always come to you with their hand out, but they need to know where you'll say "no."

Don't be afraid to tell them how hard you had to work for that money that they're getting for free. This can be a bit delicate because most kids quickly label such discussion as a lecture, but your job is to explain that spending means choices throughout the family and provide realistic examples of why that is the case.

Negotiating an allowance and chore strategy. As early as kindergarten or first grade, your kid is going to have to start paying for things, even if it's one container of milk a day. You need to understand how much money your child will need for basic school expenses. Decide whether they need to earn an amount for extras—toys and candy, for instance—then stress why working for certain treats is important. Parents shouldn't make their kids feel that they have to do sweatshop labor for every dime they receive, but there needs to be an ongoing discussion about what the parent will always cover and what is fair for a child to earn.

Take a look in the mirror. Do you drive a bigger car than you can afford? Every time you go to the store, do you pull out a credit card to pay?

Do you and your spouse or partner fight openly about money at home? Your child hears all of this. Children learn all-important lessons by example—make sure the money messages you're sending are the right ones.

Buy a piggy bank. Young children need this tried-and-true symbol of saving. They need to know there's a place to put pocket change they don't spend, and they are free to tap it only to accomplish a goal that the both of you discuss. This isn't about buying stuff, it's about setting goals.

Have them open a savings account. If small-balance passbook accounts still exist at your bank, do the old-fashioned thing and go with your child to open one. Make sure they keep their bank book or monthly statements in a safe place, and make sure they deposit funds at least once a month to get in the habit. You might also consider mutual funds geared toward young investors. Morningstar.com ranks mutual funds in all categories, but the site can help you locate mutual funds with low opening fees as little as $100 and minimum deposits of $25 or more. They rank them for quality as well.

Handling money mistakes carefully. A child is going to make mistakes with money—they'll lose it, spend it on the wrong things, or possibly give it away to others. A child needs to be taught sense and caution with money, but not fear. A little self-reflection on how you were taught about money might come in handy here.

If money is an emotional subject in your house, it's going to be emotional for the child. There needs to be a balance of firmness and understanding in any discussion of a money error, but that's what it needs to be—a discussion.

Being open about your investments. Kids are sponges. They know if their parents have investments just by watching what's in the mail. Start talking about why you buy stocks, bonds, or mutual funds to help pay for their education. If your child asks you to buy a book or subscribe to a magazine or newspaper so they can learn more, don't think twice—just do it.

Telling kids about family money troubles. If you have a sudden reversal on the job or if the family suffers an investment loss that will affect spending at home, again, there's another balancing act. Kids need to know there's a need to economize without being terrified about it. Families need to have a sit-down meeting when family finances change, and kids need to know what they can do to help.

Employing kids in the family business. Bringing your kids into the family business at legal age accomplishes two worthwhile goals. First, the child learns something about the business that's been supporting his or her lifestyle (and possibly whether they want to enter the business full-time at a later date). Second, the IRS lets you take a deduction for their reasonable compensation, which reduces the amount of taxable business income that flows through to you.

There are other benefits as well. If you hire a child under 18, you may not have to pay Social Security, Medicare, or unemployment taxes.

The amount of that compensation must fit the task, however, or the IRS will get testy. Also, your business must comply with all child labor laws.

Talking to kids about credit. It's best if kids learn about the use of credit while you're all under the same roof—not when they're off to college. Try to cosign with them on a low-limit card that they can use for agreed-upon expenses, and make sure the bill comes to them every month. Talk about the pay date so you can make sure they're paying on time.

Talk about college early. Even if you plan to pay your child's entire tuition, you need to talk about the financial investment college represents long before they go. You can also talk about whether your child will have to pay any expenses on his own and how he'll earn them. The massive investment college represents is a great opportunity to discuss what the most important things in life really cost.

In Chapter 22, we're going to talk about the family finance issues involved in divorce.

22 | *Planning for Divorce*

At best, divorce is a time of distraction in one's life, when emotional and family concerns take center stage and financial issues often take a back seat. Yet divorce is one of the biggest triggers of bankruptcy in a world where bankruptcy has gotten a lot tougher to file. That means that financial planning is crucial when a marriage breaks up.

The best time to do that planning is before the divorce is final, not after.

Anyone filing for divorce should seek the help of financial and tax advisers as well as attorneys skilled in divorce, experts say, because the financial issues that get pushed to the background eventually can take a surprising and disastrous toll on the newly single ex-spouse and his or her children.

As the following chart shows, divorce rates have plenty to do with money, race, and age, according to data from the National Survey of Family Growth from the Department of Health and Human Services.

Whether a breakup is friendly or contentious, your

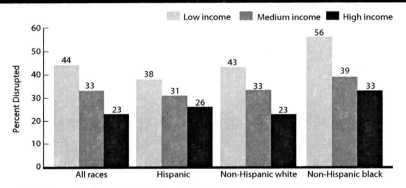

Figure 22.1: Probability that the First Marriage Breaks Up Within 10 Years by Race/Ethnicity and Median Family Income in the Community: United States, 1995

Source: National Survey of Family Growth, U.S. Department of Health and Human Services, 1995.

approach to divorce has to be strategic. This is often a tough adjustment for spouses who had previously lived a philosophy of supporting the other's decision-making at all times. In the friendliest cases, divorce is a collaborative event, but more often, it is not. It requires firmness and good advice from tax, legal, and financial experts, including CERTIFIED FINANCIAL PLANNER™ professionals.

Don't forget that divorce is a major cause of bankruptcy. Divorced people who file for bankruptcy genuinely failed to plan for all of their expenses and living costs before they made their final settlement.

UNDERSTANDING THE FINANCIAL TRAUMA OF DIVORCE

Women typically suffer the most serious financial consequences from divorce. They often earn less than their husbands, and they usually are the ones taking care of any children. Even if the husband provides full child support, often it is not enough.

Men, however, do not always escape the financial quicksand of divorce. Divorce creates two sets of expenses: two housing costs, two food bills, two utility bills, two phone bills. New expenses such as child support, child care, and new furniture and appliances add to the financial burden. Together, a dual-earning couple may have maintained a good standard of living. Apart, neither party may fare well.

Adding to the woes, one party may break promises in the divorce agreement, such as failing to help pay debts created jointly during marriage, or worse, running up credit card debts both parties are liable for. Tax consequences further complicate the process.

New rules, designed to make divorce more financially equitable, also have made it more challenging. Today, in most states, assets acquired during marriage are tossed into a common pot and then divided equally. Negotiation is fast, replacing litigation under this system, but it also means accountants, tax specialists, and property appraisers may need to be brought in.

Prenuptial agreements can minimize or avoid later financial conflicts. An inventory of assets every few years and establishment of each partner's contributions to those assets also can help smooth matters.

In the event of a divorce, the couple should consider bringing in a financial planning professional, in addition to hiring an attorney and other professional experts. The planner can help in two ways. First, they can help put together an equitable settlement by determining family assets and fair value, as well as current liabilities. Second, they can help estimate and plan for each partner's postdivorce income, tax consequences, cash flow, and retirement picture, which still need to be planned for.

START WITH A BUDGET

No matter how sophisticated you think you are about your finances, don't pass up the opportunity to do a basic financial budget for your new life as the divorce process begins. A CFP® professional can help you ask the basic questions that will help you understand what life will be like when you are living with a single job income stream or a temporary income stream provided by an ex-spouse. It's always an eye-opener. The Lilac Tree (www.thelilactree.org), an Evanston, Illinois-based not-for-profit organization for divorcing women, routinely stresses that the budgeting process is crucial, since women now outnumber men in filing for bankruptcy and their long-term earnings prospects are generally dimmer.

FIND EXPERIENCED DIVORCE ADVISERS

A good divorce attorney isn't necessarily a shark. The choice of attorneys—for men as well as women—should fit the challenges being faced on both sides. Good divorce attorneys definitely cost money, but they pay for themselves when talking with CPAs and financial planners in advocating for their clients. Some CFP® practitioners are also certified in divorce planning and can help your team with financial discovery, analysis, and long-term projections. Among other financial issues, they should understand qualified domestic relations orders— known as QDROs (pronounced "quad-rows") to ensure that pension assets will be shared fairly.

You might also want to consider mediation to work out various aspects of your settlement if things between you and your spouse are civil. Getting attorneys to work out such agreements is generally more expensive than sitting down at a table, working out the finer points, and then giving the agreement to your attorneys to review before you finalize it. Find an attorney or other adviser who is friendly toward the mediation solution first, then ask for suggestions on qualified mediators.

PROPERLY VALUE YOUR ASSETS

If you're getting the house, does it have a 20-year-old furnace and a roof that's about to cave in? A thorough inspection by a licensed inspector could help. If you're getting the family car, is it past warranty with a funny sound coming from under the hood? If your spouse runs a lucrative business that you've worked for or invested in, how do you know you're getting the right share?

Hiring a valuation expert may be necessary. Divorcing spouses need to make sure they have enough money to finance repairs and replacement of assets that they'll be paying for as a single person.

SNAPSHOT

SPOTLIGHT: SEVEN FINANCIAL MYTHS OF DIVORCE

Even though so many Americans divorce, most are misinformed about how breakups affect their money issues. Here are seven myths that many inexperienced couples face before they file:

1. **Everything is automatically split 50/50.** The standard in most, though not all states today, is "equitable distribution." What that means, however, varies from state to state and even judge to judge. Equitable does not mean "equal." Rather, how the couple's assets are divided up depends on numerous factors, including the length of the marriage, income of each party, age and health of each party, education, earning capacity, and so on. Assets each party brought to the marriage, or received separate from the marriage, such as gifts and inheritances, may or may not be included as part of the marital property.

2. **All assets are equal.** It's not as simple as "he gets the pension, she gets the house." When taxes, sales expenses, investment returns, and other factors are taken into account, all assets are not equal. A $100,000 home and $100,000 in a pension fund will not likely have the same value years from now, and the tax basis of each asset also could adversely affect the net value.

3. **Divorced women are better off financially than they once were.** According to one widely quoted study, women and children suffer an average 73 percent decline in their standard of living within one year, while men increase their standard by 42 percent. Typically, this is because women don't earn, on average, as much money as men, have more limited work experiences, are raising children, and so on. Even apparently fair divorce settlements result in driving many women into poverty within one to five years.

4. **Only divorce lawyers can work out the financial settlement.** Many attorneys are not well-qualified to determine the most equitable financial arrangements for each party. Increasingly, divorcing parties are bringing in financial specialists such as financial planners, either in the mediation process or in a judicial setting, to examine the financial data and work out a financial settlement that takes into account present and

Continued on page 200

Continued from page 199

future taxes, cash flow, inflation, investment returns, needs, and other factors. They project what the settlement will mean financially, not just now but years down the road. For example, who will pay for the children's college education years from now, and how? Or what effects will inflation have on the assets or alimony payments?

5. **The wife should get the house.** This may sound like a good deal for the wife, especially if she has custody of any children. But unless the divorce settlement or the wife's income is sufficient, she may find that she can't pay the mortgage, taxes, and maintenance on a single income. And if she sells the house, she could face a big capital-gains tax bite.

6. **My spouse will support me.** Headlines to the contrary, most divorce settlements today do not provide for any spousal support. If alimony is awarded, it typically goes to an older woman who's been married for some time and who has not worked outside of the home.

7. **My spouse will provide child support.** According to a 2001 U.S. Census Bureau study, approximately 6.9 million of the 7.9 million custodial parents with child support agreements or awards in 2002 were due payments from those awards. Among these parents who were due support in 2001, 73.9 percent received at least some payments directly from the noncustodial parent, a proportion unchanged since 1993. The average annual amount of child support received for these parents receiving at least some support was $4,300, and did not differ between mothers and fathers.

PLANNING PROPERLY FOR KIDS' WELFARE

In many states, college-age children have the right to demand financial support or college funding at the state level so their education isn't interrupted. While both parents should advocate in their kids' best interest, this isn't always the case. Be aware of your state's divorce laws with respect to secondary child support.

Get help documenting child support. Child support guidelines vary from state to state, but are generally set in the state where you and your children live, so become aware of those provisions. Also, if your state has a special program that allows a spouse to pay into a special account so child support is recorded every month, consider it. It's a good idea to enroll because it provides a paper trail and enforcement system for ensuring that kids get the money they need. Federal law requires all child support payments be made by wage assignment and health insurance by health insurance orders. Child support collection statistics reflect that only 20 percent of noncustodial parents pay their court-ordered child support monthly. That's why so many laws have been established to force compliance. Make sure you know them.

PROTECT YOURSELF FROM A TAX STANDPOINT

There are always special situations in a divorce that will determine whether a couple will need to file jointly or separately during the last year that the marriage exists. This is definitely worth discussion, since tax fraud can be a liability issue for the spouse who had no involvement or awareness of the fraud taking place.

There are many other tax issues. Regarding children, custodial parents who are responsible for the child's care more than half the year are entitled to head-of-household status that would ultimately lower their tax bills. However, the other spouse should also check to see whether they have tax advantages in this situation. Tax treatment of alimony, capital gains (from the sale of the family home), child support, pension division, and other issues need to be discussed with a tax professional.

DON'T OVERLOOK INSURANCE

Amid the emotional trauma of a divorce, and the battles over who gets the kids and what property, one important financial aspect of the breakup is often overlooked: insurance. The failure to incorporate insurance needs—health, life, disability, homeowner's, and so on—into the divorce process can have severe financial repercussions.

Health insurance. If you were covered through your spouse's plan, either at work or through an individual policy, you'll likely need to find new coverage. As part of the divorce settlement, you may be able to require your ex to continue coverage on you, but it's not likely. That leaves you with three choices.

Your first and probably best choice will be to get coverage through your own employer. If you don't have coverage through work, you probably will be able to continue coverage through your former spouse's plan for up to 36 months under the federal law COBRA. But you'll have to pay the full premiums and a small administrative fee. Another option is to buy an individual policy.

What about the children? Even if they live with you, they can qualify for coverage under your former spouse's plan until they are adults. You can make this happen through a qualified medical child support order (QMCSO), a court order that provides health benefit coverage for the child of the noncustodial parent under that parent's group health plan.

You may run into limits, however, if your spouse's plan is an HMO (health maintenance organization) and you move with your children out of the HMO's region. Then you may be restricted to emergency coverage only. Make sure you discuss all the possible causes of interruption of that coverage if you plan for your ex-spouse to cover your kids.

Life insurance. Spouses who will be paying maintenance or child support should carry adequate life insurance on themselves in order to secure court-ordered obligations. The key here is for the other spouse to make sure the insured doesn't change beneficiaries or simply drop the policy without notice (including those at the workplace).

One strategy is to ask the insurance company to send a duplicate notice of cancellation or beneficiary changes. The court also may order periodic proof from the insured that proper coverage is being maintained or that if the spouse drops the coverage, there will be penalties or an equivalent amount taken out of the deceased's estate. (This assumes there is enough in the estate to make up for the lost insurance benefits.) It is very important that your attorney advises you on how to structure this life insurance issue in your settlement so there are no tax headaches later.

You also will likely want to drop your ex-spouse as beneficiary of your own life policies, unless, of course, you're the one paying maintenance.

Even if you're receiving maintenance or child support, you may want to list your ex-spouse as beneficiary if he or she has to take on the financial obligation of raising the children should you die. Once you remarry, of course, you'll likely want to make your new spouse your beneficiary. On the other hand, if you don't have children and no one else depends on you financially, you may want to drop life insurance coverage now that you're on your own.

Disability insurance. Many divorce experts recommend that the person providing maintenance or child support payments have adequate disability coverage in order to continue payments in the event of a temporary or permanent disability. And the person taking care of the children also should have coverage, assuming he or she works. Review the policy to see whether you need to beef up the amount.

Homeowner's insurance. If you are not a "named insured" on your homeowner's policy, your personal possessions won't be covered once you divorce. And if you move out of the house before the divorce, generally, insurers will limit coverage of your personal possessions to only 10 percent of their covered value, even if you are a named insured.

Because there may be many complex insurance issues to review, consider consulting with your financial planner, who also may be able to help you with other financial issues of the divorce settlement.

ONCE THE DIVORCE IS OVER—WATCH THE SPENDING

Budgeting early in the process may cut down on the risk of overspending, but divorced spouses setting up new homes may not be able to resist. For some, spending makes them feel better, and this is one of the biggest reasons ex-spouses face financial disaster after divorce.

It's a wise idea for newly divorced individuals to work with a financial adviser to set up their initial budget. But it may be equally important for the person to set up a review visit at the one-year point after the divorce to get a fresh perspective on how their new single lifestyle has affected their finances.

In the next chapter, we'll look at another facet of family financial planning, caring for an aging relative.

23 | *Helping an Aging Relative*

Talking about an aging relative's finances needs to happen long before the elder is ill or incapacitated. In fact, the best situation is when the older relative raises the conversation first.

Recent natural disasters and national emergencies should remind us that planning makes serious emergencies more manageable. Nevertheless, many families don't discuss finances until a crisis occurs. An older relative may be unable to understand questions or express their wishes in detail. If there is no plan, family members grasp at responsibilities—or shirk them—without any idea of what the older relative would prefer.

What's critical to understand is that such talks go far beyond money. They are discussions about independence and basic preferences for the way an individual wants to live or die. And demographers believe that with the rising number of single Americans—those divorced or never married—these conversations will become increasingly complicated as they fall to children, nieces and nephews, younger friends, or designated representatives.

TALKING TO OLDER RELATIVES ABOUT THEIR FINANCES

If you are a younger relative wondering how to manage the conversation and get control of the situation, here are some suggestions:

Decide what's important to talk about first. Maybe this conversation isn't just about where the will or health-care power of attorney is. Maybe this conversation is about you noticing that a parent or loved one is moving slower, is more forgetful, is clearly looking like their health has taken a turn for the worse—and maybe that's why you want to know where the will is. Jumping into money issues first is usually a mistake. Deal with immediate health and lifestyle issues first.

Explain why you want to talk about finances. In some families, having a successful financial discussion means several attempts and some frustration. Don't let yourself become angry or frustrated—just keep starting the conversation until it catches on. It might make sense to say something like, "You've always been so independent, Mom. I just want you to give us the right instructions so we do exactly what you want."

Write down questions. When a parent or relative is unconscious or unresponsive, the younger relative is immediately in the driver's seat. That's why it's critical to make a list of questions for the elderly relative to answer in detail. The basics: where important papers are, how household expenses are paid, who doctors and specialists are, what medicines are being taken, and whether there's a will, an advanced directive, and a funeral plan (and money or insurance proceeds to pay for it). There may be dozens more questions beyond these based on your family's personal circumstances. But in creating this list, ask yourself: "What do I need to know if this person suddenly becomes sick or dies?"

Offer to get some advice. If you don't fully understand your relative's financial affairs, it might make sense for you both to talk to an attorney or a tax or financial adviser, including a CERTIFIED FINANCIAL PLANNER™ professional. A qualified adviser can offer specific suggestions on critical legal documents that should be in place and ways to make sure accounts to pay medical and household bills are accessible to the older person and the designated friend or relative who will hold the power of attorney.

Plan a caregiving strategy. You should discuss the relative's preferences and trigger points for various stages of heath care. An individual usually wants to stay in his or her home, but you should have an honest discussion about how much you can do at home as a caregiver and whether various services (home health aide, geriatric care manager, assisted living) should be introduced at various stages. Talking through what a parent will be able to live with at various health stages—and putting that information in writing—will save plenty of doubt and bitterness later.

Discuss liquidating the home. If an elderly relative becomes sick and irreversibly incapacitated, the equity in his or her home may come under consideration as a resource to pay uncovered medical or household maintenance. Since the home is both a major asset and an emotional focal point, it's best to get good advice and spell out specifically what the elderly relative wants done with his property and under what conditions.

Make sure everyone knows the plan. Once you settle on a strategy, make sure all family and friends understand the plan and their assignments.

PLANNING FOR HOME-BASED CARE

The decision to remain in the home after an accident or an illness is fairly universal. However, getting the right help for an elderly relative takes some planning and sometimes some trial and error. According to the American Association of Retired Persons, home-based health-care services may be provided by any of the following:

- **Home health agencies.** These are Medicare-certified agencies that have met federal minimum requirements for patient care so Medicare will pay for covered home health services. People who need skilled nursing home care services usually receive their care from a home health agency. Skilled nursing includes services such as wound care, giving injections, and other care that cannot be performed by a nonmedical person.
- **Hospice home care.** Hospice care is offered by skilled professionals and trained volunteers in providing end-of-life support to patients

and their families. Hospice care is based primarily in the home; check state requirements, but if your state mandates it, most hospice care home providers should be Medicare-certified and licensed.

- **Homemaker/home care aide agencies.** These agencies hire homemakers or chore workers, home care aides, and companions to help patients with basics like meals, bathing, dressing, and housekeeping.
- **Staffing and private-duty agencies.** These are primarily nursing agencies that provide the same services as homemaker agencies.
- **Registries/independent providers.** These are employment agencies for home care nurses and aides. They match home care workers with patients and collect finders' fees. In many communities, these registries find quality workers for home situations, but it's important to remember that they are not usually licensed or regulated. In many states, registries are not required to screen or do background checks on the home care workers. Check your own state's regulations on these matters first.

To get coverage under Medicare, the following must be in place:

- A doctor's recommendation that an elder needs medical care in the home and a doctor must prepare a plan for that care. The doctor has to review that plan every 60 days or more.
- One of the following care options is required—intermittent (not full-time) skilled nursing care, physical therapy or speech language pathology services, or the need for continued occupational therapy.
- The home health agency must be approved by Medicare.

THE GERIATRIC CARE MANAGER OPTION

For anyone who has ever lost sleep worrying how their parents are doing from across the country, hiring a geriatric care manager (GCM) might be a worthwhile consideration. Baby Boomers should be thinking about them as part of their own long-term care strategy.

Who are geriatric care managers? They are located in communities around the nation and they come from diverse backgrounds in nursing, social work, psychology, and finance. They provide service in all levels of the geriatric care process:

- They are the eyes and ears of children and friends who can't be on the ground to support an older relative. For example, if a senior suffers a sudden, debilitating stroke, they are the go-to people to find that community's best rehabilitation and long-term care options.
- If a child simply wants to make sure his or her parents are checked on a couple of days a week to make sure that the house is clean and they're eating properly, geriatric care managers can coordinate that too.
- They also serve a watchdog function over billing and whether a senior is getting proper health-care services in a hospital, nursing home, assisted-living facility, or at home.
- Sometimes, their most valuable service is providing mediation between siblings and other relatives who can't agree on how to care for their loved ones.

It makes sense to start your search for a geriatric care manager when there's not an emergency. As of this writing, GCMs are not regulated by states and it's definitely worth taking the time to find a good one. Their services range from $80–$200 an hour based on their assigned tasks, and those are predominantly out-of-pocket expenses, since some long-term care insurance policies only pay a portion of the cost.

The National Association of Professional Geriatric Care Managers (www.findacaremanager.org), the field's trade association, is a good starting point to find GCMs in a particular geographic area. Many GCMs have earned certifications that train and certify them to do various tasks. NAPGCM recognizes the following: Care Manager Certified (CMC), Certified Case Manager (CCM), Certified Social Work Case Manager (C-SWCM) and Certified Advanced Social Work Case Manager (C-ASWCM).

An experienced geriatric care manager will readily tell you their specialty and where they find it necessary to bring in help. For instance, a

GCM who senses a family doesn't have a plan to pay for care or access the senior's assets will generally suggest the family bring in its own tax or legal help, or suggest help on the ground in the community.

Bringing in help. Optimally, the first step in hiring a GCM or any other assistance for a senior relative is to talk to the senior first, preferably while everyone is healthy and willing to talk. Here's what should be discussed between the senior and their chosen decision-maker:

- What is your preferred choice for long-term care (home-based care, assisted living, nursing home)?
- How do you want your assets used to pay for your care?
- Is your health-care power of attorney up to date?
- Do you have any particular choices of professionals or facilities in mind?

If that discussion settles on the need for a geriatric care manager to enter the process, then here are the questions that need to be asked:

- How long have you been in this field and what is your professional background?
- My relative has the following health conditions and wishes for dealing with them. What is your experience in this area, and how would you deal with such a client?
- Are you available for emergencies? What, in your view, constitutes an emergency?
- Does your company provide home care services? Are they licensed?
- How do you communicate with family members?
- What are your fees, and how do you prefer payment?
- If my relative were in a hospital/nursing home/rehab facility/their own home, what would your visitation schedule be, and what would you do while you were there?
- What are your various certifications, and what do they mean?
- Are you qualified to interpret billing statements, and how do you

handle payments for expenses that my relative needs?
- What is your liability coverage? Have you ever been sued?
- Can you provide references?

AFFORDING NURSING HOME CARE

The average annual cost of nursing home care today is $55,000 or $150 a day, and in major metropolitan areas, that cost can be upwards of $65,000 a year. That's the price *today*.

And except for a few short days in a skilled nursing facility after a hospital stay, Medicare won't pick up any of the cost.

We'll have a more detailed discussion of long-term care insurance in Chapter 35, but given that the average nursing home stay is less than three years, that means that unless an elderly person has at least $150,000 set aside strictly for end-of-life care, they must depend on the state to help them afford that care. And very few quality nursing homes have more than a few Medicaid beds.

This is an expense that you must plan for in addition to retirement, and most Americans are not anywhere near that level of preparation.

In the next chapter, we'll discuss planning for the death of a spouse.

24 | *Planning for the Death or Disability of a Spouse*

Death and disability know no date on the calendar. The names Christopher and Dana Reeve as well as Terry Schiavo are uncomfortable reminders that young lives as well as old can be cut short after debilitating illnesses of varying length. You can't control death, but you can control the length and extent of your care.

WHY FACING THE WORST IS IMPORTANT

Like most people, you probably would like your wishes and values respected, even when you are physically or mentally unable to express them. The combination of a living will and a durable power of attorney allow you to formalize your wishes ahead of time.

Despite the fact that the vast majority of American adults recognize the importance of these two "advanced medical directives," only 20 to 30 percent of American adults have them, according to the National Council on Aging. Unfortunately, every few years, a case captures national attention regarding why such documents are critical for adults of all ages.

A living will is a person's written expression of what life-sustaining medical treatment they wish to receive or not receive, should they become terminally ill or on life support and unable to physically or mentally express that decision to their medical providers. Ideally, the living will should cover such issues as resuscitation, life-support technologies, use of artificial nourishment, medication and pain management, and organ donation.

All 50 states allow for living wills, though the laws differ on what language can be used. You can buy "off-the-shelf" living will documents, and some employers are even offering them as employee benefits. But it's usually best to hire an attorney to draft or at least review the document so it is tailored to your desires and conforms to your state's laws. The last thing you want is something open to misinterpretation or challenge.

Once you've drafted the proper paperwork, give a copy to your primary physician and discuss your wishes with them. Also give a copy to the person who holds your designated health-care power of attorney and make sure you have the same discussion. While hospitals and nursing homes often will accept copies, it's still best to keep the original in a place your agent can get to easily—for example, don't put it in a safe-deposit box unless the person has access to the box. It's also wise to discuss the living will with all those close to you, so that the person who ends up making medical decisions on your behalf won't be battling siblings or other relatives.

And don't wait until you're older to draw up a living will. Terry Schiavo was only 26 years old when she became incapacitated.

The second key advanced directive, and one that's often overlooked, is the durable power of attorney for medical care, sometimes called a health-care proxy or medical directive. With this document, you appoint a person to act as your agent (the proxy) to make medical decisions on your behalf in the event you are incapacitated.

This document is broader than just for living will situations. For example, it might be used for someone in a medically induced coma who needs an unanticipated procedure in the middle of surgery, or for treatment of an Alzheimer's patient. While you can be as explicit and as limiting as you like in such a document, it usually is better to arm the agent with broad powers so he or she can handle unforeseen situations.

As with the living will, an attorney should draft this document. You also may be able to have the living will and the health-care proxy drafted into a single document, saving you some money.

The medical community has become much more accepting of living wills and durable powers of attorney for health care. But if the medical provider refuses to accede to the agent's instructions and those expressed in the living will, the agent has the legal right to appeal within the health-care institution or change providers.

Ultimately, the keys are to complete these documents in advance, be sure they are drafted or reviewed by an attorney, and discuss them thoroughly with those closest to you. Also, be sure to review existing documents to be sure they are up to date with law changes. Only then can you be reasonably assured your wishes will be carried out under such difficult circumstances.

PREPLANNING YOUR FUNERAL

Preplanning a funeral isn't something most of us actually look forward to. But think about how much easier you can make life for your family if you do.

Here are a few tips for preplanning a funeral so that you have the funeral that you (or the terminally ill person for whom you are planning) desire at the best price.

The average cost for a funeral, according to the American Association for Retired Persons, is around $6,000, but it doesn't take much for the numbers to go higher. Choosing expensive options can easily push the cost of a funeral over $10,000.

Survivors have to make decisions very quickly after death and sometimes that leads to expensive mistakes. It's common for them to "prove their love" by buying an expensive casket and service, even though they may end up spending far more than the deceased would have chosen. That's why preplanning can help make this inevitable event far less stressful for your loved ones.

Preplanning doesn't mean simply telling your family what you want for your funeral. You need to actively shop and price. Otherwise you may

SPOTLIGHT

MY SPOUSE HAS DIED—WHAT DO I DO ABOUT OUR FINANCES?

Dealing with personal finances is difficult following the death of a spouse. Although the surviving spouse needs time to adjust and grieve, important financial decisions often must be made—or in some cases, not made—soon after death. Here are some questions commonly asked by surviving spouses.

What do I do first? Making funeral arrangements and taking care of any organ donations are priorities. Get 10 to 15 copies of the death certificate from the funeral director. You'll need them to claim life insurance, Social Security benefits, employment benefits, investment accounts, and so on. Also notify any financial advisers you have.

The other major thing to be done, as difficult as it may be, is to sort through your important financial documents—your spouse's will, insurance policies, household bank statements, investment accounts, trusts, deeds, debts, bills, employee benefits, checkbooks, safe-deposit box, and so on. Look for cash resources, such as money market and saving accounts. You'll probably need cash to take care of funeral expenses, estate settlement, and ongoing living expenses. Sufficient cash reserves also can help you delay some financial decisions until you are ready to address them.

What do I do about the insurance? Send a death certificate copy and the benefits claim as soon as possible. The claims process can take several weeks—discuss it with your agent. While it's best not to make major financial decisions soon after the death of a spouse, you may need to decide fairly soon how you want to receive the insurance benefits. Payout choices might include a lump sum, interest payments, or an annuity, and some of these choices are irrevocable. You could delay your decision for a while if you don't need the money immediately, or collect interest for now and the principal later. If you take the money in a lump sum, put it into a short-term, interest-paying investment such as Treasury bills or a money market. Nothing risky at this stage.

What about my spouse's employee benefits or pension? Learn what benefits you are entitled to, such as medical coverage. Contact the retirement plan administrator to learn your survivorship benefit options. Pay attention to deadlines. You may need to

Continued on page 217

make decisions regarding pension benefits fairly soon. But don't rush decisions sooner than necessary.

What about my spouse's estate? Determine if probate is required. Even simple probate can take six months. Many assets legally pass to survivors without the need to go through probate, such as life insurance proceeds, pensions, trust assets, and jointly owned property. Jointly owned property passes to the spouse free of federal estate tax. However, this can cause tax problems later when you die. If a good estate plan is already in place, fine. If not, you may still have some options left, such as disclaiming property. This essentially means you refuse to accept it so that it passes to someone else, such as your children. You must disclaim property within nine months and before you take possession of it. You'll also likely need to retitle assets, change beneficiary designations and perhaps trustees. Review your own estate plan.

Should I change my investments? Not right away, unless you have reason to believe investment money is tied up in something excessively risky. In time, however, you will want to reexamine your investments. Your needs as a single person will have changed and some of the investments may no longer be appropriate. You may need more income, for example, or feel uncomfortable about the portfolio's risk.

What about my house? It's generally best not to make major changes for a while. While it is tough to continue living in a home where you and your spouse lived for years, major, sudden financial moves can lead to emotional and monetary mistakes that you might make later.

What other financial steps should I take? Establish or revise a household budget. Household income and expenses usually change with a spouse's death, with income often declining. A budget should be done in the context of changes you may want to make to your overall life goals. Another step is to consider putting your credit cards in your own name, especially if you need to establish or re-establish your own credit.

What about professional advice? You may need an attorney to handle estate issues, and a financial planner to advise on important financial decisions, such as how to handle pension benefit options. Whoever you work with should be competent, trustworthy, and sensitive to your personal needs at this difficult time.

SPOTLIGHT

WHY JOINT TENANCY ISN'T ALWAYS THE BEST IDEA

Love isn't always the best thing when it comes to estate planning.

Out of love and financial expediency, the vast majority of couples own their assets jointly. Most commonly this takes the form of "with rights of survivorship." Under such rights, each owner has an undivided interest in the property and can't sell it without the consent of the other owner(s).

Couples usually take this route because (a) it seems the natural and "loving" thing to do, (b) financial institutions such as banks tend to push it, and (c) it avoids the expense and delay of probate when one of the spouses dies. However, warn financial planners, holding all marital property in joint tenancy is not always a great idea, for several reasons:

- **Estate taxes.** When one spouse dies, the surviving spouse receives all jointly owned property without going through probate and without gift or estate taxes through the unlimited marital deduction (the exception is noncitizen spouses). That's what makes joint tenancy so appealing. Unfortunately, in the case of larger estates, that can be a tax disaster. It definitely makes sense to consult with financial and tax experts first.
- **Remarriage.** Jointly titled property in a second marriage means the property goes to the surviving spouse, and, perhaps ultimately, to the children of the surviving spouse's first marriage. That means that children from the first marriage of the spouse who dies first won't be able to inherit the asset that their parents acquired. That's why estate issues really need to be addressed before any second marriage, particularly when children are involved.
- **Liability.** Jointly owned property is open to creditors of either spouse. That means income and assets contributed by one spouse to their joint accounts could be confiscated in the event of a liability judgment or business debts owned by the other spouse. Some experts say couples shouldn't even own cars jointly. Holding property in the other spouse's name isn't foolproof protection against claims, but it's far better than joint ownership.

Continued on page 219

- **Self-protection.** Should one spouse become incapacitated, the other spouse cannot sell, borrow against, or gift jointly owned property without permission from the courts (unless the couple had enough foresight to have prepared powers of attorney in advance). Also, all too common is that one spouse handles all the family's finances and the other spouse doesn't know what to do when that spouse dies. Owning at least some property separately compels both spouses to take some responsibility for money.

Careful titling and the use of trusts and other estate planning techniques can solve or mitigate many of these problems. For example, if you and your spouse each have more than $2 million in your own names, then the first to die can pass his or her estate assets to other heirs free of tax with the proper trust arrangement. The surviving spouse can do the same thing. Some examples:

A bypass trust (sometimes called a credit-shelter trust) allows the assets from the estate of the first spouse to die to go into the trust. The surviving spouse receives income from the trust, but the principal remains outside the estate of the surviving spouse and goes to the heirs at death. Except in community property states, however, a bypass trust cannot be funded with jointly owned property. If that's the case, with a properly drawn will, the surviving spouse can disclaim jointly owned property and it will be put into the bypass trust.

A qualified terminable interest property trust (QTIP) is useful for seeing that jointly owned property goes to children from a first marriage. The surviving spouse receives all income from the trust, and can get at some of the principal. But at death, the remaining trust assets will go to the designated children.

One fear couples have for divvying up property for individual ownership is divorce. The partner who's earned the money may be reluctant to put some of it entirely into the spouse's name, even as a way to protect against lawsuits. Financial experts say the fear is largely unfounded, since the courts generally care less about how property is owned than in determining an equitable distribution of the property (it's divided 50-50 anyway in

Continued on page 220

Continued from page 219

community property states). However, laws vary from state to state regarding what constitutes equitable distribution.

Also be aware that joint tenancy usually supersedes any prenuptial agreements regarding jointly owned property.

want a funeral that is far more expensive than you realize or that your estate can afford.

Start with a funeral home's price list. Federal rules require all funeral homes to provide a specific, detailed price list for their goods and services. You don't have to select every item on the list, either.

Keep in mind that most states don't require the use of a funeral home for a service. You or your church may want to simply hold a memorial service without the body present, thus eliminating the need for embalming, an expensive casket, or attending funeral staff.

Shop around. The cost of funeral home services can vary widely. Caskets are a particular area where costs can be dramatically cut, without sacrificing the deceased's desires. The cost of caskets at a large Midwestern funeral home, for example, runs from a low of $700 to a high of $15,500. Third-party casket stores, including some online, have entered the market in recent years, selling caskets well below the cost of what many funeral homes charge. And the funeral home must use that casket without charging a handling fee.

Know what you are required by law to have and what isn't required. Two examples are embalming and "grave liners." State laws typically don't require embalming, at least within two to three days of death. As for grave or vault liners, or what the funeral industry calls "outer burial containers," state laws again typically don't require it. Most cemeteries require some sort of liner so that the ground doesn't eventually settle over the grave, but that can be relatively inexpensive. Yet as with caskets, liner costs range widely, from less than $1,000 to over $8,000.

Consider cremation. It's generally less expensive than a "full-service funeral" that includes a casket and burial, though this increasingly popular choice is certainly not for everyone.

To prepay or not. There are several ways to prefund a funeral, from paying the funeral home directly to buying a dedicated life insurance policy to establishing your own investment account for that purpose. Each has their pros and cons. But what is certain is that preplanning presents the opportunity to set aside money for the inevitable expenses, again potentially saving your loved ones money and stress.

Look for financial help. Social Security pays its beneficiaries a small death benefit. Also, veterans are entitled to a free burial and grave marker in a national cemetery.

Ultimately, the issue of preplanning your funeral isn't what you spend for it but whether what is spent buys the type of funeral and burial that you want and can afford. If you desire a lavish funeral with an expensive casket and a high-cost location within the cemetery, and you can afford it, that's fine. If you prefer cremation or a "party" without the traditional funeral, that's fine too.

What you don't want is to force your surviving loved ones into guessing your wishes and making potentially expensive financial decisions under severe stress.

LETTERS OF INSTRUCTION

When a loved one dies, there are moments of confusion and sometimes anger when survivors try to interpret the deceased's wishes on a variety of issues. Letters of instruction—written while you're healthy—are a way to avoid that.

A letter of instruction can be a single letter submitted with your will and on file with your attorney or financial planner that addresses multiple subjects or a series of detailed letters that accompany various points in your will and overall estate plan. It is wise to speak with an estate attorney or your financial adviser before you start putting these letters together. Some people even reinforce these documents by reading them on video, on the theory that pictures don't lie.

Issues you might want to address in letters of instruction:

- Funeral plans
- An index of all relevant investment and savings accounts
- Social Security and VA benefits
- Vehicle titles
- Outstanding loan information
- Access to computerized financial files
- Instructions for business associates
- Plans for surviving pets
- Who will get specific items in the home (furniture, jewelry, etc.)
- All insurance policies and health-care insurance records

Last point. All the best-laid plans are worthless if your executor or designated individuals holding power of attorney don't know where to get their hands on what you've written. Make sure you keep key friends and family members updated with the same information on where these documents are located and who to call for off-site copies.

In the next part of this book, we'll be looking at planning for college and making smart borrowing decisions.

Part VII

Affording College

College Savings—Not Just for the Kids Anymore

Tim Wyman, CFP®

Saving for college will always be an issue for parents, but as people change careers, it's an issue for everyone. A planner can help you look ahead to what your child's education will cost and whether you'll need to upgrade your skills at some point.

Tim Wyman, a CERTIFIED FINANCIAL PLANNER™ professional from Southfield, Michigan, stresses the importance of thinking about higher education as a family issue, not just something for the children.

"If you look over the lifetime of any worker, the difference in wages between college graduates and high school grads is very dramatic, but it's also going to become a greater issue in future years as mid-career education becomes more common," said Wyman.

A planner can help you negotiate the triangle between college savings for your kids, college savings for yourself, and your retirement. "In 17 years, a four-year public university education will cost well over $100,000, and a private school over $300,000. After I pick people up off the floor, we start breaking down those numbers into a monthly goal. And I stress how important it is to start immediately, because the cost of waiting is substantial."

Wyman also points out that today and in the future, parents will need to be aggressive about negotiating tuition, room, and board at colleges where either they or their children have been accepted. "Planners can have an important role in training parents and individuals to understand what college costs will be in the future and how to meet those obligations through savings, financial aid, and other funding sources."

He stresses that people can't ignore their retirement goals to meet the high cost of education. "You can always borrow money for college, but you really can't borrow for a 30-year retirement. Most of us will need help to meet those goals."

25 | *Starting Early*

Two hundred dollars a month. Focus on that figure for a moment. The day your child is born, you begin setting aside $200 a month until his or her eighteenth birthday. Assuming investment gains based on a compounded rate of 8 percent, by the end of 18 years, you'll have $97,071.03. That's assuming you never add another dime and the rate never changes.

The above example assumes that you built a diversified portfolio that meets that return. Of course, it's possible to build a portfolio that exceeds that return or at least protects you from serious dips in the market.

The prevailing wisdom still holds—the earlier you start saving for a college education, the better.

AN 18-YEAR JOB

We covered this briefly in Chapter 20, but it's worth a refresher. The College Board estimated that in 2005–2006, annual average tuition and fees were $5,491 at four-year public colleges and $21,235 at four-year private colleges. And for room and board, the cost was $6,636 at four-year public colleges and $7,791 at four-year private colleges.

So for tuition, fees, room, and board, at *2006 levels*, you would be paying an average of $48,508 for four years of public college, and $116,104 for private school. Fast-forward to 2024, when the College Board estimates that four-year public school number will be $129,845 and private school will be $314,674.

Some people might ask the question, "At these prices, is college really worth it?"

The answer is a resounding "yes." Your kids can't afford not to go to college. For that matter, you can't afford not to upgrade your skills over the length of your career. In December 2000, the U.S. Census Bureau reported that the average income for students with a bachelor's degree is $45,678, almost twice the $24,572 income of a student with just a high school diploma. That's a difference of almost $1 million in lifetime earnings. Here's the most important point: you get that bump even if you don't send Junior to Harvard.

THE ONE-THIRD RULE

Most agree that the days of parents footing the full bill for college are over, even for upper-income parents. Today, there's a discussion about what's right for parents to pay and what's right for students to pay. It's called the "One-third Rule," and it means the following: parents save enough to pay for one-third of the total expected cost; they pay one-third out of their income and add it to financial aid while the student is in school; and the student borrows or somehow funds the rest.

What's the principle behind the One-third Rule? That you'll be spreading the total cost of college over an extended period of time, which is a more efficient way to save. It also allows you to distribute assets in a way that will maximize the student's chances of obtaining the best financial aid package.

To figure out a savings and investment strategy that truly fits our situation, you consult with a financial adviser such as a CERTIFIED FINANCIAL PLANNER™ professional. Affording college and retirement requires a strategy because though they might be tempted, a parent can't sacrifice retirement

---

SPOTLIGHT

THE COLLEGE SAVINGS REALITY GAP

A March 2006, WSJ.com/Harris Interactive personal-finance poll showed that nearly one-third of parents who expect to pay for some or all of their kids' college costs haven't saved any money for that purpose.

Over two-thirds of parents who expect their child to attend college say they plan to pay a portion of their child's college costs, according to the poll, while another 12 percent plan to pay for all of their child's education. At the same time, about 69 percent of those parents who expect their child to attend college say they expect financial aid or scholarships to pay all or a portion of college costs.

Of those who plan to pay some or all of their child's college costs, about a quarter expect to pay between $10,000 to $19,999 annually for their child's education, including room and board, and 17 percent expect to pay $5,000 to $9,999 a year. Another 16 percent expect expenses of about $20,000 to $30,000 a year.

Despite these expectations, about 68 percent of these parents say they've saved money to help pay for college. About a quarter of those polled say they have saved less than $5,000, and nearly a third of those polled say they haven't saved any money specifically for college.

The poll, which surveyed 579 parents or legal guardians of children aged 18 or younger, found that about 97 percent of the parents expect their child or children to attend college.

---

savings for their child's education.

GREAT WAYS TO START SAVING WITH SMALL AMOUNTS

One of the biggest challenges for families saving for their children's college education is that there are so many options for saving, and one size does not fit all. Which options are right for you depend in part on the age of your child, family income, potential for financial aid, and the expected cost of college. Here are the major college-savings options to consider

Figure 25.1: Weekly Savings Required to Reach Savings Goal

The following table shows how much you'd need to save weekly in order to reach various savings goals at 8 percent interest. On one hand, with time on your side, the impact seems relatively painless; on the other hand, some years might be easier to earn 8 percent than others.

Goal	1 Year	4 Year	8 Years	12 Years	17 Years
$5,000	$92.29	$20.38	$8.58	$4.77	$2.66
$10,000	$184.58	$40.76	$17.16	$9.54	$5.32
$25,000	$461.45	$101.92	$42.88	$23.86	$13.28
$50,000	$922.90	$203.84	$85.76	$47.72	$26.56
$100,000	$1,845.82	$407.68	$171.53	$95.42	$53.11
$250,000	$4,614.54	$1019.20	$428.81	$238.56	$132.78

Source: FinAid.org (2006).

while you're getting help to make the right choices.

In 2006, there were plenty of important changes in education savings instruments.

529 college savings plans. President Bush eliminated the 2011 expiration date on the popular tax-free features of these accounts, and experts were already pointing to cheaper and more diverse choices for parents investing in these plans for the future. Here is what these popular state-run plans provide:

- Investments grow tax-deferred and withdrawals for qualified college expenses are free of federal tax
- Some states give tax breaks on the contributions
- Over $200,000 can be invested in many plans, and as much as $110,000 at one time
- Investor retains control and can change beneficiaries
- No income restrictions
- Their impact on financial aid is smaller than many alternatives

We'll get into 529 plans in more detail in the next chapter. The bottom line is that 529s can be an especially good alternative for high-income families wishing to save a substantial amount for college, investment options usually are limited, and management fees are sometimes high.

Coverdell education savings accounts. This type of account got bad news in 2006; its tax-exempt treatment was reset to expire at the end of 2010. Given the amount of pressure exerted to make tax benefits permanent on 529 plans, there is reason to hope that these may ultimately be made permanent as well. You can contribute up to $2,000 a year per child, but there are income restrictions ($190,000–$220,000 for married couples in 2006). Earnings are federal income tax-exempt if used for qualified education expenses including private elementary and secondary schools.

Coverdells can be a good option for people who can save only a small amount each year, or who may want to fund a Coverdell before moving on to other alternatives. Their impact on financial aid is now the same as that of 529 plans—the account is considered the parent's asset instead of the student's, resulting in more aid.

Other characteristics of Coverdells:

- **Account ownership.** Coverdell accounts may be owned by the student or the student's parent.
- **Contribution age limit.** Contributions may be made until the beneficiary reaches age 18.
- **Withdrawal age limit**. The money must be used by the time the child reaches age 30, or the earnings will be taxed as ordinary income plus a 10 percent penalty.
- **Rollovers.** Coverdell accounts may be rolled over to the Coverdell account of a family member of the previous beneficiary.
- **Income restrictions.** Contributions are phased out for incomes between $95,000 and $110,000 (single filers) or $190,000 and $220,000 (married filing jointly). These phase-outs may be bypassed by giving money to the child through UGMA/UTMA and having the child contribute to his or her own Coverdell account.
- **Corporations may contribute to your account.** Corporations, including tax-exempt organizations, may contribute to an individual's

Coverdell account, regardless of income level.

- **Contributions must be in cash.** Contributions must be in the form of cash. Stocks, bonds, or other investments are not permitted as contributions.
- **How they affect financial aid.** Amounts are treated as assets of the account owner, but it's better to have the assets in the parent's name.
- **Income tax implications.** Contributions are not deductible on federal or state income tax, but earnings accumulate tax-free. Qualified distributions are exempt from federal income tax. This may change at the end of 2010, when these tax advantages are set to expire. Contributions may be made until the due date of the contributor's tax return (normally April 15 of the following year). Nonqualified withdrawals are taxed as ordinary income at the donor's rate and subject to a 10 percent tax penalty. (Nonqualified distributions remain tax-free in cases of death or disability of the beneficiary.)
- **Estate tax implications.** Contributions are removed from the donor's gross estate but included in the beneficiary's gross estate.
- **How the funds can be used.** Primary, secondary, and postsecondary education expenses, including tuition, fees, tutoring, books, supplies, related equipment, room and board, uniforms, transportation, and computers.
- **How they coordinate with 529 plans.** You can contribute to both a Coverdell account and a section 529 plan in the same year, but there may be gift tax implications if you give more than $12,000 per beneficiary.
- **How they coordinate with education tax credits.** You can claim a Hope Scholarship and/or Lifetime Learning tax credit in the same year as you withdraw funds from a Coverdell account, so long as the credits are claimed using different qualified education expenses than those paid from the Coverdell distribution. You can't use the same expenses to justify two different programs.
- **Elementary and secondary payments.** Coverdells not only pay for higher education expenses such as tuition and fees, but also for tuition and fees in elementary and secondary school.

Prepaid tuition plans. Under these plans, you can buy part or all of a school's future tuition bill at today's prices. Once offered only by some states, a coalition of nearly 200 private schools now offers prepaid tuition plans through a program called the Independent 529 Plan. Earnings from either private or public plans are tax-exempt.

It's a good option for conservative investors who want to lock in tuition costs and who know what college their children will likely attend (there are penalties for changing your mind about a state school, but there's more flexibility under the private plan). Also, under current rules, prepaid plans reduce financial aid dollar-for-dollar.

Custodial accounts. Investments are held in the name of a minor, but are managed by the custodian (such as a parent). This arrangement provides some tax benefits, especially for higher-income families because they shift capital gains taxes to their lower-income children. Unlike some other college funding alternatives, there are no income restrictions. But contributions over $12,000 a year per parent (as of 2006) are subject to gift tax, and the assets remain in the parent's estate in some instances.

Custodial accounts present three major drawbacks. One, the gifts are irrevocable. Two, the child assumes control of the assets when he or she becomes a legal adult (legal age is set by the resident's state), and thus may spend the money on something other than college. Three, the assets typically count more heavily against financial aid, though some colleges are changing their policies in this area.

Series I and EE U.S. Savings Bonds. The interest earned from these bonds is free of federal tax as long as it is used to pay for tuition and fees, the parents hold the bond title, and parental income isn't too high. But the benefits may be reduced by other education tax breaks such as the HOPE Scholarship. To learn more, go to www.treasurydirect.gov.

Taxable investments in the parent's name. The advantages include nearly unlimited investment options, no income restrictions, retention and control of the assets, and the flexibility of using the assets for something other than college if necessary. The major disadvantage is the taxes on earnings. You can minimize that by gifting the assets to your child when it's time for college and having them sell the assets, though you could face *gift* taxes in such a situation.

Individual retirement accounts. Money taken out of a traditional IRA is free of the 10 percent early withdrawal penalty (but not ordinary taxes) if it's used for qualified education expenses. Withdrawals of Roth IRA contributions are tax-free, and even the earnings may be tax-free in some situations. Yet, pulling money out of retirement funds is always very risky and should be considered a last resort.

BOOST YOUR BARGAINING POWER

Nearly one-third more high school graduates are applying to college than there were 25 years ago. Yet colleges and universities feel the pressure of magazine and other college rankings as part of their overall marketing plan, so their competition for top graduates has gotten cutthroat. That's good news for parents and prospective students.

How do you get your student into a good school with the best chance of affordability? It pays to negotiate, but only if you have something to negotiate with. Here's what you'll need:

- **A child with great credentials.** It helps if your child is a bright student, with a high grade point average, high SAT and ACT test scores, and extracurricular activities that help top schools take notice. They want the best and the brightest to keep their image golden. Increasingly, schools are handing out scholarships based on merit instead of need, a controversial issue, but beneficial nonetheless if you have one of those bright students.
- **The right school.** Even if your kid isn't a National Merit scholar, pick a school with a good reputation where your student's grade point average and test scores rank above the average of incoming freshman (these scores are often published in various college-rating guides). The school will be more prone to offer you a better deal.
- **Acceptances at several schools**. Have your child apply to several similar schools where you think he or she stands the best chance of

getting in (as well as one or two "safety" backups and a couple of "long shots"). That way, if the child is accepted by more than one school, you can use the financial aid package of one school to barter with another school. Aid packages vary widely from school to school.

- **An eye on the endowment.** Some schools, particularly private, simply have more money—called an endowment—to offer for grants and scholarships. That's aid you don't have to pay back. Dividing the number of students into the school's endowment fund provides one rule of thumb.
- **A firm guarantee on aid.** Some schools offer freshmen what amounts to "teaser" aid. The package is great in the first year, but those discounts, grants, and scholarships turn to straight loans in succeeding years when students are reluctant to leave. Try to get a four-year commitment to the aid package.
- **An application strategy.** While grant and scholarship money generally goes on a first-come, first-served basis, talk to other parents with children at that school to find out what they know about the aid application process. Earlier is better at some schools and not at others.
- **Extenuating circumstances.** Make sure the financial aid officer knows of additional reasons your student will need aid, such as a job loss, other children in school, and so on. The officer may beef up the package accordingly.

Ultimately, the most important thing to remember is to pick the right school for your child and then worry about the money.

In the next chapter, we'll discuss 529 plans and how they work.

26 | *College Savings Plan*

At this writing, some big questions have recently been answered about 529 plans, not the least of which is the extension of their tax-free status by Congress. Uncertainty on these issues had slowed contributions to these once wildly popular plans. According to Boston-based Financial Research Corp., growth in the number of new accounts slowed to an average quarterly rate of 4 percent in 2005 from an average of 21 percent in 2002.

529 plans are complex to sort out without some sort of help, and it's tougher still to determine whether one state's plan is invested more competently than another's.

Currently, 62 senators and more than 120 members of the House of Representatives have been co-sponsors of bills to make the legislation permanent, according to the National Association of State Treasurers.

WHAT IS A 529 COLLEGE SAVINGS PLAN?

The 529 college savings plans—named for the federal law that created them in 1996—allow a parent to open a tax-deferred college savings plan with as little as $25 to start, in some states.

One important note: A 529 college savings plan is *not* the same thing as a 529 prepaid college tuition plan.

Prepaid tuition plans are just that—tax-deferred savings plans that allow you to save for tuition for in-state schools (though some plans allow you to transfer out a portion of those assets to out-of-state schools). Also, it's important to note that prepaid tuition plans are not an automatic guarantee a student will get into that college.

All 50 states now offer their version of a 529 college saving plan, and you can usually access the details through your state treasurer's office.

THEIR CURRENT TAX ADVANTAGES

Under the tax law passed by the Bush Administration in 2001, any withdrawals from 529 college savings plans after 2002 are tax-free if the account holder uses them to pay for a beneficiary's college tuition, fees, books, supplies, and—for students enrolled at least half time—room and board. (Previously, withdrawals were taxed at the beneficiary's tax rate.) The 2002 federal tax law change also allowed 529 account holders to roll over funds from one state's 529 plan to another state's plan once every 12 months for any reason. It's possible to transfer funds to another 529 plan at any time if you change the beneficiary as well. In August 2006, Congress made permanent the tax advantages of 529 plans, which had been set to expire at the end of 2010.

There are gift and estate tax benefits too. Federal tax law allows for a general accelerated gift option that allows individuals to average gifts over $12,000 per beneficiary ($24,000 for married couples, based on 2006 levels) over a five-year period without incurring federal gift tax. So an individual can contribute up to $60,000 per beneficiary in one year and a married couple up to $120,000 per beneficiary without incurring gift tax. If you give the full amount, you will not be able to give any gifts to the same individual during the five-year period without incurring gift tax or using up a part of their lifetime exclusion.

Contributions at or below the annual gift tax threshold are immediately removed from the donor's gross taxable estate and included in the estate of the beneficiary. Unlike certain types of trust funds, contributions to section 529 plans are considered a completed gift, which means the amount is excluded from the donor's estate. The only exceptions are if you cancel your 529 account or if the donor dies during the five-year averaging period.

HOW A FAMILY BENEFITS

Everyone up and down a holder's so-called "lineal family tree"—parents, aunts, uncles, brothers and sisters, as well as your kids—can benefit from the tax breaks and educational rewards of these plans. In fact, if your child gets a full scholarship to Harvard, that means any close family member on the aforementioned list can use the money in that account to go to school themselves— which can be a great option for career-changers. Better still, parents, grandparents, siblings, and friends can make deposits to these plans and get a tax benefit. And no, neither you nor your designated beneficiary have to go to school in the state where the plan is located.

WHO CAN CONTRIBUTE?

This is a very attractive aspect of a 529 college savings plan. Anyone can contribute money on behalf of a beneficiary. Relatives, friends, colleagues, even complete strangers can kick in.

Federal law requires that a 529 college savings plan must have safeguards to prevent contributions in excess of those necessary to provide for the qualified higher education expenses of the beneficiary, but does not otherwise specify a limit on contributions. That means each state sets its own limit. Most states use a limit that is based on an estimate of the amount of money that will be required to provide seven years of postsecondary education (including both undergraduate and graduate school). Even so, there is considerable variation in state cumulative contribution limits, which in 2006 ranged from $146,000 to $305,000. The median limit was $235,000.

The 529 plans require cash contributions that can be transferred from your checking or savings account. Automatic payroll deduction is becoming more frequent as well, so check your plan's options.

WHO PICKS THE INVESTMENTS?

Each state typically selects qualified, nationally known investment managers to create the plan choices. Most state treasurers' offices feature direct links off their Web sites to their particular in-state plan, with instructions on how to open accounts. The funds can be invested in a variety of investments from low-to-moderate risk. It is important, however, to check the performance of these investments against other states' offerings.

WHO RETAINS CONTROL OF THESE FUNDS?

This is one of the more attractive aspects of the 529 plan—the person who opens the account retains control of the funds. That means that parents can keep control of this substantial asset until the funds are spent.

HOW TO EVALUATE A 529 PLAN

Your financial adviser or your CERTIFIED FINANCIAL PLANNER™ professional can help you sort through the details of various state plans. There are various services that now rank the offerings of each state's plan. SavingforCollege.com and finaid.org are leading sites to help educate you in how these plans work.

Today, some states will allow you to put in close to $300,000 over the life of the plan.

Fees vary from state to state, and they're very important to watch. Management fees of 2 percent or more are common in some states, and if you wouldn't settle for that in a mutual fund, you shouldn't settle for it in a 529 plan.

529 PLANS AND FINANCIAL AID

The 529 plans could affect financial aid, depending on the school and how they value these assets. If your child qualifies for a fabulous financial aid package, don't be surprised if the school requires full disclosure of 529 funds—a portion of which could be deducted from that total aid package. It's worth some research ahead of time with your schools of choice.

WHEN 529 PLANS GO BAD—AN OVERVIEW OF PROBLEMS IN THE 529 WORLD

In all truth, investors in 529 plans face the same market risks as those who invest in 401(k) plans. When poor investment choices are made, these critical funds can be in jeopardy.

529 plans also face the 401(k) dilemma—too many choices and a need to watch fees. However, with the proper research and advice, it is now easier to shift from one state's plan to another. In the past, that was allowed only when changing the beneficiary of the account. Now, you can move money as often as once a year for any reason without triggering tax penalties. Yet some plans place their own restrictions on withdrawals.

In May 2006, the National Association of Securities Dealers issued an alert "that investors may be shortchanging themselves by investing in 529 college savings plans with high fees, plans that currently do not offer them state tax benefits, or both." The organization pointed out that some brokerage firms offered only a limited number of plans and barred more attractive options from other states that could have lower sales charges, expenses, or the possibility of better tax advantages.[1]

A 2004 study by the University of North Carolina at Wilmington showed that state-sponsored 529 plans with the highest fees ironically seemed to draw the most investors.

WHY PREPAID TUITION PLANS NEED TO BE CHECKED CAREFULLY

Prepaid tuition plans allow you to pay into a state or regional tuition savings plan to insure yourself against full increases in tuition in the future. If you're sure Junior will attend a state school or a school within a particular group of colleges with prepaid plans, they make some sense.

But these plans have had their share of woe, even more than 529 college savings plans.

During the last market slump, many of these tuition plans lost money and couldn't meet the annual tuition increases being made at those schools. As a result, participants had to cough up more cash for the tuition bill they thought they had locked in at a lower rate. Second, prepaid tuition plans got nastier treatment by financial aid officers than 529 savings plans—aid counselors looked at 529 savings plan assets as property of the parent, while 529 prepaid tuition plan assets were viewed as student assets. That meant that withdrawals from a prepaid tuition plan reduced federal financial aid eligibility dollar-for-dollar.

There's been an effort to remedy this. As of July 1, 2006, the federal financial aid formulas will no longer discriminate against prepaid plans. As far as federal grants and student loans are concerned, 529 prepaid tuition plans will be considered assets of the parents, just like 529 college savings plans. Yet there is still some dispute on how universities will distribute their own institutional aid money to students, particularly at private schools, which distribute a larger part of their endowment to students to cover tuition.

It's all very complicated, and it underscores why you should get help with any 529 savings strategy. But here are some general questions to ask of any prepaid program you're investigating:

- How solvent is the state or regional plan?
- How is the plan's money invested?
- How has the plan done since inception?
- Has the plan ever had to return principal to investors because it wasn't meeting obligations during a market downturn?
- Check the fine print. If a plan guarantees your tuition costs as long as annual tuition costs don't exceed 5.5 percent a year, and then the actual tuition increase turns out to be 6 percent, then what happens?
- Under what conditions might the prepaid tuition plans liquidate? What happens to participants' principal if it does?
- What happens if your kid decides he wants absolutely nothing to do with the schools in the plan?

In Chapter 27, we'll look at financing options for parents and other college savers who have started late in the game.

ENDNOTE

1. www.nasd.com/InvestorInformation/InvestorAlerts/529Plans/CollegeSavings Plans-SchoolYourselfBeforeYouInvest/index.htm.

27 | *Starting Late—College Financing Options*

As we've noted, a staggeringly large percentage of families haven't planned adequately for their children's college tuition. Of course, with tuition rising between 5 and 8 percent annually over the last decade, inflation certainly hasn't kept up with one of our most crucial expenses in life.

It's easy for a parent—or a child—to feel depressed about inadequate savings for college as little as two or three years before graduation.

To that, we offer three words: Get over it.

The bottom line is that it's tough for any parent, even higher-income parents, to pay full freight for their kid's tuition these days. In truth, every dollar you save for college is one less dollar you have to borrow.

That said, the watchwords for late starters are diligence and creativity.

FINANCIAL AID, SCHOLARSHIPS, AND FOUND MONEY

The savings-to-tuition gap is coming at a perilous time for federal college student assistance in general. At the time this book was published, the Bush Administration held the maximum Pell Grant (the federal government's major college grant program for students in financial need) at $4,050 for the fifth year in a row and kept spending flat on the Work Study and Supplemental Educational Opportunity Grants Programs, among others.

The current trend in federal support of college funding is toward merit funding and away from financial needs-based assistance. What does that mean? Merit-based assistance usually takes the form of scholarships, while need-based aid typically appears as grants, loans, work-study, etc. Without getting into the political and class ramifications of this, it's important to know that today's student looking for help needs to come to the game with a higher record of academic achievement to qualify for the maximum amount of help.

What this means for parents who have come late to the college savings party is that they need to focus on a combination of savings, loans, and scholarship/grant opportunities to close the gap. It's important to know that every family's situation is different, and this chapter will serve only as an overview of options, not a specific answer guide to fit each student and family.

For a better barometer of where you stand, consult a financial adviser such as a Certified Financial Planning™ professional. Some CFP professionals have specific training in college planning and can help you at any stage of the savings game. For more information, go to www.Planner Search.org to help you find a member of the Financial Planning Association in your area with specific skills to match your needs.

The College Board, the 106-year-old not-for-profit organization that involves colleges, secondary school districts, and higher education nonprofits in providing information for prospective college students, has several calculators on its Web site (www.CollegeBoard.com) including a financial aid EasyPlanner (http://apps.collegeboard.com/fincalc/ep/wizard-home.jsp) that allows a visitor to see if he or she has saved enough for college, then what their options might be from direct aid, scholarships, and loans.

FINANCIAL AID MYTHS

Millions of college students miss out on valuable financial aid every year simply because they mistakenly believe they won't qualify for aid or they are intimidated by the process. Yet applying for financial aid can make the difference between affording the school you want to attend and attending the school you can afford. It can even make the difference of being able to stay in school once you're enrolled.

A study released in October 2004 by the American Council on Education found that during the 1999–2000 school year, half of all undergraduate students enrolled at colleges that participated in the federal financial aid program didn't bother to apply for aid. And among those who applied, some missed application deadlines, often resulting in no aid awards.[1]

While some students would not have qualified because they had sufficient financial resources, many left money on the table. In fact, the study concluded that 850,000 low-income students would have qualified for federal Pell Grants, which is money that students don't have to pay back.

The first key for overcoming the myths about financial aid is to understand exactly what "financial aid" means. Aid is actually a mixture of loans, grants, scholarships, and work-study (the student works a certain number hours a week at the school). To calculate how much aid your student qualifies for, start with the total cost of attending a particular school: tuition and fees, books, room and board, transportation, and miscellaneous expenses. The school then determines how much of that total cost your family can reasonably be expected to pay, known as the expected family contribution (EFC).

Typically, the calculation of the EFC starts with completion of the Free Application for Federal Student Aid, known as the FAFSA. This assesses the student and parents' income, investments, and other financial resources, and arrives at an EFC number. Additionally, some colleges, particularly private, gather further information to see if the student qualifies for nonfederal (institutional) financial aid. Theoretically, the shortfall between what the family is expected to pay and the total cost of that institution is made up by financial aid.

WHO QUALIFIES?

Don't assume that because you are a middle-income or affluent family you won't qualify for aid. According to the College Board, the share of family income required to pay college cost has gone up for all groups but the wealthiest over the last 20 years. Students received almost $90 billion in financial aid in 2001–2002, an increase of 11.5 percent over the preceding year, or 10.0 percent after adjusting for inflation.[2]

And while you might not qualify for aid from a lower-cost college, you might qualify for aid from a more expensive—and perhaps for you, more desirable—school.

The majority of financial aid comes in the form of loans, so you will have to pay it back. But the loans are often subsidized, meaning you don't have to pay interest or principal on the loan until after the student graduates or quits school. It's also worth noting that student loans bear lower interest rates than other forms of loan debt and have repayment terms of ten years or more, a big help to cash flow. Furthermore, the student may receive work-study for 15 or 20 hours a week. Many colleges, particularly private schools, kick in grants or merit scholarships from endowment funds.

Aid packages can vary substantially among schools, and even region to region, so compare them carefully—especially the nonloan portions. Don't consider the packages written in stone. Sometimes errors are made or important financial information is left out. Did you overlook mentioning special financial circumstances, such as high medical bills or a disabled child at home, or that you have multiple children in college?

And just because you don't qualify for aid one year doesn't mean you won't the next. The school's aid pool or criteria may have changed, or your circumstances may have changed, such as a second child entering college.

Perhaps the greatest myth about financial aid is what impact savings will have on it. *How* you save—such as a custodial account versus a 529 savings plan—will influence a family's EFC, especially for affluent families on the margin for aid. The Harvard study, for example, shows that saving in certain types of college investments reduces aid more than an identical amount saved in different types. A CFP professional can help you sort out which options are best for your particular circumstances.

The key, however, is to not skip saving for college because you don't want to risk reducing financial aid. Remember, the majority of aid these days is loans. It's usually better to save in advance and *earn* interest than to borrow later and *pay* interest.

OTHER IDEAS

Home equity lines. Many parents choose home equity loans or second mortgages because they are readily available—assuming they have equity in their home and good credit. Home equity loans are tied to the amount of equity the borrower has in his or her home.

Age-based funds. These funds have investments that grow more conservative as the child nears college age. Many 529 plans feature such one-stop, "age-based" options.

Make sure you're watching fees. If your investment horizon is short, you need to watch how much you're paying to invest. Focus on stock funds that charge less than 1 percent in annual operating expenses and select bond funds with expense ratios of 0.75 percent or lower.

In Part 8, we look at buying your first home and real estate invest-ment—in fact, two very different things.

ENDNOTES

1. www.acenet.edu/AM/Template.cfm?Section=CPA&Template=/CM/ContentDisplay. cfm&ContentFileID=642.

2. www.collegeboard.com/press/cost02/html/CBTrendsAid02.pdf.

Part VIII

Bricks and Mortar

How Real Estate Can be Part of a Lifetime Financial Plan

Nancy Flint-Budde, CFP®

Buying your first home—or your fifth requires re-education every time you do it. Why? Because markets and opportunities change.

Nancy Flint-Budde, a CERTIFIED FINANCIAL PLANNER™ professional from Salem, New York, says individuals have gotten quite an education in investing from 1999 to 2006. "See what various markets have done. In 1999, everyone wanted to be in the stock market. By 2000, nobody wanted anything in bonds. And in 2005, the real estate market, which had been galloping at double-digit gains for more than ten years, was starting to go that way as well."

What a financial planner can bring to the real estate process is a clear view of mortgage options, debt management, and most important, planning for the day when an individual or family moves from home ownership into real estate investment.

"People have been looking at their homes as a source of cash in recent years, and as markets slow, we're going to see that point of view change," says Flint-Budde. "Planners are important because they help people avoid excessive risk and keep them diversified."

28 | *Buying Your First Home*

Whether you're in your twenties or much older, buying your first home is possibly the biggest single financial decision of your life. Yet home ownership is not for everyone. You not only need to understand the money side of the transaction, but your personal needs as well.

This book was written at a very interesting time in the real estate market. After more than a decade of annual double-digit price gains in many markets, the U.S. residential real estate market was starting to cool. This was particularly worrisome for several reasons. Housing debt—fueled by easy access to home equity loans—was eating away equity in a large number of American properties.

The Federal Reserve's Survey of Consumer Finances, released every three years, reported in February 2006 that average family incomes fell 2.3 percent between 2001 to 2004, dragged down by the sluggish recovery from the 2001 recession.

Real net worth—the difference between family assets and liabilities—rose only slightly from 2001 to 2004. Median net worth rose only 1.5 percent to $93,100 during the period, versus a 10.3 percent gain from 1998 to 2001. And liabilities rose faster than assets, due largely to a big rise in mortgage debt.

WHY BUY?

Generally, there are three primary reasons why people buy homes:

- **They want to cut their income taxes.** With a mortgage, you may be able to deduct the interest you're paying and property taxes from your taxable income. This cuts your income tax payment, and may make home ownership cheaper than renting.
- **They see it as an investment, not a long-term residence.** Some people buy housing they plan to live in as an investment (a concept we'll discuss further in Chapter 30). They live in it while they fix it up and then sell. Recently, the market was hot enough to do that and guarantee attractive profits. But markets slow and investors always need to be aware of that.
- **They want to build equity.** As a mortgage loan is paid down and housing prices head up in an area, homeowners build value in what they have bought. This provides an ownership stake that can be used for a home equity loan or line of credit or profit when the home is sold.

HOW MUCH DOWN PAYMENT DO YOU NEED?

A decade ago, mortgage loans were fairly traditional. There was little or no talk about home equity lines or interest-only loans, which we'll get to in more detail in the next chapter. A 20 percent down payment generally waived the added expense of private mortgage insurance (PMI), a requirement at banks in cases where they lend money to borrowers who obtain loans that are more than 80 percent of their new home's value. PMI plays an important role in the mortgage industry by protecting a lender against loss if a borrower defaults on a loan and by enabling borrowers with less cash to have greater access to homeownership.

While it is still good to deliver some level of down payment, with the aggressive rise in home prices over the last decade, fewer people can afford such a hefty chunk at the outset. Check with your lender to see how much less PMI will cost you based on how much down payment you can afford.

There's another alternative to paying PMI: the 80/10/10 loan. Here's how it works—you take out a first mortgage for 80 percent of the sales price, a second mortgage (or home equity loan) for the next 10 percent of the sales price, and put down 10 percent in cash. This means taking on significant debt, so discuss this choice with a financial adviser first.

WHAT TYPES OF PROPERTY ARE AVAILABLE?

While single-family homes, condominiums, and rental apartments top the list of real estate most people buy, other people increasingly buy property for rehabilitation and resale and out-of-town rental as well. Here's an overview of the key categories of properties most people buy and for what purpose:

- **Single-family home.** This is the most common form of residential property, the single-family detached house. Houses come in all shapes, sizes, and price ranges, but their physical characteristic is that the home sits by itself on its own piece of property. They are generally easier to finance than properties the owner does not live in, because the belief is that they will be better maintained and easier to appraise for value.
- **Condominium.** Condos exist in virtually every community of any size. Condos became popular in the 1970s, when state legislatures passed laws allowing their existence. When you purchase a condo, you are purchasing an actual unit, as some say, "from the inside paint in." That means the person who owns it also owns the walls, ceiling, and floor of the unit, and may also own the plumbing and perhaps a parking space if one is allotted to that unit. The buyer also owns a share in common elements of the building in conjunction with the other unit owners. Common elements may include the roof, plumbing, lobby, laundry room, garden area, or the garage. When it comes to

the outside structure of the building and common elements, there is a joint governing body, called the condominium association, that gathers facts, bids, and decides how money for repairs and other projects will be collected and paid out. Financing a condo purchase is similar to obtaining a mortgage on a single-family home, except that your lender may have restrictions on types of condos approved for FHA financing. Some lenders may grill you if you are not planning to live in the development because they like to see owners on site. Why? Because renters sometimes mess up the property or skip on the rent, which destroys your cash flow as an investor.

- **Cooperative apartments.** A housing co-op might look like an apartment or a condo, but the ownership structure is much different. Co-ops (short for "cooperatives") are apartment buildings owned by a corporation that's formed by developers or the original tenants of the building. Each resident owns shares of stock in a corporation, not their own unit. Co-op housing residents have the same potential tax benefits as other homeowners, including taking their share of the mortgage interest and real estate taxes as a deduction on their income taxes. While co-ops might be more affordable than similar condominium dwellings, their ownership structure requires that new buyers be approved, something that doesn't happen in a condo situation.

- **Townhouses.** Like condominium and co-op dwellers, town home-owners typically share a wall in common with neighborhoods. But townhome property may be held in a variety of ways. Most row houses built in the 20th century were held "fee simple," meaning that owners hold legal title to their structure and the land it sits on, and are personally responsible for all taxes assessed to that property. Some townhouses may be held as condos, but most are a hybrid, falling somewhere between condos and single-family homes.

- **Mobile homes.** These are a relatively cheap housing option, but they can become complicated to own. When buying or investing in a mobile home, it is almost more important to check out where you'll be placing the home, because management structures vary widely.

Mobile homes are not necessarily treated as any single-family home. It depends on the land-ownership structure underneath. In some parks, you must buy the lot for your home; in others, you can lease instead of buying it; and in others, you don't buy the land at all, but instead purchase a share in a corporation, much like buying a co-op. Property taxes are handled in various ways based on these distinctions. Like condo communities, co-op buildings, and town homes, mobile home parks have rules that must be followed by the residents. Banks and credit unions may lend for mobile homes, though most manufacturers do as well.

WHAT TYPE OF FINANCIAL SHAPE SHOULD YOU BE IN BEFORE YOU START LOOKING?

Before you make any major purchase, you need to do two things. First, extinguish as much debt as you can, and that certainly means credit card debt. Second, you need to make sure your credit reports are free of inaccuracies.

As tough as it might be, you'd also be wise to get your emergency fund in shape before a big home purchase. That means three to six months of income that needs to be set aside for emergencies—not down payments. It will be your insurance against an unexpected home repair in the future or the loss of a job that could impair your ability to meet your mortgage.

WHAT EXPERTISE DO YOU NEED?

Since sellers pay the real estate commission, not first-time buyers, you're not going to be stuck with a 4 to 6 percent commission on your first home. But that shouldn't stop you from making contact with a real estate agent in a community or neighborhood where you really want to buy. Knowledge is power. If you don't want to consult an agent, there are other resources:

- **Check local newspaper Web sites** for access to property transfer data in various neighborhoods right down to the specific street

SNAPSHOT

REAL ESTATE SEARCH TOOLS

The Internet has created a world of property search and management resources that puts individuals in the driver's seat as never before.

Web resources are spread throughout this book, but here's a summary of some of the most useful real estate investment sites you'll find on the Web:

Associations:
- National Association of Realtors
  www.Realtor.org
- National Association of Housing Cooperatives
  www.coophousing.org

Construction Assistance:
- RS Means Project Cost Estimator
  www.rsmeans.com/calculator/index.asp
- Hanley Wood (provider of specialized paid reports on specific home renovtion and construction projects)
  www.hanleywood.com

Credit Sites:
- Credit reports
  www.myfico.com

Economic Information:
- UCLA Anderson Forecast
  http://uclaforecast.com
- U.S. Census Bureau/Census of Housing
  www.census.gov/hhes/www/housing/census/histcensushsg.html

Financial/Tax Planning:
- Financial Planning Association
  www.fpanet.org
- Securities and Exchange Commission EDGAR database (to look up all public securities filings)
  www.sec.gov/edgar.shtml
- For 1031 exchanges:
  www.1031.org

Foreclosure Information:
- RealtyTrac.com
  www.RealtyTrac.com

Mortgage Trends:
- HSH Associates, Financial Publishers
  www.hsh.com

address. Start checking "comparables" (comparable prices) on property in the neighborhood where you want to buy. Check to see how far back you can trace transactions on particular properties to see how they've appreciated—or not.

- **Consult various lender Web sites** to see to trends for local mortgage rates and mortgage products. A good independent site is www.Bankrate.com, which lists current mortgage rates in various local markets.
- **Schedule a session with a financial adviser** such as a CERTIFIED FINANCIAL PLANNER™ professional for a holistic view of your financial picture before you start your search. He or she might also have a line on real estate attorneys to help you approve the paperwork when you do buy.

In the next chapter, we're going to take a closer look at home financing.

29 | *Home Financing— The Good, The Bad, and The Ugly*

Borrowing more money than you've ever seen in your life is definitely a memorable experience. There are smart ways to get there…and dumb ways too.

FIGURING OUT HOW MUCH HOME YOU CAN AFFORD

When people think about buying a home for the first time, only careful study and advice keeps them from overpaying. Generally, a housing payment shouldn't be more than 25 to 30 percent of a family's gross income.

The housing payment includes the actual mortgage payment (principal and interest), property taxes, and homeowners' insurance; commonly referred to as PITI. So, if your gross income is $4,000 a month, your monthly housing payment shouldn't be more than $1,200.

These days, most lenders will tell you that you can easily go 30 percent or more, and when housing prices were going up at a steady gallop, that might have been true because equity was following at a similarly brisk pace. But you have to consider the weight of a mortgage payment in good markets and bad. You also have to consider whether you could carry the payment if:

- You or your spouse lost your job
- You suddenly had to replace a car and needed to take on a car payment
- Your income and property taxes rose

That doesn't include paying expenses for yourself, your kids, and of course, saving for retirement. If you've forgotten the trouble that problem debt can cause, go back and read Chapter 8 and consider all of these things before you consider a home you can't afford.

RISKY LOANS—WHY YOU NEED TO AVOID THEM

A July 2005 study by LoanPerformance, a San Francisco-based mortgage loan research firm, showed that one of every four new mortgages was an interest-only loan—a loan that delays principal payments for three years or more to guarantee a borrower a lower monthly payment.

Skyrocketing real estate values, other forms of high-rate consumer debt, and a trend toward get-rich-quick real estate investment has driven supply and demand for loans that allowed lower monthly payments in exchange for slower growth of equity in property, or in some cases, no growth at all. Former Federal Reserve Chairman Alan Greenspan issued his own concerns in 2005: "There's potential for individual disaster here."

Are these new mortgage loans ticking time bombs? It depends on your financial situation and how you use them. It's best to get some advice before you respond to these offers. Based on your situation, some of these loan options may actually be good choices. Your tax adviser or CERTIFIED FINANCIAL PLANNER™ professional not only can help you understand these options, but he or she can assess your overall financial picture to see if they're right for you.

Whether they come from your current lender or a late-night infomercial, here's an overview of several nontraditional loan options on the market and their potential risks and rewards:

Interest-only loans. This immensely popular loan option allows a borrower to pay only the interest on the mortgage in monthly payments for a fixed term. After the end of that term, usually five to seven years, the borrower can refinance, pay the balance in a lump sum, or start paying off the principal, in which case the payments can rise. They do work for some people—for instance, those who expect their income to jump considerably in the next few years. Some types of interest-only mortgages have been around for decades and used by wealthy borrowers who were sophisticated and disciplined enough to find profitable uses for money saved on monthly payments. But today's loan products are increasingly marketed to ordinary homebuyers and, in many cases, to "sub-prime" borrowers who could not have qualified for standard loans in the past. That's where the risk comes in.

Zero-down mortgages. An increasingly common option for borrowers with less-than-perfect credit, these loans allow borrowers to buy with no money down. It gets a borrower into a home, but any chances of acquiring equity in a home will have to come from rising market values, and that's not something every borrower can count on. It might be better to ask for a low down payment alternative—such as FHA financing—that allows a borrower to have some small amount of equity at the start. A lack of equity in a property exposes a homeowner to greater foreclosure risk.

Piggyback loans. Some borrowers who can't make a 20 percent down payment may consider an end-run around private mortgage insurance by taking out a first and second mortgage concurrently. Typically, a piggyback loan works as follows: the most common type is an 80/10/10 where a first mortgage is taken out for 80 percent of the home's value, a down payment of 10 percent is made, and another 10 percent is financed in a second trust at possibly a higher interest rate. Some lenders may allow a piggyback loan for less than a 10 percent down payment.

100-plus loans. Also known as loan-to-value (LTV) mortgages, lenders promote these mortgage loans of 100 percent or more of appraised market value as a way to draw in customers who can't make a down payment. An overly high appraisal value in a sliding market, a loss of home value, or even worse, the loss of a job can lead very quickly to rising debt and possible loss of the home.

Negative amortization loans. Negative amortization means that a loan balance is increasing instead of decreasing. With a negative amortization loan, if a payment isn't enough to cover the interest and principal payment, the shortage is added to the loan balance, which means you never really start paying off the loan. Again, this may work for people in short-term housing situations in markets with rising rates, but those conditions are never guaranteed.

WHEN THE TIME COMES TO REFINANCE

In a rising interest rate environment, thoughts turn to refinancing. Many people try to go for fixed-rate mortgages or long-term adjustables to keep their payments from rising out of control. Some tips on doing it right:

Dispose of as much debt as you can. Obviously, getting the best rates is based in part on the debt level you're carrying now. Try to pay off as much high-rate debt as you can before you begin the process.

Make sure your credit reports are clean. Before you start applying to refinance, make sure your credit reports are free of errors. This will take at least a month, so the best strategy is to plan the process ahead of time.

SPOTLIGHT

Questions to Ask Loan Officers Before You Borrow

If you're planning to buy an investment property with this new crop of low down payment loans, you should ask your loan officer:

- How much will I have to pay each month?
- How much will I pay when (or if) this loan converts?
- Is this a negative amortization loan, and if so, how much will I owe on the loan balance when the super-low interest rate expires?
- What happens if rates rise?

Start with your goals. If you plan to stay in a home for a lifetime, steer toward fixed-rate loan options so you're not squeezed by rate increases.

Focus on in-house fees. By now, most conventional lenders have gotten wise to the notion that most consumers can spot extraneous fees. However, that doesn't mean you shouldn't ask about fees when you have questions. The chief culprits are application fees, document preparation, and loan-processing fees. Since most of these functions are paper-handling tasks done in-house, it's worth asking to see if you can bring those fees down.

Figure out how much that appraiser and credit report really cost. It gets a little tough to figure up the markup on these items, but see if the appraiser will tell you what his hourly rate is when he comes by to appraise your property. As for the credit reports, those are pretty easy—see what TransUnion (www.transunion.com), Experian (www.experian.com), and Equifax (www.equifax.com) charge for more than one credit report in a year. Then ask your lender where those fees are on your statement to see how closely they match.

Make rate comparisons on level ground. Say you have an offer for a 6.5 percent rate with one point and another lender has the same type of loan available for 6.5 percent and zero points. Review the numbers yourself or consult with your adviser or CERTIFIED FINANCIAL PLANNER™ professional in your area. Make sure you understand the tradeoffs and at what point in time, given your personal circumstances, one loan would have been preferable over the other.

What's Uncle Sam getting? It might be worth a call to the city clerk's or assessor's office to see what they charge lenders for recording, transfer, or tax-related fees, and again, double-check those fees on your statement.

Check for predatory practices. As rates go higher, conventional lenders get choosier about who they'll work with. That pushes more people down the food chain of lenders who are willing to take on riskier business. Make sure the lender you're working with doesn't add prepayment penalties or erroneous fees during the process.

See if going fixed-rate makes sense. Over the past few years, many lenders have been marketing adjustable-rate loans as a way for borrowers to keep payments down and draw on home equity. However, as short-term rates have moved beyond long-term rates, lenders are attempting to get more borrowers into fixed-rate products. Again, evaluate how long you plan to stay in the property before you agree.

Keep an eye on the rate horizon. If economic growth slows, the Federal Reserve could begin lowering short-term rates. There are no guarantees, but borrowers with longer-term adjustable mortgages might want to sit tight based on that scenario.

Know when to pull out of a bad deal. If you find something wrong with your refinancing deal at closing, you have three business days from the date of closing to mull it over. If you decide to reject the deal, you must notify the lender in writing within the three-day period. The lender then has 20 days to return your fees.

FIXING THE DAMAGE

During that floating cocktail party that was the 1990s, people weren't all that worried about tapping their home equity to pay off bills or do home improvements. Inflation was in check, investments and wages were still on the rise, and recession hadn't yet dampened the job picture.

The new century has brought new realities, and for many, a new view of the reality of borrowing against their homes. As the prime rate has risen since 2004 from a rate around 4 percent, the interest debt from home equity borrowings has sliced the cash flow of many households.

There are two primary kinds of home equity debt.

A home equity loan is a one-time, lump sum that is paid off over a particular amount of time with a fixed rate and number of payments. **A home equity line of credit** (also known as a HELOC), works more like a credit card because it has a revolving balance—interest is due on the out-standing balance and that rate may vary over time.

The bad news with the reliance on HELOC debt is that many more homeowners who have used the lines to make major purchases and pay off debt have not been able to wean themselves from continued use of credit cards and other spending while doing so. Add that combination to rising rates, and you see an increasingly large group of homeowners facing the risk of foreclosure, being forced to sell or downsize, or at best, staying in debt well into their senior years.

In the past few years, homeowners who have relied heavily on HELOCs have discovered that they don't have a useful spending tool but another big loan balance in the tens of thousands. Minus the plastic, rising interest rates have made HELOC debt feel like just another credit card eating through borrowers' wallets.

Ways to cope with the threat of rising debt:

Refinance into a fixed-rate first loan. If you have a good credit rating, are planning to stay in your home for awhile and otherwise have low debt, make every attempt to combine your first and second mortgages into a fixed-rate first mortgage and attempt to pay a little more than the minimum balance each month.

Cut up all but one emergency credit card. The term "emergency" now means what your parents meant—such as a car-breakdown emergency, not an emergency latte. Fixing long-term debt problems means redefining one's entire relationship with spending and credit.

Start tracking spending. If you've never bought a personal accounting program for your computer, now might be the time. Even if you total up your expenses the old-fashioned way (with boxes of receipts and sheets of paper), computerized tracking allows you to categorize your spending in ways where you can immediately see changes in spending patterns that you can correct. It makes it easier for year-end tax preparation too.

Make shopping lists for everything. Impulse buying is fine on birthdays, but not the rest of the year. Start creating lists not only for the grocery, but for necessary trips to the mall, drugstore, and discount store. Forcing yourself to list what you'll be buying gets you thinking about what you really need—soon, you'll be scratching things off.

Add to minimum payments. Get in the habit of paying amounts above the stated payment on mortgages, car loans, or any remaining credit card balances. You'll eliminate debt faster with minimal pain.

Set a budget. It may be the $4 trip for your mid-morning coffee or those extra cable channels, but once you make a decision to cut debt, it is also necessary to cut spending. Take a cold, hard look at everything nonessential in your daily spending, write down what you plan to live without, and stick to it.

Re-evaluate energy use. Cut back on the car trips, turn off the lights when you leave the room, and get used to wearing a sweater around the house. Current energy crises should build lifelong conservation habits that will save you money.

Cut back on unnecessary insurance. Cut out unnecessary coverages and raise deductibles on home and auto. What's unnecessary coverage? Generally anything you can easily pay out of pocket in an emergency.

In Chapter 30, we'll discuss real estate investment—a world different from real estate ownership.

30 | *Real Estate as an Investment*

According to the National Association of Realtors (NAR), nearly 40 percent of all home sales in 2005 were for second homes, up from 36 percent the year before. Of that number, 27.7 percent were for investment, compared with 23 percent in 2004, and 12.2 percent were bought as vacation homes.

NAR reports that the buying of investment properties continues a trend that started with changes in tax laws in 1997. Previously, when homeowners sold their primary residences, the only way to avoid capital gains taxes was to roll over gains into another, more expensive home. Now, couples can claim a $500,000 exemption on sales of primary residences, enabling them to downsize into less expensive houses and apply the difference to second home purchases.

THE DIFFERENCE BETWEEN INVESTMENT AND OWNERSHIP

The first thing you need to know about real estate investment is that it has nothing to do with home ownership. Your residence may represent a healthy portion of your personal wealth thanks to the real estate run-up of the last ten years, but it is not an investment. It is a home, a place of emotional and physical attachment.

Investments are meant to be bought and sold when market conditions warrant. The level of commitment you have to a real estate investment should be dependent *only* on the profit you can extract from it.

WAYS TO INVEST IN REAL ESTATE

- **Direct ownership of individual property.** Many people already own real estate—their home. In fact, it often is the single most valuable financial asset they own. But homes typically aren't counted as part of their investment portfolios because people usually don't use their home as an investment. It is a place they live in for personal reasons, and while they hope to sell it for a profit when they move, it commonly is with the intent to move into another, and presumably more expensive, home. (Some retirees sell and move into a smaller home or apartment, and use the profits to help fund their retirement.)

  A more likely way to invest directly in real estate is to buy individual properties, such as rental homes, apartment buildings, or office buildings. You then can generate income through depreciation-sheltered rent and sale for profit. This type of investing requires knowing the market well and being a landlord—not something the average investor may want to pursue. But it can be highly lucrative if done well.

- **Public and private limited partnerships.** These involve a limited number of partners investing in property managed by a general partner or sponsor (such as a brokerage firm). They are illiquid long-term investments, as there is a limited resale market. Limited partnerships were especially popular in the 1970s and 1980s until tax law changes, mismanagement, poor real estate values, and high fees killed the market. However, they are showing signs of life again.

- **REITs.** In existence since 1960, real estate investment trusts have become very popular in the last decade. These companies pool investor money, much like a mutual fund company does, to invest in real estate. **Equity REITs** buy income-producing property such as apartment buildings, office buildings, and shopping centers. REITs often specialize in certain regions or types of properties, such as self-storage buildings or health-care facilities. Income generally comes from rents, though there may be profits from the sale of the properties. **Mortgage REITs** buy mortgages and construction loans on commercial properties. **Hybrid REITs** buy property and mortgages. Buying a REIT is like buying and selling stock, and REIT prices fluctuate like stock prices. REITs pay out 95 percent of their net taxable income. Unlike limited partnerships, the over 200 REITs are easily traded on stock exchanges and over the counter.

- **Mutual funds.** There are a number of mutual funds that focus on real estate. They invest primarily in REITs or real estate-related industries such as homebuilders or building supply companies. Funds that invest primarily in REITs tend to be income-oriented. Some mutual funds invest in real estate overseas. The biggest advantage of mutual funds over other types of real estate investments is that they provide greater diversification and they are easier to select than the more specialized and complex REITs and limited partnerships.

THE FLIPPING PHENOMENON

There have always been "flippers" in real estate—people who buy distressed properties with cash and sell them to a waiting buyer. Yet the real estate frenzy of the last few years bears little resemblance to the cash-based process that provides the biggest opportunities for gains.

In the past few years, people have attempted to get into this field with debt, not cash, and those with the right skills did okay. Actually, some did more than okay in the right situations. But as real estate began slowing in late 2005 and interest rates began to accelerate, many flipper wannabes found out that the lure of easy profits blinded them to the potentially devastating financial risks of being in too much debt with property they couldn't sell at the price that would secure them a profit.

The bottom line is that real estate moguls aren't made in a day, no matter how many infomercials you watch.

In fact, real estate investment is either a career you can devote yourself to full-time, or in small, careful increments with a minimal dependence on debt. In fact, many newbie investors have found that a less-than-thorough once-over on a property can reveal expensive repairs that need to be done before the property can be resold. Sometimes, a buyer's financing falls through, the market cools, and you, the investor, are left with holding costs that far outstrip your cash flow until the property can finally sell.

So the question is—do you want to flip or do you want to invest for the long haul?

WHAT IT REALLY MEANS TO BE AN INVESTOR

Successful investing is informed investing. It also means having the money and time to be patient and to rescue yourself when things go wrong—and in the beginning, many things can go wrong. Here are characteristics of successful real estate investors:

- **They are students of finance, construction, and neighborhoods.** They spend anywhere from three months to a year learning all they can, until they feel comfortable making the move. If they miss an opportunity, they miss it.
- **They get to know bankers and other key property players personally.** For those who plan to get into the foreclosure market, they get to know bankers and courthouse staffers personally so they understand how the process really works. Infomercials and Web sites don't know what's going on in your community. People do.
- **They get their advisory team together first.** CPAs, attorneys, financial planners—the decision to invest in real estate cannot be isolated from your personal financial circumstances. Your personal finances and business finances will be connected to the moves you make in real estate investment whether you are planning for it to happen or not. Don't wait for the IRS to point that out.
- **They often start as owner-occupiers.** If you are handy, continue becoming a real estate investor as an owner-occupier. Learn to do the bulk of the renovation and fix-up work yourself, and be realistic about more dangerous or complicated jobs you know you cannot do. Owner-occupiers generally get more favorable loan and tax terms.

- **They try to have some cash in the bank.** Problems always crop up that lengthen time frames in renovation and selling. Real estate investors have to have a sizable emergency fund for that purpose alone.
- **They understand their investment limits.** While real estate deals are far from uniform, there are some rules of thumb for setting a dollar investment in a property or walking away entirely. For many, that means a target purchase price of at least 30–50 percent below the market value you'll create after you've fixed them up. That way, after you subtract rehab expenses, commissions, financing, and miscellaneous costs, your target is a minimum 20 percent profit margin.

TAX IMPLICATIONS OF REAL ESTATE INVESTMENT

If you start going crazy buying properties, don't be surprised if Uncle Sam knocks on your door wondering why you're not doing it as a formal business. Your advisers will point out that thin line between investor and business owner. It's a fairly expensive one. If investors hold the property for a year or more before selling, sale proceeds are considered long-term capital gains and are taxed at a 15 percent rate. If the IRS renders your property transactions as a business or a trade instead of ordinary investment, that could mean a tax hit as high as 35 percent.

Without planning, you'll quickly be scratching your head wondering why you ever made the first step. So be careful.

1031 EXCHANGES AND HOW THEY WORK

If you plan to buy and sell real estate as a long-term asset or retirement strategy, it's worth understanding the 1031 exchange.

Also known as "like-kind" exchanges, 1031 exchanges allow an investor to defer capital gains taxes if he or she sells a big asset, such as a rental vacation home, and invest the proceeds immediately in a similar asset. Although 1031 exchanges can apply to many types of exchanges, they are most often used for real estate. The advantage? The investor can delay tax consequences when upgrading the investment property he or she owns.

How 1031s got started. Named for their place in the U.S. tax code, 1031 exchanges were created in the 1920s for businesses and big-league investors who owned many assets and wanted a way to defer taxes over the long term. Until a few years ago, those groups were still the main customers for 1031 transactions— but skyrocketing real estate values and the rising number of Baby Boomers headed for retirement have made 1031 exchanges popular for smaller investors too. However, these are complex transactions and almost always require assistance from tax advisers and intermediaries required to facilitate each deal.

How 1031 exchanges work. The 1031 exchanges have strict time frames for buying and selling real estate if the exchange is not simultaneous, so it's important to find a broker and tax adviser who understand exactly how these complex transactions work. The simplest form of a "forward" 1031 exchange works like this: a person with available property identifies a property of "like-kind" value for an exchange. Because of the IRS's broad definition of "like-kind," the property doesn't have to be identical or for the exact same purpose—in other words, a six-unit apartment property could be exchanged for a warehouse, strip mall, or even undeveloped land. Under the basic rules of 1031 exchanges, investors have 45 days to identify up to three properties of equal or greater value that they plan to exchange for the old one and a total of 180 days to close the deal. The 1031 exchange transactions require the involvement of a third-party intermediary—often a tax or real estate professional—to hold the money while the exchange is done so the tax advantage doesn't evaporate.

What's a reverse exchange? It allows the replacement property to be purchased and closed on before the relinquished property is sold. Usually the intermediary takes title to the replacement property and holds title until the taxpayer can find a buyer for his relinquished property and close on the sale under an exchange agreement with the intermediary. Subsequent to the closing of the relinquished property (or simultaneous with this closing), the intermediary conveys title to the replacement property to the taxpayer.

What kind of property doesn't qualify under 1031? A personal residence; land under development; construction or fix/flips for resale; property purchased for resale; inventory property; corporation common stock, bonds, notes, and partnership interests.

Are there other restrictions? A person may be disqualified if they don't handle their 1031 strategy properly. An investor who buys and sells frequently may be declared a "dealer" of real estate and be subject to ordinary income taxes instead of capital gains. Consult an adviser.

Is there an easier way to buy? Qualified commercial real estate agents are often good at continually spotting properties that would qualify for a 1031 exchange. But keep in mind alternatives that may save money in brokerage costs. Major retailers that do a good job of scouting locations may also have an outreach function for attracting individual investors for syndicates formed to own their real estate. This type of ownership can also be done as a 1031 strategy, but again, with the right advice. Even the most established real estate opportunities have risks.

Keep abreast of the tax code. Even if an investor doesn't have as much expertise in tax issues as the average CPA or real estate attorney, it's important to have a basic understanding of the tax issues that affect real estate transactions. The IRS Web site (www.IRS.gov) is a good book-mark to help investors start that education.

In Part 9, we're going to move to the topic of insurance and what personal coverage you should carry.

Part IX

Understanding Insurance

As Individuals Take On More Risk, Insurance is a Critical Investment

Jim Barnash, CFP®

"Risk management is the foundation of the financial plan," explains Jim Barnash, a CERTIFIED FINANCIAL PLANNER™ professional based in Chicago. "And it takes many forms besides insurance."

A financial planner can take an individual or couple through their basic insurance needs—life, health, auto, disability, and eventually, long-term care insurance. "It's fairly easy to comprehend the value of protecting one's stuff," Barnash says. "But nonproperty coverage is tougher for people to understand, and a planner can really help with that."

A planner can also help coordinate other key plans and paperwork that need to be part of an individual or family's overall risk management plan. "Since 2001, we've seen 9/11, the Terry Schiavo life-support court battle, and Hurricane Katrina affect the way we look at disaster and risk," Barnash notes. "A planner can help you consider medical directives, home inventories, and most important, up-to-date estate planning to make things easier for your family to carry out your wishes exactly."

Insurance issues really need to be part of a broader disaster plan that need to be part of a broader disaster plan that should be reviewed every few years.

31 | *Life Insurance*

Life insurance is generally seen as a product for families, and to a big extent, that's correct. If you have someone who depends on your income and you're not a millionaire with plenty of cash to provide them after your death, then life insurance is a useful tool to help them pay expenses.

When is life insurance a good idea for single people without dependents? Only if your friends or family members don't have enough cash on hand to cover debts and funeral costs.

Most financial planners, including CERTIFIED FINANCIAL PLANNER™ professionals, would tell you that insurance is not a replacement for a long-term savings or investing strategy, but a supplement to it. For instance, life insurance and its ancillary products can have some very attractive tax characteristics, which we'll get to a little later.

WHO NEEDS IT?

Generally, those who need life insurance are people:

- With dependents: either children, friends, or family members with special needs
- With a nonworking spouse or spouse with an income substantially lower than yours
- With significant debts that would be too great for one income to pay off

HOW MUCH DO YOU REALLY NEED?

There are several rules of thumb on this issue, but here's some prevailing wisdom among most financial experts.

The right amount of life insurance will allow your dependents and beneficiaries to invest the insurance payout and then draw down the account over time in a way that matches the income you would provide if you were still around.

That's actually a better way to look at the issue than the "five or ten times annual income rule," because it not only settles on a dollar figure, but a strategy through which to invest and eventually spend the proceeds.

What factors enter into this calculation? Far more than a family's basic living expenses. Also consider:

- College funds needed for each child
- Money to cover special health expenses for a family member already diagnosed at the time of the insured's death
- Funds for child care if the surviving spouse needs to keep working

TYPES OF LIFE INSURANCE

Term. Term life insurance is the simplest kind of life insurance because it pays if death occurs during the term of the policy, which is usually from 1 to 30 years. There are two kinds of term life insurance: **level term** means that the death benefit stays the same throughout the duration of the policy, and **decreasing term** means that the death benefit drops in one-year increments over the duration of the policy. Most term policies are decreasing term policies.

Whole life/permanent. Whole life or permanent insurance pays a set amount at death and the insured pays a fixed premium as long as they live. For this guaranteed benefit, whole life is usually the more expensive choice because it front-loads its costs into the early premium years of the policy to invest the money to pay for death benefits at the end of several years or decades. At a certain point, the policy owner will pay enough to start accruing cash value on that money, which can be withdrawn if the policy owner decides to cancel the coverage. There are four types of permanent insurance:

- **Whole or ordinary life.** This is the most common type of permanent insurance policy, offering a fixed death benefit with a savings account. You agree to pay a certain amount in premiums on a regular basis for a specific death benefit. The savings element grows based on dividends the company pays to you.
- **Universal or adjustable life.** This variation offers a little more flexibility, such as the possibility of increasing the death benefit if you pass a medical exam. The savings product attached to this kind of account generally earns a money market rate of interest, and after you start accumulating money in this account, you'll generally have the option of altering your premium payments. This helps if you lose your job or have some other financial misfortune. However, there's no free lunch—if you use up your reserve fund for this feature and are forced to stop paying a premium altogether, there goes your coverage.
- **Variable life.** This policy lets you invest your cash value (the savings element of a permanent life insurance policy, which represents the policy owner's interest in the policy) in stocks, bonds, and money market mutual funds, which is good if those investments go up. If they go down, your cash value and death benefit will probably shrink, but you need to make sure there's a guarantee that your death benefit won't fall below a certain level.
- **Variable-universal life.** This choice allows you the flexibility of premium payments with a more aggressive investment scenario for the cash value of the policy.

ANOTHER OPTION: RETURN-OF-PREMIUM TERM LIFE INSURANCE

One of the big gripes people have about buying any kind of insurance is that they'll never see their premium dollars again. Well, if you think you're the one policyholder who's going to beat the odds health-wise, there might be a way to buy coverage and get your money back too.

In recent years, insurance companies have promoted a concept called return-of-premium term life insurance, which pays back in a lump sum all the premium dollars insured people pay into their policy, as long as they keep the policy for its full term. It sounds like a good deal, but some financial planners and insurance experts express caution.

Here are the catches:

- **Higher cost.** The annual premiums for the return-of-premium policy are 47 percent higher than the premiums for the standard term policy. The shorter the term, the more you'll pay. Also, the older you are when you buy this coverage, the higher your premiums are going to be.
- **You might risk being underinsured.** Financial planners strongly recommend that the first priority for life insurance is to have sufficient coverage. If you can't realistically afford ROP coverage for the amount you need, but you can for regular term, you probably should go with the regular term. You also don't want the higher ROP premiums derailing contributions to retirement plans or excluding other insurance needs, such as disability coverage.
- **You're stuck for the whole term.** Historically, holders of term insurance keep their policies for an average of only eight or nine years before they either drop coverage or switch policies. Yet over 20 or 30 years, you might go through some difficult financial times and be forced to drop the steeper-priced ROP policy.

Some critics of these policies argue that people would be better off buying a cheaper standard term policy and investing the difference that would have gone to ROP premiums, particularly if they can invest in a tax-deferred retirement account.

Proponents counter that many people are not disciplined enough to consistently and wisely invest the difference. They claim you'd have to earn 6 to 8 percent annually to accumulate an amount equal to the amount of the return of premium. Furthermore, that invested amount will eventually be taxed, unlike the ROP refund.

LIFE INSURANCE'S INVESTMENT AND TAX ADVANTAGES
Life insurance proceeds don't generally go into Uncle Sam's collection

plate, which makes life insurance an attractive purchase for many individuals hoping to maximize the amount to give to heirs. Yet life insurance can also be purchased in a way to give the living policyholder tax-free income during retirement.

One of the popular vehicles to do this is at the time this book was published was the revocable life insurance trust. This 2006 example from the *Journal of Financial Planning* indicates how the purchase of life insurance can provide considerable investment and protection value to individuals who aren't particularly wealthy:

> Consider the case of a young married couple, Bob and Susan. Both are employed, and they have two children, ages five and three. Bob and Susan do not have estate tax issues, but they are concerned about the costs of their children's education, especially if either parent dies prematurely.
>
> Although Bob and Susan have some life insurance to cover part of the income-replacement problem, they are particularly risk averse about investment return and the inflation rate of future educational costs. They estimate that the cost of education would be $150,000 for both children. Bob and Susan each buy a $150,000 term insurance policy and name a revocable trust as beneficiary.
>
> The revocable trust provides broad investment powers and directs the trustees chosen by Bob and Susan to hold the proceeds in a common trust fund until the younger child finishes college. The trust document directs the trustee to distribute income or principal as needed for education costs. After the younger child graduates, the trustee is directed to hold the remaining fund in equal separate shares for later distribution—for example, when the beneficiary reaches age 30. The trust is also named as contingent beneficiary of the other policies, including any group term life insurance Bob and Susan have from their employer.
>
> Revocable trusts can allow investment of the proceeds to be much more creative and appropriate for the time horizon than under

a court-supervised guardianship for the minor children. In addition, distributions can be delayed beyond the age of majority. In some states, a nominal amount of funding may be required to create a valid living trust. Alternatively, a testamentary trust created under their wills could be designated as the beneficiary or contingent beneficiary of life insurance policies to accomplish a similar purpose. Again, state probate law should be examined to make sure that paying life insurance to a testamentary trust doesn't cause any disadvantages, such as greater probate costs or exposure to creditors. In addition, some states require nominal funding of a living trust in addition to the mere designation of the trustee as beneficiary of a life insurance policy.[1]

Since we're talking about estate issues here, getting proper advice is critically important. The federal government's current estate tax ceilings were set to expire in 2010, and this fact alone could affect the attractiveness of this strategy for your situation.

SHOULD YOU BUY LIFE INSURANCE FOR YOUR KIDS?

There is plenty of debate on this topic. Some planners believe life insurance is a good purchase on behalf of your kids since, at the very least, it provides burial funds if something horrible occurs, or at best, it provides a way to set aside cash to draw on for the future. Others believe that life insurance is a lousy way to set aside money for burial expenses and an even lousier way to invest for their kids' futures, given the current popularity of 529 college savings plans and other kinds of investment accounts.

Some experts believe that life insurance might be a good investment for kids if there's a poor health history in the family and money may be needed to draw on for medical or death expenses.

Ultimately, this is a discussion for you and your financial adviser.

In the next chapter, we'll discuss purchasing insurance for your home.

ENDNOTE

1. David Cordell and Ted Kurlowicz, "Life Insurance Trusts Aren't Just for the Wealthy," *Journal of Financial Planning*, May 2006, pp. 42-44.

32 | *Home Insurance*

Horrible disasters not only wipe out property, but lives. Particularly at times when so many homeowners are significantly leveraged with mortgage and credit card debt, the amount and quality of home insurance can make the difference between normalcy and financial ruin.

WHAT SHOULD HOME INSURANCE COVER?

If you own, you need to insure:

- The replacement value of the physical structure of the home, not including the value of the land
- The replacement value of your personal possessions (including significant quantities of jewelry, technology, art, or other objects that may require additional insurance on their own)
- The cost of living expenses off-site if your home is too damaged to live in
- Your liability to others

Most leading insurers assign values to these coverages, and, for the most part, they meet local standards. But your agent needs to know about renovations and additions to the property as they're added so you can truly replace what you have.

Standard homeowners' policies provide coverage for disasters such as damage due to fire, lightning, hail, explosions, and theft. They do not cover floods, earthquakes, or damage caused by lack of routine maintenance.

Flood insurance is available from the Federal Insurance Administration (www.fema.gov) and earthquake coverage is available from private insurance companies or, in California, through the California Earthquake Authority (www.earthquakeauthority.com).

In the wake of Katrina, some insurers were starting to curtail hurricane coverage, so it's important to know what individual insurers are offering in your area and whether they're referring coverage to other insurers. Obviously, when fewer companies are competing for customers, premiums go up.

WHAT IS REPLACEMENT VALUE?

Insurance with the correct replacement value would cover the amount it would take to rebuild your home thoroughly right on the same piece of land.

Beware of any home insurance policies that base coverage on "fair market" or "cash value." That means the company will cut their payment based on the wear and tear they believe the item had, and on top of that, you'll be forced to substantiate the value of the item when it was lost or destroyed.

Replacement value replaces what was lost. Period. However, there are certain stipulations. Some insurers will pay only if you replace items within a certain time period; if you are out of your home for six weeks and your policy stipulates replacement of covered items in four, you have a problem. Also, if you choose not to replace a covered item for any reason, how will you be reimbursed for the covered loss?

To be safe, designate a weekend to photograph the interior and exterior of your home—in sections so it can be clearly seen. Take tight shots of appliances and other valuable items. If you haven't bought a digital camera, consider one that not only photographs a wide area, but one that can take tight shots of jewelry and other small items you know you'll want replaced. Burn these photos onto a CD that you can keep in a safe place, and if you feel the need to show any of these items to an agent for special coverage over and above your existing coverage, bring the CD to his or her office.

The Insurance Information Institute says you can start estimating the replacement value for the structure of your home by multiplying the total square footage of your home by local building costs per square foot. You can find out this information from your local real estate agent, builder's association or insurance agent.

There are other factors you need to consider:

- The type of exterior wall construction—frame, masonry (brick or stone), or veneer
- The style of the house (ranch, colonial)
- The number of bathrooms and other rooms
- The type of roof and materials used
- Other structures on the premises such as garages, sheds
- Fireplaces, exterior trim, and other special features like arched windows
- The cost of custom-built kitchens, bathrooms, or other improvements

See if you can add an inflation guard feature to your homeowner's policy to cover increases in construction costs.

WHAT ARE ENDORSEMENTS?

People are investing in expensive entertainment centers, computer systems, and other costly possessions that take a lot of money to replace. That's on top of jewelry, cameras, and other traditional valuables that homeowner's policies may not cover completely in case of lost or theft.

You may need to buy an endorsement for those goods. Endorsements, sometimes called "floaters," are additional coverage you can purchase for your homeowner's insurance policy. They cover specific risks that are not included on a standard policy and as such are dependent on your needs and lifestyle.

Ask your agent what's right for you. And make sure you have that equipment photographed as well, including serial numbers and other identifying features.

INSURING CONDOS, CO-OPS, AND APARTMENTS

Home insurance isn't only for freestanding homes. Condo owners and apartment dwellers also need to insure their property and belongings.

For condos and co-ops, you need to know what areas are covered by the condominium and co-op and what areas you'll need to insure. You'll obviously need to insure your own belongings and certain designated areas of the structure. Check with your association to make sure your policy covers the right elements.

Renters should invest in insurance for their possessions since landlords don't cover those losses. Some landlords will also require you to carry liability insurance, in case someone is hurt inside your apartment while visiting or working there.

WHAT ARE DEDUCTIBLES?

Deductibles are the amount of out-of-pocket cost you pay before the insurance kicks in, and just like auto and health insurance, home insurance gets cheaper when you raise the deductible.

But here's the point about taking on a higher deductible for your insurance. Make sure you sock money away—or put that difference in your emergency fund—to make sure you have enough money to pay your deductible if you need to.

WHAT IF YOU HAVE TO MOVE TEMPORARILY?

If you are put out of your home by some natural disaster, fire, or other insured cause that makes your home unlivable, make sure you have coverage to pay your living expenses. This is called loss-of-use coverage. Be very precise about what this will cover—hotel, food, utilities, and transportation.

WHAT'S AN UMBRELLA POLICY?

An umbrella policy is critical coverage if you keep your home, auto, and watercraft (if you own a boat) insurance at one carrier. Individual coverage in each of those areas has limits on liability insurance. Umbrella policies are designed to give a person added liability protection above the limits on those individual policies. Depending on the company and your record, you can add an additional $1 to $5 million in liability coverage.

WAYS TO SAVE

Carriers who insure both home and auto will sometimes offer a discount for customers who buy their home and auto policies at the same place, so in addition to umbrella coverage, see what that grouping will save you.

Other factors that save or cost money on home insurance:

- **The way your home is constructed.** If you live in a wooden home with wooden siding, you're going to pay more because wood is less resistant to fire.
- **The kind of pets you have.** Some insurers are penalizing homeowners for certain breeds of dogs and other animals believed to be more violent than others, thus raising the risk of liability.
- **Your proximity to the fire department.** Premiums may be affected by the distance between your home and fire department, the quality of the department's fire-fighting equipment, level of training, and response history.
- **The crime rate in your neighborhood.** High-crime neighborhoods are more expensive to insure.
- **The likelihood of natural disasters.** Hurricanes in the Gulf and East Coast, mudslides, wildfires, and earthquakes in the West, tornado alleys in the Midwest. If there's a pattern of weather or geological behavior where you live, you're going to pay higher premiums that cover likely damage.
- **The age of your home.** Older homes are susceptible to breakage, erosion, and other risks.

- **Your claim history.** If you file claims for every little problem, you'll pay more.
- **Your credit rating.** The less attractive your credit rating, the more you'll pay because high debt and shaky payment behavior suggest that you might let a property deteriorate or delay payments on mortgages or other home-related debts.
- **Your deductible.** One of the few things you can directly control. If you pay a higher deductible, you'll get a lower premium. However, you need to make sure you can afford the deductible if a loss happens.

In the next chapter, we'll look at disability insurance and why most American workers need it.

33 | *Long-Term Disability Insurance*

Disability insurance protects your ability to earn an income. It pays your rent or mortgage, and all your basic living expenses if you are injured or sick for an extended period.

Think your employer's coverage is enough? Think again. You'll have whatever sick leave you have coming, and then short-term disability that at most employers usually doesn't last more than 12 weeks. There are employers that offer long-term disability coverage, but if you've never checked the terms of that coverage, you should.

It never hurts to consult a financial adviser with expertise in this subject, such as a CERTIFIED FINANCIAL PLANNER™ professional.

BASIC COMPONENTS OF LONG-TERM DISABILITY COVERAGE

Total benefits. Long-term disability insurance is structured to pay 60 percent of your income. See if the policy you're buying offers you the chance to buy more insurance as your income increases in future years.

Benefit term. For each disabling incident, your policy may pay benefits for a certain period—two years, five years, or until retirement. Most disability insurers don't pay for life because this coverage is intended to pay

293

disability during your working years.

Buying younger is better. Like health and life insurance, the younger you buy, the less you'll pay. For women, that's an exception because they currently live longer than men. Occupation enters into the picture because high-risk jobs (where disability is a greater work-related factor) tend to draw more claims. Like health insurance, it will consider your medical history and your lifestyle, including whether you smoke or drink to excess.

CONSIDERING SELF-EMPLOYMENT?

You'll especially need long-term disability insurance because you'll be out on your own. But buy before you quit your current employer—you'll be priced on your long-term employment, wage, and health history. It's going to get tougher to buy that same level of coverage when you're on your own.

Premium cost. Like most types of health and life insurance, the younger you get a policy, the better deal you'll get on the premium. But there are no simple charts in this category of insurance like there are for term life insurance. The premium will depend on a wide array of factors and can vary dramatically from person to person. It will consider such things as your age, your sex (women pay more for DI because they tend to live longer, sicklier lives than men), your job (librarian: good; dynamite handler: bad), your income, your medical history, and your lifestyle, including the use of tobacco and alcohol.

Cancellation policy. Make sure that once you're approved, the insurer can't cut your coverage unless it decides to stop writing coverage for everyone in your job class. It should also state they can't raise your rates.

Guaranteed renewable. Like the category above, it means you can't be canceled, except if the insurer stops writing insurance for your job category. They can, however, raise the rates for everyone in the category.

Own occupation vs. any occupation. If you have "own occupation" coverage, it goes into effect if you can't perform the functions of the job you're now in. "Any occupation" coverage pays only if you can't work at any job where you've been reasonably trained to do the tasks. For example, if you're a writer, you could be easily transferred to a receptionist's job or some other function within a company that involves using a computer and answering phones—tasks you did in your original position. That could significantly interfere with your recovery time, so specify "own occupation" coverage.

Elimination period. Like a deductible in home, health, or car insurance, the elimination period is a big cost determinant in disability coverage. Most policies will kick in after 30 days after you've been declared disabled.

 TIP: **DISABILITY POLICY CHECKLIST**

America's Health Insurance Plans (AHIP) provides the following checklist on reviewing any disability policy before purchase:

1. How is disability defined? Inability to perform your own job? Inability to perform any job?
2. Does the policy cover accidents? How about illness?
3. Are benefits available for total disability? For partial disability? For residual disability? Only after total disability?
4. Are full benefits paid, whether or not you are able to work, for loss of sight, speech, hearing, or use of limbs?
5. What percentage of income will the maximum benefit replace?
6. Is the policy noncancelable, guaranteed renewable, or conditionally renewable?
7. How long must I be disabled before premiums are waived?
8. Is there an option to buy additional coverage, without evidence of medical insurability, at a later date?
9. Does the policy offer an inflation adjustment feature? If so, what is the rate of inflation? Is there a maximum?

But if you specify an elimination period of 60, 90 or 120 days, your premium will drop. An important point about the 30-day elimination period is that the benefits don't start accumulating until you've been laid up a month after the ruling date, and you won't get your payment until a month after that. Be very clear with your insurer about when you'll get your first check based on what elimination period you choose, and funnel the money you'll need in the meantime to your emergency fund.

Partial payments/residual benefits. Some policies may offer you "residual benefits" or a partial payment if you're less than 100 percent disabled, but still can't perform all the duties of your job.

Rehabilitation riders. Carriers are doing more these days in the area of benefits for rehabilitation and job retraining. (It makes sense—the faster they get you back on the job, the sooner they can stop paying benefits.) Ask whether the policy includes a rehabilitation rider.

Business recovery benefits. Some policies give business owners compensation for certain office expenses and payments after you come back to the job and have to spend most of your time re-establishing your customer or client base.

Make sure you take stock of all the disability benefits owed you—from your employer, from your state, from the U.S. Department of Veterans Affairs if you've served in the military, or Social Security. Do the same fact checking you'd do on private insurance to see when those benefits would start and how much you'd get.

In Chapter 34, we'll take a look at buying auto insurance.

34 | *Auto Insurance*

After taxes and the addition of the most basic of options, today's entry-level new automobile can easily cost more than $20,000. If you're involved in an accident, you're facing thousands of dollars—sometimes tens or hundreds of thousands of dollars—in liability, in health-care and property costs if you're ruled negligent behind the wheel.

Is that the kind of cash you have on hand?

Those who risk driving without insurance not only risk immediate financial ruin, but they endanger their credit rating, which gets noticed by lenders and future employers.

Auto insurance isn't just about being able to fix a few dings on the car.

WHAT AUTO INSURANCE COSTS

The cost of auto insurance varies based on your gender, age, where you live, what you drive, your existing credit rating, and your accident record. It also varies significantly by carrier, so you need to check with several types of insurance companies on comparable coverage before you make a choice.

There really is no national average for pricing on auto insurance, but experts maintain that six-month premiums between various carriers can vary widely.

How best to check? About a month before your next premium bill is due, gather the names of insurers suggested to you by friends and relatives. Make it a mix of major carriers as well as high-quality smaller carriers. You can go to A.M. Best's Web site (www.ambest.com) to check out the ratings on the various carriers you choose—Best rates insurers on their financial strength, which is a good indicator of their ability to pay claims.

Check with your state insurance department to find out if any of the carriers on your list have had regulatory problems—it's a good indicator of whether they respond to customers and pay warranted claims.

And here's one more important tip—check all these details before you buy your dream car.

What you'll pay is linked to the following:

- **The make and model of the car you're driving.** If you're buying or leasing a particular automobile, check the rates first—SUVs, convertibles, and other performance cars typically cost more to insure. Of course, you might find a wide range of rates within certain model categories, so that's another good reason to widen your selection of vehicles before you buy.
- **Your age.** Adult drivers with clean driving records generally pay less than people in their teens and twenties.
- **Your gender.** Until the age of 25, there is a wide disparity between what males and females will pay, as most parents know. A female teen driver may add 50 percent to a family's annual auto premium, but an under-25 male driver may easily double the family's premium. Why? Young males generally have worse driving records than young females.
- **Where you live.** Higher-crime areas boost premiums for all insured property—cars, homes, and businesses.
- **Safety devices on the vehicle.** If your car has anti-lock brakes, side and front air bags, automatic seat belts, and plenty of safety lights on the car, that has the potential to lower your premium.

- **Your driving record.** If you've had frequent tickets, particularly for moving violations, alcohol-related offenses, or other driving-related run-ins with the law, that will add to what you pay if a carrier agrees to insure you at all.
- **Your claims history.** Frequent claims raise your premium, period. Most people drive around with dings because fixing them will ding their insurance rates.
- **Security issues.** Anti-theft devices will cut dollars off your premium, as will a commitment to parking in a locked garage or other safe area.
- **Your deductible.** One of the few things you can directly control. If you pay a higher deductible, you'll get a lower premium. However, you need to make sure you can afford to pay the deductible if a loss happens.

WHAT YOUR POLICY COVERS

Your auto policy covers two things: liability and property damage. Here's what that means:

Liability coverage. Most policies cover bodily injury, property damage, and uninsured/underinsured motorists. Bodily injury liability insurance protects you if you're sued by someone who was injured in an accident in which you were ruled at fault. They might claim medical expenses, lost wages, and pain and suffering.

Liability for property damage coverage pays for any damage you cause to other people's property. This not only includes other vehicles, but stationary property like walls, fences, and equipment. Meanwhile, uninsured motorists coverage protects you if you're injured in a hit-and-run or by an uninsured driver.

Property damage coverage. This is apart from property liability coverage. It includes collision coverage and comprehensive coverage. Collision coverage pays for the physical damage to your car if you hit an object or another car. This coverage is generally not required by law, but if you have an outstanding auto loan, your lender might require it. If you have an older car, insurers might "total" it rather than pay the full value of the repair because that cost may exceed the actual worth of the car.

Comprehensive coverage, meanwhile, pays for damage to your auto from almost all other causes, including fire, severe weather, vandalism, floods, and theft. The law generally doesn't require you to carry this coverage, but again, check with your lender.

INSURING YOUR FIRST CAR

Whether you get your first car in your teens or after you start your first full-time job, there are many ways to trim the staggeringly high cost of insurance under the age of 25. Some of the primary ways are listed above, but here are a few more.

If you still live with your parents, you might consider staying on their policy and paying the difference, because your parents—if they're drivers with a good record—will generally keep your portion of the payment lower than if you bought your own policy. Another tip—pay your parents on time.

To control your premium, see if you can commute to work most days by public transportation and confine the bulk of your car use to the weekend. That's a money-saver on premiums at any age.

If you purchase a used car or if parents give you their old car, consider dropping collision coverage, but check to see what the car's service record is and whether dropping collision is going to make that big a difference in the premium. Depending on the make and model, sometimes the collision portion of the policy isn't that big a deal. It all depends on the car and your desire and ability to replace it.

BUYING COVERAGE FOR A FAMILY

You probably already know that insuring teenagers is going to be expensive. But there are ways to keep what you'll pay under control.

- It's going to be a big hit, but put your kids on your policy. It'll be cheaper than insuring them separately.
- If your child goes to college without the car, alert your insurer. You'll get a discount for the time they're away from the car.

PLANNING TIPS: IF YOU'RE A DIVORCED PARENT WITH A TEEN DRIVER...

You and your ex need to coordinate auto insurance coverage before your child gets his driver's permit. In most cases, experts advise the parent who has the child in residence for the most time to add the child to his policy. However, if the living situation is split into large chunks of time in different municipalities, each parent might want to add the child to his or her policy during the relevant timeframe.

It might make the most sense to discuss this issue with an expert such as a CERTIFIED FINANCIAL PLANNER™ professional, to make sure you both get the best deal on coverage with no danger of lapses.

If you're caught letting your teen drive without coverage, you'll risk losing your own insurance.

If you're a parent who carpools your nondriving kids and their friends to all sorts of activities, you might want to consider additional liability coverage in case an accident happens with a full car.

Take a tip from our chapter on home insurance and buy umbrella coverage for your home and auto that will provide additional protection if you are constantly transporting nonfamily members.

- Make sure your child takes a drivers' training course and keeps his or her grades up. Kids with good grades are generally considered more responsible and more likely to be safer behind the wheel. You'll get a discount for that.
- Choose that family sedan with the extra airbags. If you're going to insure a teenager on the family policy, make sure you do it on a car with the best safety rating you can afford.
- Talk to your kid about safe driving. You talk to your children about the dangers of drugs, alcohol, and sex—make sure you've added this important issue to the list.
- Lead by example. If you haven't figured this out already, your kids

watch everything you do. If you cut corners on the road, chances are excellent they'll do so as well.

In the next chapter, we'll investigate the basics of finding individual health coverage.

35 | *Health Insurance*

A generation ago, nobody talked much about having to buy their own health insurance.

Employers found it easier—and more affordable—to supply coverage to their workers. Self-employment was not as popular as it is today, so the demand for independent coverage wasn't as great. And the information age had not matured to the point where financial and health data was so accessible to insurance providers in helping them decide the health haves and the health have-nots.

The search for health insurance today is challenging

Figure 37.1: Percent of Households "At Risk" at Age 65 by Age Group and Income Group

Number of Self-Employed Business Owners
Current Population Survey, Outgoing Rotation Group Files (1979–2003)

Source: University of Chicago, Santa Cruz.

for healthy people and much more so for people with pre-existing conditions—conditions and diseases that predate the current search for coverage and may prove expensive to the insurer down the line. Whenever you search for coverage, the results are usually a rude awakening in terms of cost and availability.

People who are planning to become self-employed should definitely review their insurance situation *before* they step out on their own. That means they should check out independent options even if they plan to temporarily buy insurance through COBRA (Consolidated Omnibus Budget Reconciliation Act).

COBRA permits employees to continue group health benefits provided by their group health plan for limited periods of time under certain circumstances such as voluntary or involuntary job loss, reduction in the hours worked, transition between jobs, death, divorce, and other life events. Qualified individuals may be required to pay the entire premium for coverage up to 102 percent of the cost to the plan.

Because COBRA isn't exactly cheap, it makes sense to check outside coverage as well as COBRA for the best price and offerings.

WHERE TO START

The ability to buy health-care coverage should start with an examination of insurance availability in your state. "Guaranteed issue" is the term given in states that guarantee that insurance for all or most health conditions can be written for every individual who wants it, no matter what their condition. That sounds good until you realize that insurers can charge what they want to meet this requirement, and that often means that independent coverage can be unaffordable in those states that have that provision.

Call or check the Web site of your state insurance department to see what the conditions are for acquiring independent coverage in your state.

THE NEXT STEPS

Once you check out the state situation, these are generally the next steps toward finding the best coverage.

Find two health insurance brokers who know your market. You might be able to find brokers who deal in health benefits through your company, professional organizations, or entrepreneurial message boards on the Internet. You might also have luck finding local brokers through friends, colleagues, and your chamber of commerce. Let them bid out coverage based on your health and age particulars, and see what they bring back.

Reputable brokers will tell you how various insurers behave; whether they're swift at paying claims or if they multiple-query every claim that comes in. Brokers should also know what health histories and pre-existing conditions are automatic grounds for rejecting your application.

Countersurf. Generally, you should be extra cautious when you shop for anything on the Web, and health insurance is no exception. However, you can gain some perspective by going to such sites as eHealthInsurance.com (for individual coverage) and DigitalInsurance.com (for group insurance). These sites will quote basic rates (your rates may differ) based on your age and location, and give you a summary of coverage, co-pays and other details. You can use these sites to better understand any broker quotes you're given.

Investigate requirements for your state's high-risk pool. If you've been turned down for insurance, your state provides a last-resort solution, and that's the state insurance pool. Check it out at your state's insurance regulation site and go from there. Warning—prices will undoubtedly be steep.

See if you can form a group. Again, this is something you need to check out with your state and then your tax adviser if you are self-employed and can prove it. Some states will allow you to buy group coverage with as few as two employees, and some states may even allow the formation of a group of one. The coverage will likely be cheaper, but there's going to be plenty of paperwork.

Join an association with coverage. Some chambers of commerce and professional organizations offer the opportunity to join up for group coverage. Chambers of commerce tend to be a better bet because they insure a wide variety of people and not necessarily the sickest.

If all else fails. Consider going back to work for a company with a decent health plan. You might have to wait three to six months to get on the plan, but if you have a serious health condition, it might be necessary.

CONSIDERING HSAS AND HIGH-DEDUCTIBLE POLICIES

Health savings accounts (HSAs) are a way for people considering high-deductible policies—about the only way to get an affordable premium these days—to get a tax break while they save to cover the cost of that deductible.

Here's how they work:

What is an HSA? Health savings accounts were created as part of the Medicare Modernization Act of 2003, but have not been wildly popular because they're complicated. Anyone under age 65 who buys a qualified high-deductible health plan (HDHP) can open an HSA. However, you can own an HSA and be covered under other types of insurance policies that cover liability, dental, vision, and long-term care needs, as long as the same expenses are not covered by both your HSA and the insurance policy.

How do I find a qualified policy? If you're employed, your employer obviously selects a qualified option and makes that available to you. However, for individuals or sole proprietors buying such policies, you need to put in some search time since HSAs haven't gotten much of a marketing push. Obviously, ask if your current insurer has a qualified plan, and there are Web sites you can search for ideas—www.hsainsider. com and www.healthdecisions.org.

What are the minimum deductibles for qualified policies? For 2006, the minimum deductible for high-deductible health policies is $1,050 for individual coverage (increased from $1,000 for 2005) and $2,100 for family coverage (increased from $2,000 for 2005). Policies must also not have an out-of-pocket maximum (including deductibles and co-pays) greater than $5,250 (single) and $10,500 (family).

If I find a policy, should I automatically buy it? No. Since this is a tax issue as well as an insurance issue, it makes sense to discuss this decision with your tax or financial adviser, such as a CERTIFIED FINANCIAL

Planner™ professional.

How much can I contribute to an HSA? Your maximum contribution is the lesser of your insurance plan deductible or the maximum allowed by the IRS. For 2006, the maximum annual HSA contribution for an eligible individual is $2,700. For family coverage, the maximum annual HSA contribution for 2006 is $5,450. Similar to IRAs, there is also a catch-up provision for individuals 55 or older—$700 in 2006.

What's the difference between an HSA and a medical flexible spending account (FSA)? One important difference is that HSAs allow balances to be rolled over from year-to-year, growing on a tax-free basis as long as they're used for medical expenses. On the other hand, medical FSAs require that the money you contribute each year be spent by year-end or you'll lose it. But in certain cases, such as when you incur medical expenses early in a year, you can be reimbursed by your FSA without having to fully fund it—so FSAs might be a better deal. Get help from your tax or human resources professional.

Can I have both an HSA and a flexible spending account? It depends. If your FSA provides for limited reimbursement for items not covered by your health insurance plan (such as dental, vision, or wellness care), you can use an HSA for items covered by your plan and your FSA for medical expenses that are not. Obviously, double-check this with an expert.

What happens if I need to use my HSA dollars for any nonmedical reason before age 65? You'll get hit with a 10 percent penalty, plus any withdrawals will be taxed at ordinary income tax rates. After age 65, you're free to use the funds for any purpose without penalty, but nonmedical withdrawals are still taxable.

In the next chapter, we'll discuss long-term care insurance.

36 | *Long-Term Care Insurance*

Long-term care (LTC) insurance is not just a subject for people over 55. The earlier you start thinking about the kind of coverage you'll want and need, the better.

Why consider LTC insurance? The MetLife Mature Market Institute provided some sobering statistics in 2005:

- The average daily cost of a private room in a nursing home in the United States is $203 per day or $74,095 annually, representing an increase of 5.7 percent from 2004's $192.
- The highest nursing home rates, once again, were reported in Alaska, where the cost is $531 per day. The lowest were in the Shreveport area of Louisiana at $115.
- The cost of a home health care aide averaged $19 per hour nationally, an increase of $1 or 5.5 percent.
- The national average for homemaker/companion care averages $17 an hour.[1]

WHAT IS LONG-TERM CARE INSURANCE?
Long-term care insurance pays benefits when a physician prescribes them. Usually, LTC policies cover all levels of

care in state-licensed nursing homes, and many cover assisted living and home health care.

What services are covered? Generally covered are nursing care, therapy, personal care, and homemaking administered by agencies and providers that are state-licensed. For example, a policy may cover $150 a day in a nursing home. If the total cost of a day in the nursing home is $190, you would have to pay the difference. A policy may not cover all expenses.

Many policies now offer an inflation-adjustment feature that increases your per-day benefit to cover higher costs. For example, the daily benefit amount might increase each year at a compounded or simple rate of 5 percent.

Premiums can vary widely based on your age, your health, and the exact benefits you buy. Plus, the inflation feature will make your policy more expensive, but at the rate health care costs are going up, it may be worth the money.

A policy purchased in your early fifties may be relatively inexpensive, compared to one purchased at age 70. In general, premiums remain fixed each year, unless they are increased for a class of policyholders at once.

It makes sense to speak with a financial adviser, such as a CERTIFIED FINANCIAL PLANNER™ professional *before* you make a commitment to this type of insurance. Why? Because premiums can be considerable, and you want to make sure you're buying the best insurance to cover your particular needs in the future.

WHAT DOES LONG-TERM CARE ACTUALLY COST?

As of 2005, MetLife reported that a month in a semiprivate room in a nursing home ranged from a low of $3,000 in Shreveport, Louisiana, to a high of $9,250 in New York City, according to a survey by the MetLife Mature Market Institute (MMI).[2]

That would mean a year-long stay translates to $36,850 in Shreveport and $112,400 in New York City.

MetLife also estimated costs of assisted living and home health care. In August 2005, the lowest average monthly base rate for an assisted-living facility was $1,650 in Jackson, Mississippi, area and the highest was $4,300 in the Stamford, Connecticut, area.[3]

FACTORS TO CONSIDER WHEN YOU'RE BUYING A POLICY

Your age. The younger you are when you buy it, the less expensive the premiums. You can pay off the premiums over a set period, such as ten years, or pay level premiums for the remainder of your life, assuming you keep the policy in force. (Your state insurance commission can approve rate increases for an entire class of policyholders.) Some professionals recommend buying LTC insurance as early as your thirties or forties. Most recommend mid-to-late fifties or early sixties.

Daily benefits. Determining how much daily benefit you need should take into account several factors. First, what does LTC care cost where you expect to receive care? A CFP professional can help you find the answers to these questions.

Are you insuring for two people or one? If one moves into a nursing home, remember that you still have expenses associated with the spouse who's still at home. What if both of you end up needing care at the same time? Some companies offer "shared benefits," where two people are covered by a single policy, or discounts may be available if both spouses buy separate policies with the same company at the same time.

What can you afford out-of-pocket? You need to consider other financial resources, such as retirement income or savings, if you end up needing care. You can reduce premiums by planning to pay a portion of care out of pocket. But will those resources be adequate when you need them? What if they are resources you want to leave to your children or may otherwise need?

Inflation protection. This is a very important feature, especially for younger buyers. Nursing home rates have been going up five percent or more a year, according to the American Council of Life Insurers.[4]

That means a nursing home that costs $180 a day today would cost $480 a day 20 years from now—a likely scenario for a 60-year old buying a policy but not needing it until he or she turns 80. Be careful which type of inflation protection you buy. Some policies offer a choice between a compounding inflation rider and a simple inflation rider. The simple version will cost less but results in smaller annual increases in the daily benefit, potentially leaving you short.

Benefit period. How long do you want the policy to pay for coverage: two years, three, five, eight, a lifetime? The longer the period, the more expensive the premiums. According to MetLife, quoting government estimates in 2005,[5] the average stay in a nursing home is 2.4 years, but of course, some patients remain much longer. Some experts recommend buying lifetime benefits if you can afford them; others feel comfortable with five to eight years. You should consider your family health history in this. For example, if your family has a history of Alzheimer's disease, you might want to consider a longer benefit period because Alzheimer's patients in the early stages of the disease may live a decade or more.

Elimination period. This is the number of months you choose to wait before benefits begin. Benefits might begin immediately or within 30, 60, or 90 days, or half a year or longer. Unless coverage begins immediately, you'll have to pay out of pocket until coverage begins. As these policies evolve, you need to keep advised on various crediting options that may save you money in this area. You do need to run the numbers, though. Say the period is 90 days. At $180 a day, you'll pay out of pocket $16,200. But 20 years from now, at five percent annual inflation, that 90-day period could cost $43,200! Will you have the funds?

One of the most important things to keep in mind is that the long-term care policies continue to evolve and they're complicated. It makes sense to get advice on the best options for you.

In Part 10, we'll be focusing on catching up with retirement savings.

ENDNOTES

1. Metlife Mature Market news, news release, Sept. 27, 2005.
2. Ibid.
3. Ibid.
4. www.acli.com/ACLI/Newsroom/News%20Releases/Text%20Releases/NR06-019.
5. Metlife Mature Market news, news release, September 27, 2005.

Part X

Funding an Underfunded Retirement

NOTES FROM A PLANNER:

Making Up for a Late Start

Marc Freedman,
CFP®

Poor planning, late starts, financial emergencies along the way—people have many reasons for failing to plan well for retirement. So how can a planner help you catch up?

Marc Freedman, a CERTIFIED FINANCIAL PLANNER™ professional based in Peabody, Massachusetts, notes that it's not all that tough to fall behind. "It's very interesting when I meet people for the first time and they say they want to focus on retirement. They want investment advice, and that's actually the easiest part. They say, 'Make me money,'" Freedman explains.

"But the retirement planning process is more about defining the big goals. It's not my job to tell my client what the next ten years of their life is going to look like. It's their responsibility to tell me, and we need to work together to determine how that will happen."

Freedman notes that based on today's figures, the

average Baby Boomer is going to live into their nineties. "Today's 65-year-old looks younger than he or she ever has. Why would you assume that you will only have to provide for 15 or 16 years of income once you retire? You may end up having to provide 30 years or more."

The first thing a planner does is get a client focused on that reality. They'll ask for a net worth statement to determine what you own and then they'll ask for statements and documents to verify the accuracy of your statements. Then, the planner will ask the client about dreams and goals. "Not until those things are clear can a planner address the catch-up question," said Freedman.

37 | *Do You Have Enough?*

In the late 1990s, relatively few people were worried about how much money they had socked away for retirement. Before the tech wreck of 2000 and the economic fallout after the 9/11 terrorist attacks, the Internet boom was marching upward and stocks in most investment categories were galloping along at double-digit gains. It seemed that no matter what mistakes were made along the way, the market would eventually save us all.

Today, that picture is much different. The Center for Retirement Research at Boston College has introduced some frightening numbers on the subject. In June 2006, it unveiled the National Retirement Risk Index, which showed that almost 45 percent of working-age households are "at risk" for being unable to maintain their preretirement standard of living in retirement. For retirees facing a sudden loss of pensions and benefits, there are really very few options save going back to work or turning home equity into a personal bank. So the time to start taking on the lion's share of your retirement responsibility is

Figure 37.1: Percent of Households "At Risk" at Age 65 by Age Group and Income Group

Income Group	All	Early Boomers 1946–1954	Late Boomers 1955–1964	Generation Xers 1965–1972
All	43%	35%	49%	49%
Top Third	36%	33%	35%	42%
Middle Third	40%	28%	44%	46%
Bottom Third	53%	45%	54%	60%

Source: Center for Retirement Research at Boston College, www.bc.edu/centers/crr/press/pr_2006_06_06.pdf.

now, whether you're 5, 10, or 20 years away from hanging it up, if that's your plan.

One general tip. If you're not really certain where you stand, get some help. If you've never sat down with a financial adviser, it may be time to get a second opinion on your retirement readiness. The meeting may yield some ugly news, but it's better to know the options than cross your fingers.

HOW MUCH WILL YOU NEED?

You'll probably need about 70–80 percent of your last paycheck before retirement. Then think about how far out you are from your chosen retirement date, and then the numbers will get interesting. The official terminology for this target amount is "replacement income," and it's drawn from what you've saved in your own IRA and 401(k) self-directed accounts, other investments, Social Security, and any other pension assets you might still have out there when you retire.

Too complicated? That's why you shouldn't be ashamed to ask for help. Here are some things you may want to discuss:

What does "retirement" mean to you? It's arguable that traditional retirement is going to be dead for many of us because we haven't saved enough or because our investments haven't performed as well as we hoped they would. So you may want to start thinking about a second part-time career or new ways to earn. There's no shame in doing this—in fact, many people are structuring their retirements to include new careers or other forms of paying work that they would like to do until the end of their lives.

Think about an annuity. Annuities are investments that provide fixed or variable payments to the investor over a set period of time. (See Chapter 38.) The collapse of traditional plans is putting new focus on the annuity business, and it's worth talking about with an expert because it's easy to make mistakes.

Do a retirement-spending dress rehearsal. In the last few years before retirement, see how much you can live like you're already retired. Give up the lattes and the pricey clothes and dinners; see if you can live with a smaller car or a used one. Retirement is easier if you can down-shift into it, both from a monetary and activity standpoint.

Get in shape physically. It may be strange to hear health advice tied to your financial well-being, but it should be one of the first things you consider. That's because the numbers on a bathroom scale, blood pressure monitor, or cholesterol report can dramatically affect the cost of your health-care and insurance premiums going into retirement. You'll find that pre-existing conditions can boost your premiums—or possibly deny you coverage. That's a very ugly surprise going into the years when you're going to need health-care coverage the most.

Consider a career shift. It may be a bit extreme to switch careers just because a particular employer has better benefits and savings options. But if the job appeals to you and you can make a move without endangering what you've already accrued, why not consider it?

Use your catch-up options. Various IRA and 401(k) options allow you to make additional contributions over standard savings limits above the age of 50. Make sure you know what those additional amounts are and take full advantage of them. (We'll get into more detail about them in Chapter 40.)

Do an investment inventory. In a 30- to 40-year career, you may have gathered bits and pieces of pension benefits and personal savings and investments along the way. Likewise, insurance policies, savings bonds, and other small investments may have slipped your attention. A re-evaluation of retirement options should begin with a full accounting and reorganizing of all investment and savings assets, preferably in an organized outline that's easy for you and your adviser to access.

Think about health savings accounts. Today, there are strict limits and spending rules for health savings accounts, but if some lobbyists get their way, there might be a day when health savings accounts can become a long-term savings solution similar to a 401(k) plan. Getting into the pre-tax savings habit with health-care dollars is a good plan, in case there's more flexibility awarded to these accounts in the future.

EIGHT WAYS TO MAKE THE MOST OF YOUR 401(K)

Let's get one thing straight: 401(k) plans and similar employee-funded retirement plans are here to stay.

These plans have been battered by the sour stock market of 2000–2002, corporate scandals, and the mutual fund scandals that occurred around the same time. Despite this, employee-funded retirement plans, in one form or another, will remain the primary source for building retirement assets for millions of workers. Here are eight key ways to make the most of your 401(k).

1. **Join.** One in four eligible workers doesn't participate in their employer's 401(k) plan, and rates tend to decline during market downturns, which actually may be the best time to start. So either join or stay in.

2. **Hold steady or even increase contributions.** Many workers reduce their 401(k) contributions because of difficult economic times or their fear of the market. Echoing the point above, see if you can make a significant contribution when markets are low. You'll get to take advantage of the upswing through dollar-cost averaging. Need to know how that works? When stocks are down, you're able to buy more shares or stock for the same amount of money. As the market rebounds, any securities that lost value after you bought them will stand to regain that

value. Dollar-cost averaging allows people with smaller amounts of money to get into the market while keeping their risk relatively low. Always confer with a financial expert before you embark on such a strategy to see if it fits your long-term investment goals.

3. **Make the match.** At the very least, contribute enough in your 401(k) plan to meet the minimum company match—typically 3 percent of salary. This is free money! Though some employers have suspended matches, most are maintaining their previous match percentages.

4. **Create an investment plan.** One reason many eligible 401(k) plan participants don't join, bail out of their plans, or reduce their contributions is that they don't have an overall investment plan. By having clear goals, investment objectives to reach those goals, and an understanding of investment risk and your own tolerance for risk, you are less apt to get caught up in the temporary ups and downs of the market.

5. **Diversify...maybe.** If most of your investment portfolio is tied up in your 401(k), it's even more important to diversify your account. Yet many 401(k) participants concentrate their investments in only one or two investment options at most, usually large-cap stock mutual funds or fixed income.

   That advice may change if your 401(k) is part of a much larger investment portfolio. The reason is that many 401(k) plans offer a limited range of investment choices, so you might need to leave your 401(k) mostly in large-cap and fixed income while you use other investment vehicles, such as taxable accounts, for alternative investments such as real estate investment trusts, small-cap stocks, and international funds.

6. **Don't overload on company stock.** As Enron illustrated, loading up your 401(k) primarily on an employer's stock can be disastrous. Both your job and your retirement are riding on a single employer. Financial planners typically recommend keeping company stock to no more than 10 or 20 percent of your account's value. But it can be difficult to keep the percentage that low if the company match is

only in employer stock and you're restricted regarding how soon you might sell it and buy other types of investments. Again, you may have to diversify your overall portfolio by buying other assets outside of the 401(k) plan.

7. **Avoid borrowing from your plan.** The first drawback from borrowing is that you reduce the ultimate size of your 401(k) nest egg because you're not allowing the money to grow tax- deferred. You also run the risk of facing taxes and penalties if you fail to repay the loan—say, due to being laid off.

8. **Don't cash out.** A 2005 survey by Hewitt Associates found that 45 percent of employees taking 401(k) distributions cashed out of their plan when changing jobs. This normally results in taxes, possibly penalties, and definitely the loss of tax-deferred growth. Hewitt's study showed that young people were the greatest "cash-out" offenders. The highest incidence of cash distributions (66 percent) was among employees age 20–29. However, more than 42 percent of workers age 40–49 elected to cash out of their 401(k) plans upon leaving their jobs.[1]

WHAT DOES END-OF-LIFE CARE COST?

As we discussed in Chapter 36, the main reason people might be interested in buying long-term care insurance is to cover the potential cost of nursing or home-based home care, which could run hundreds of thousands of dollars. This is particularly important for someone who wants to leave some money to their heirs and doesn't want it spent in a nursing home.

It bears repeating that this is an issue you should discuss with your financial adviser, because unexpected medical expenses can wipe out a portfolio. And if such an illness comes long before the end of life, that leaves an extraordinary gap in your finances. Think about it.

PLANNING A WORKING RETIREMENT

Some people actually want to work in retirement, and not just because they have to. There's much discussion today of a "new" type of retirement, where people transition into new careers, part-time work, and causes. It's critically important to plan for this option if your ambition and health support such a goal.

Why? You may want to move around your retirement dollars in such a way that you'll be able to defer a lot of that income while you work so when the time comes to finance a "real" retirement, you'll have all the money you'll need.

REBALANCING A PORTFOLIO OVER TIME

It's not enough to save. Every once in awhile, you have to pull a rebalancing act.

Rebalancing a portfolio involves periodically readjusting its mix of assets. Smart investors start by establishing an initial asset allocation, assigning percentages of the portfolio to assets such as stocks, bonds, and cash, and perhaps other types of investments such as real estate and commodities. The allocations are further broken down by subcategories, such as different types of stocks and bonds.

The target allocations should be appropriate for that investor's investment goals and financial circumstances, as well as comfort level with certain types of investments. Someone older with no children and nearing retirement, for example, will likely have a different mix than a family in its early accumulation years. Smart investors also readjust the target allocations to reflect major changes in their personal financial circumstances (but not changes in the markets).

Why rebalance just because a portfolio no longer matches its original allocation? Why not just let it ride—especially if the market's going up? Because if you don't, you increase the risk that you won't achieve your investment goals. Say you had 55 percent in stocks and 45 percent in bonds in the early 1990s. Unless you rebalanced along the way, by the end of 1999, that mix might have become "unbalanced"—say, 80 percent in stocks and only 20 percent in bonds.

You know what happened next. This stock-heavy portfolio, especially if it was loaded with tech stocks, suffered more when the stock market declined steeply over the next three years than it would have had it maintained its original 60/40 balance through periodic rebalancing.

How much to allow a specific asset category to shift before readjusting it is up to you, but a common guideline is 5 percent. To rebalance, consider directing future investment funds into those underrepresented categories until it's back in balance. You also can readjust by selling off some of the overrepresented assets (the winners) and buying the underrepresented (the losers)—selling high and buying low. It is usually better to execute this strategy within tax-favored accounts to avoid taxes on gains, but if you need to rebalance taxable accounts, don't let tax concerns derail you.

As always, consult an expert if you're unsure how your portfolio needs to be adjusted.

In the next chapter, we're going to look at annuities and how they can fit into a retirement portfolio.

ENDNOTE

1. www.hewittassociates.com/Intl/NA/en-US/AboutHewitt/Newsroom/PressReleaseDetail. aspx?cid=2015, Hewitt Associates Release, "Hewitt Study Shows Nearly Half of U.S. Workers Cash Out of 401(k) Plans When Leaving Jobs," July 25, 2005.

38 | *Annuities—Are They Right For You?*

If you want to start a debate among financial professionals, just bring up the subject of annuities. It doesn't matter whether the parties involved have ever bought them or even investigated them. There are simply strong opinions about this investment option.

So let's talk about what they are and how they work.

WHAT IS AN ANNUITY?

An annuity is an investment contract between an investor and an insurance company. Most often, it is used as a vehicle for saving for retirement or to guarantee an income for life. The investor pays a lump sum in exchange for future periodic payments immediately (known as an immediate annuity) or at some future date (a deferred annuity) that can continue as long as your lifetime if you choose.

Many experts think that putting a lump sum of money—no more than half your assets—in a guaranteed annuity that will pay you monthly until you die allows you to free up the rest of your money to invest (and spend) more aggressively.

Where does the controversy come in? Over fees,

investment mission, the flexibility of the agreements, and tax issues. Some people wonder whether an annuity is a better choice than a Roth IRA invested in conservative no-load funds. But everything depends on the type of annuity and whether it fits your needs. Before you invest in an annuity, you should consult a financial expert who knows your entire tax and retirement picture.

There are ever-changing flavors of annuities that deliver steady income, growth, and savings opportunities. Annuities are purchased with lump-sum payments, typically $5,000 or greater. Yet once you're in an annuity, prepare to be in for the long haul— it's very expensive to get your money out in an emergency.

TYPES OF ANNUITIES

Most discussions of annuities begin with the following important distinction: fixed vs. variable.

Fixed annuity. This type of annuity guarantees the principal (the amount you invest) and a minimum rate of interest for the term of the agreement, assuming the insurance company that issues the annuity stays financially healthy. That's why it's always important to check the insurance company's A.M. Best rating before you invest. For all fixed annuities, the growth of the money invested is tax-deferred, but annuities can be purchased with pretax income and be tax-deferred, or they may be purchased with money that has already been taxed.

Variable annuity. The money you put in a variable annuity is invested in a fund, similar to the way a conventional mutual fund operates. The fund has a particular investment objective and your money—less fees and expenses—will move with the market. There is no guaranteed return as with a fixed annuity.

The following types of annuities come in fixed or variable forms.

Deferred annuities. Deferred annuities tend to be the most frequently chosen annuities because investors put in their money well before they need it and they accumulate value—more or less guaranteed—over time.

Immediate annuities. While deferred annuities are designed to help you maximize your investment over time, immediate annuities begin paying you an income from the moment you invest for as long as you designate. These annuities are commonly used to provide pension benefits to retired employees, and you'll often see them offered to teachers or other public or nonprofit employees.

Life annuities. There are many flavors to this type of annuity, but in its simplest form, it gives the person who buys one payments for life. The differences come in the way the annuity contract is structured. Life annuities get more expensive as you add features. For example, a life annuity that designates a beneficiary—someone to collect the remaining payments of the annuity if the original holder dies—costs more than a "straight life" annuity that simply pays the holder until he or she dies.

Term certain annuities. This annuity has a fixed payment with no opportunity for adjustment and only for a specific period. If the investor dies before the term of the annuity is up, the insurance company gets to keep the money.

Single premium annuities. This form of annuity is funded by a single payment and usually invested for the long term.

Flexible payment annuities. A flexible payment annuity allows for many payments over a particularly long period of time for the maximum chance of growth.

WHAT QUESTIONS SHOULD YOU ASK?

1. What's the health of the insurance company offering the annuity? Check with A.M. Best to see how the company is rated.
2. How have the investments performed within the annuity you're thinking about?
3. Are there surrender charges for this product? How much are they and when do they disappear? (Many annuities don't drop surrender charges until your eighth year of ownership; bad news if you need the money in a hurry.)
4. What are the initial fees and annual fees on the annuity?

Have the annual returns exceeded the fees you'll pay on the annuity? If they don't, there go your gains.

5. How much do you pay in extra fees for extra features? If your annuity has a guaranteed minimum income benefit, for instance, what will that cost you?

6. If you have a few years until retirement, how does an annuity choice compare to a competing investment vehicle, such as the coming no-income-limit Roth or other choices?

7. If there's a bonus credit feature on a variable annuity—which adds more to your contract value if you pay certain amounts in—are there additional fees that might offset those gains?

In the next chapter, we'll look at spending your retirement savings wisely.

39 | *Spending Your Retirement Savings Wisely*

Saving and investing for retirement is a challenge, but most people don't think enough about the second important phase of retirement planning—how you'll sensibly withdraw the money. This is one of the best reasons in support of bringing a financial adviser—such as a CERTIFIED FINANCIAL PLANNER™ professional—into the process in the years before you retire.

Disorganized spending of retirement assets can spell disaster for all the hard work you've done.

THE STARTING POINT
Many financial advisers agree on this particular idea: based on a successful saving and investing strategy over time, you should be able to withdraw about 4 percent of your nest egg the first year of retirement and increase that amount by 3 percent a year to cover inflation and still have enough money to live on until you die.

In reality, life happens. Cars break down. Roofs leak. In the first year of retirement, people spend more than they allot because they're still dealing with common expenses and emergencies while trying new things. That's why you need to plan for a retirement that's not based solely on withdrawal of funds you've accrued. You have to continue to invest for growth to handle the unexpected. Generally, most retirees spend down their taxable investments first, then move on to their tax-deferred investments so they can continue to grow.

VISUALIZING THAT FIRST YEAR OF RETIREMENT

There are thousands of resources that tell you how to manage your retirement savings while you're still working for that nest egg. So why are so many new retirees suddenly paralyzed with financial fear when they finally quit working?

Some of it is natural; retirement is a big lifestyle change and many people question whether they're spending too much during that first crucial year. Surprisingly, freedom can be very expensive. But that nervousness may also be an indication that an individual hasn't received as much instruction in how they will spend during retirement as they've received saving for it.

A huge nest egg—or a nest egg that seems huge—sounds great. But the death of traditional pensions and the rise of (often-underperforming) self-directed retirement plans have made it tough for individuals to easily predict what they'll actually have to spend. And without a complete plan that takes into account personal circumstances, financial goals, inflation, the rising cost of health care, increased longevity, and ultimately long-term care, retirement money probably won't last as long as you do.

As the official Baby Boomer retirement wave begins, some financial advisers have begun to elevate the discussion to postretirement spending and investing as a way to repair preretirement planning. Individuals who have worked with financial and tax advisers, including CERTIFIED FINANCIAL PLANNER™ professionals, should have a much clearer picture of how they should manage their spending in the first five years of retirement.

If you haven't, it's time to get some help.

For potential retirees who want to eliminate those first-year jitters, here are planning ideas to implement as soon as possible:

Define a vision of retirement and revisit it every year. Anyone who has worked successfully with an investment manager or financial planner has addressed the kind of retirement they want and how old they'll be when they start it. A retirement that includes world travel and a general increase in leisure-time spending may cost significantly more than a preretirement lifestyle with a 60-hour workweek built in. A retirement with rewarding part-time work built into the picture might make the other goals more affordable. A person who manages his or her finances or works with an expert needs to revisit those goals annually to assess whether they will still be able to afford a particular style of retirement at the age they plan to start it.

Track working-life expenses for three to six months. This is where that vision of retirement starts getting real. Knowing for the first time what an individual spends on lattes and late-night carryout may cause a radical shift in behavior—from spending to saving.

Create a worst-case health scenario. For many, the biggest spending issue postretirement is end-of-life care. That may mean paying for expensive experimental treatments to fight disease or long-term assisted or nursing home care. Some projections put annual nursing home costs at more than $100,000 a year in the next two decades, compared to their current annual range of $45,000–$60,000. While public aid picks up medical expenses for those who exhaust their assets in most states, most of us want more than minimal standards of care.

Build several annual budgets. There are many rules of thumb that govern retirement spending. A popular one is that no one should spend more than 4 percent annually of the present amount in their nest egg. Another is that retirees only need 70–80 percent of their last working year's income to be comfortable. There really is no one-size-fits-all solution because spending decisions are different at all stages of retirement. Every investor might consider doing one or more annual budgets that build various risk scenarios into their plan, since computers offer the opportunity to do so time effectively.

Shift into a retirement investment strategy in stages. Because a clear majority of investors have inadequate retirement funds in place at or near retirement age, it may seem silly to talk about investing postretirement. But the younger an investor is, the more valuable the conversation. As investors tried to recover from the 2000–2002 stock market slide, many ran to real estate or any strategy that looked like a quick gain. In good markets and bad, balance is still key. Good advisers can help build more balanced portfolios that fit the exact needs of the investor as retirement nears.

THINK ABOUT HOW YOU'LL SPEND YOUR IRAS

Individual retirement accounts are one of the most popular ways Americans save for retirement. Yet many IRA owners make critical mistakes that can needlessly cost them or their heirs money or thwart the owners' plans. Here are eight ways you can ensure that your IRA works as you designed it.

1. **Begin your required minimum distributions on time.** Some people heading into retirement try to avoid withdrawing from their retirement accounts as long as possible to keep them growing. Yet regardless of whether you are still working, you must begin taking an annual minimum required distribution from your traditional IRAs (not Roth IRAs) no later than April 1 following the year you turn 70½. If you don't withdraw enough or you don't withdraw it on time, the IRS will penalize you 50 percent of the difference between the amount you took out and the amount you should have taken out.

   The IRS has simplified the calculation of the minimum distribution. Furthermore, the law now requires all IRA custodians and qualified plan administrators (such as 401(k) plans) to inform the owner of the upcoming required distribution and to offer to calculate the minimum distribution amount. But it's still up to you to take out the money, which you can draw from any or all accounts you own, as long as the total minimum amount is distributed.

2. **Don't wait until the last moment.** Some IRA owners wait until the April 1 deadline to take out their *initial* minimum withdrawal. But remember, you'll have to make another withdrawal by December 31 of the same year. Two minimum withdrawals in the same year could bump you into a higher tax bracket and increase your tax liability. Also, owners of large accounts may actually reduce their tax bite by taking some withdrawals during lower-income tax years well before they turn 70½.

3. **Name a beneficiary.** Failure to name a beneficiary usually means the assets go to your estate and that will cost your heirs money. That's because if you hadn't already started taking distributions yourself by the time of your death, the IRA assets must be distributed to your estate's heirs within five years of death. Or if you had started, distributions must be paid out to the heirs over what would have been your remaining life expectancy. Either way, this deprives the heirs from "stretching out" the tax-deferred assets over their own lives and creates a bigger tax bite.

4. **Name a contingent beneficiary.** This allows the primary beneficiary to "disclaim" (reject) the IRA inheritance if he or she doesn't need the money, so that it automatically passes to the contingent, who typically is younger and can stretch out the inheritance longer.

5. **Name the right beneficiary.** Your choice of beneficiary for your retirement accounts should be reviewed on a regular basis not only to make sure your retirement funds go to the right person after your death, but to make sure those assets travel in the most tax-efficient way possible for them. Your beneficiary situation is part of your overall estate plan, so it makes sense to consult a financial advisor.

6. **Changing your beneficiary.** Don't forget to change, in writing, your beneficiary in the event of a marriage, divorce, birth of a child, death of a beneficiary, or similar circumstances.

7. **Have the right number of IRAs.** For example, if you have a single large IRA but want to bequeath its assets to multiple heirs and a charity or two, consider separate IRAs for the charities and perhaps

for each heir (especially if their ages are significantly different). Lumping them into a single IRA accelerates the required minimum distribution rate the heir(s) are required to take each year. On the other hand, if you have multiple IRAs but not multiple heirs or charities, consolidating them can reduce paperwork and custodial fees and make it easier to track investments and calculate minimum distributions.

8. **Check to see what your IRA custodian allows.** Just because federal law allows you to choose certain options with your IRA doesn't mean the IRA custodian does. The custodian might not allow you to stretch out the payments with your children or grandchildren, for example, or allow the descendants of a deceased beneficiary to receive that heir's share if the IRA has other named heirs. The options are spelled out in the custody agreement.

DON'T FORGET OTHER KEY MONEY ISSUES ON THE WAY TO RETIREMENT

While you're planning how you'll use your money in retirement, make sure key financial safeguards are in place:

Insurance. Health, home, auto, long-term care and life insurance coverage is particularly important to check before you retire. As income declines in retirement, all of these insurance products become much more important. It is best to sit down with your insurance professional to determine whether your coverage is adequate.

Check key dates. Retirement requires us to become experts in government programs and other benefits issues that can be complex, particularly based on individual circumstances. Here are some key dates you should be aware of according to the Social Security Administration:

- **Social Security benefits.** People who want to start collecting benefits at age 62 need to apply when they're 61 and nine months old. To collect at 65, you need to apply at 64 and nine months, and to receive benefits at age 70, you should apply at age 69 and nine months.
- **Medicare.** Americans receiving Social Security benefits before age 65 are automatically enrolled in Medicare. Otherwise, most experts

advise you to apply for Medicare benefits at age 64 and nine months even if you won't be using Medicare benefits.

• **Retirement accounts.** Refer to the information above.

In the next chapter, we'll discuss catch-up provisions for retirement saving.

40 | *How to Catch Up*

A 2005 study from the Vanguard Center for Retirement Research noted that while the overwhelming majority of age-50-and-older participants in company-sponsored retirement plans are eligible to make catch-up contributions to their accounts, they don't bother to do it.[1]

Why? Vanguard said the strongest influence tended to be household income—or the lack of it.

WHAT'S A CATCH-UP PROVISION?

Passed in 2001, the Economic Growth and Tax Relief Reconciliation Act contained a number of provisions designed to encourage retirement savings in the United States. Among the provisions was a higher contribution level for older workers in defined contribution retirement savings plans, such as 401(k) and 403(b) plans.

Under the law, plan participants age 50 and older were permitted to contribute an additional $5,000 to their retirement accounts in 2006.

How many people took advantage of this great way to shore up retirement savings before retirement? Only 13 percent. The Vanguard study showed that those likeliest to take advantage of the catch-up provisions already had healthy balances in their accounts.

WHO NEEDS TO CATCH UP?

Here's an idea. If you're 50 with an annual income of $60,000 and your financial assets (not including your residence) equal or are less than your annual income, you're way behind. But if you have three or four times your salary in assets, you should continue saving, but you don't necessarily need to shell out for catch-ups.

The best way to determine what shape you're really in is to sit down with a financial adviser who can take the whole picture into account: not only what you've saved and what you need to save, but what you plan to do in your retirement. Your decision to work—or not work—in retirement will help you answer this question.

By the way, these catch-up provisions may not always be around. Unless Congress extends the provisions or makes them permanent, the act will sunset at midnight, December 31, 2010.

OTHER IDEAS

If you're running behind in your retirement savings, there are solutions:

- **Work more.** Yes, it sounds silly, but as long as you discuss the tax implications in advance with your financial or tax adviser, get more money coming in the door and sock that cash away.
- **Rebalance.** Again, get some advice, but depending on where your savings stand, see if your portfolio is exactly where it should be at this point in your life and whether it is correctly balanced against the number of years you'll have until you start drawing on those funds.
- **Take a hard look at company stock you own.** This is an extension of the rebalancing idea, but if you work for a company where you've amassed a considerable amount of stock, think carefully and unemotionally about whether you should continue to keep a stake that might be an uncomfortably large part of your portfolio. In other words, remember Enron and the number of people whose life savings were wiped out as a result of the fraud and financial failure of that company.

In the next part, we'll be looking at the basics of investing.

ENDNOTE

1. https://institutional2. vanguard.com/VGApp/iip/Research?Path=PUBNEWS&File=NewsCatchUp Contributions.jsp&FW_Event= articleDetail&FW_Activity=ArticleDetailActivity& IIP_INF=ZZNewsCatchUpContributions.jsp.

Part XI

The Basics
of Investing

What Can a Financial Planner Teach You about Investing?

Louis Barajas, CFP®

Louis Barajas, a CERTIFIED FINANCIAL PLANNER™ professional based in Santa Fe Springs, California, looks back at the 2001–2002 market year and sees diversification as the main benefit of an investment planning strategy.

"A properly diversified portfolio, in our case, was down only about 6 percent that year in a year where you saw a double-digit drop on most markets," explains Barajas, a planner who works with primarily middle-income clients in the Hispanic community. "What planners can do is get to know the client, his long- and short-term goals, and design an investment strategy that will deliver the most realistic reward with the least amount of risk."

At his firm, Barajas and his staff do PowerPoint presentations and one-on-one discussions with clients to determine their investment goals and risk tolerance, and then design an investment plan around that.

"You want to keep the client away from 'investment noise'—whatever is hot at the moment," he explains. "Planners, unlike a lot of financial professionals, have the chance to get to know the financial DNA of the people they serve, and that produces investment strategies they're comfortable with."

41 | *What Is Investing?*

Investing is the commitment of money or capital to make a profit. That's an easy definition and many of us know it. So why are so few of us truly good at it?

Because investing lessons are among the toughest we'll ever learn. When it comes to money, we can be tempted by greed, overenthusiasm and our own ignorance; mostly we learn our lessons through the mistakes we make.

But it doesn't have to be this way.

Before you consider a move into stocks, real estate, or another kind of investment, it helps to understand what sensible investment strategy is and how various investments may perform over time. It's also worth considering getting help from a financial adviser or tax expert such as a CERTIFIED FINANCIAL PLANNER™ professional. Many people come to the financial planning process expecting dramatic gains in their portfolio. Gains are great, but in a down market, most people appreciate a portfolio that shows resilience and allows for flexibility in protecting capital.

WHAT IS ASSET ALLOCATION?

Asset allocation is how you divide your investments

among different categories—such as stocks, bonds, real estate, precious metals, collectibles, and cash—so your risk tolerance is in balance with your investment goals.

What's interesting about asset allocation is that it's less cut-and-dried than it used to be because people are living longer, in some cases working longer because they want to, and in others, taking breaks from work throughout their working lives. It used to be the case that someone approaching 65—what used to be known as the "traditional" retirement age, began to downshift their investment portfolios into bonds and cash equivalents to protect their principal. After all, if they lived another 20 years, they'd be lucky, right?

Today, asset allocation is a whole new ballgame. It's a lifestyle issue, not merely a money issue. It starts with examining life and career goals throughout a life and career that may end at 50, at 65, or much later. And then it involves balancing the investments and other assets an individual has to minimize specific risks that could happen in that individual's situation.

In general terms, asset allocation is a risk-management tool that fits you and your goals.

Where do you start? Start with a financial and tax expert (it makes sense to talk to both) who can review your current finances and ask you important questions about your goals. If they're good at their jobs, they'll ask you about what you want to do with your life, not simply when you want to retire. They'll ask if you plan to have kids. They'll ask if you want to own more than one home, or if you want to own one at all. They might ask you if you want to build "sabbaticals" into your working life over the decades. They should behave a bit like shrinks—getting you to admit goals you never really knew you had, money problems you never knew existed, or sources of cash you never realized could be channeled into something more productive. With all this knowledge in place, then you begin to allocate your assets.

What changes an asset allocation? Sudden or expected changes in life events. A family member gets seriously ill. A child gets ready to go off to college. You quit work to go back to school. You lose your job and are unemployed for months. We're talking about dozens of variables based on an individual's unique situation.

The reason so many people are disappointed with their investments is because they don't have a unified plan that links those choices to what they really want out of life.

Whatever the media tells you, only the foolish walk into an investment without an overall idea of how it should fit into their total financial picture. Nobody starts a new job expecting every day to go perfectly, but it's amazing how many people expect their investment ideas to be fool-proof going in.

But to get whatever you want, you have to ask yourself how soon you want those things and what risks you're willing to take to get them. Take a minute and do the following quiz.

LEARNING TO LOOK AROUND YOU

Investing isn't just about making money. It's learning to learn all about the world around you. If you've never read a business page in the newspaper or watched the daily stock market roundup on TV, it might

---

A RISK QUIZ

Getting involved in any type of investment should start with a definition of what you're willing to risk for a profit. Ask yourself the following:

1. Am I more concerned about maintaining the value of my initial investment or about making a profit from that investment?
2. Am I willing to give up that stability for the chance at long-term growth?
3. How would I feel if the value of my investment dropped for several months?
4. How would I feel if the value of my investment dropped for several years?
5. Am I in a financial position to handle any losses at all?

Completing the above quiz doesn't mean you have an investment strategy. It's a starting point to help you develop your investment strategy.

---

not be an automatic source of fascination. But you need to try. That's because what happens in business and the economy will affect pretty much everything you invest in.

If you are reading this, it's a good start. But set aside 20 minutes a day to learn what happened in the business world. That will get you thinking not just about investments to buy, but why they go up and down.

However, as you learn about the daily movements in business and markets, that doesn't mean *you* should change your money strategy on a daily basis. The critical benefit of a solid financial strategy is diversity that can protect a portfolio for the long haul.

DOLLAR-COST AVERAGING

When people talk about the time value of money, they mean that it's generally cheaper to start investing today than five years from now. Why? Because good investments will appreciate over time without you doing anything.

Dollar-cost averaging is a technique designed to reduce market risk through the systematic purchase of securities at predetermined intervals and set amounts. It's also a good way to invest if you don't have a lot of money. Instead of investing assets in a lump sum, the investor works his way into a position by slowly buying smaller amounts over a longer period of time. This spreads the cost basis out over several years, providing insulation against changes in market price.

If you are working alone or with an adviser, you should discuss not only what investments you plan to buy, but when you should buy them. Some advisers believe in dollar-cost averaging, some don't. Make sure you discuss the concept, though.

INVESTMENT CHOICES THAT MAKE UP A PORTFOLIO

A balanced portfolio is typically made up of a variety of different investments that have their own behaviors. Here are descriptions of asset categories that may make up a diversified portfolio:

Stocks. A stock is a share of ownership in a corporation. Stocks are generally the "go-to" investments for long-term retirement and college savings because they blend the greatest risk and highest returns among the three leading asset categories that make up most investors' retirement plans and investments. As an asset category, stocks generally offer the greatest potential for growth, and for those who remember 2000, the greatest potential for loss. Stocks hit home runs, but also strike out. The volatility of stocks makes them a very risky investment in the short term. Large company stocks as a group, for example, have lost money on average about one out of every three years. And sometimes the losses have been quite dramatic. But investors who have been willing to ride out the volatile returns of stocks over long periods of time generally have been rewarded with strong positive returns.

Cash. Cash and cash equivalents—such as savings deposits, certificates of deposit, Treasury bills, money market deposit accounts, and money market funds—are the safest investments, but generally offer the lowest returns. The chances of losing money on an investment in this asset category are generally extremely low.

Bonds. Bonds are "debt instruments"—meaning that each bond entitles the holder to a portion of the company's borrowings that are typically paid back with interest. But bonds aren't issued only by corporations—nonprofit entities as well as governments also issue them to fund programs and expansions. Bonds are generally less volatile than stocks but offer more modest returns. Some people hold bonds of high quality to offset volatility in stocks.

Real estate. Real estate investments can include houses, office buildings, apartment buildings, condos, or other types of commercial and residential properties. They can also be held in a real estate investment trust (REIT). Real estate can be risky in overheated markets, but investors who hold properties in good or improving neighborhoods generally see returns over a substantial period of time.

Precious metals. This category includes gold, platinum, even precious coins. People view precious metals as wealth that can be carried, held in their hands. People who have lived through the Great Depression have a particular love for it and have been known to put it in safe-deposit boxes.

There is a school of thought that jewelry, bullion, or any other form of precious metal can be used as currency in an emergency. Yet most experts will tell you that despite price spikes during national and international emergencies, metals can be among the most stagnant investments out there.

Energy. Energy stocks sometimes behave like precious metals. When there is world strife, particularly in oil-producing countries, people like to hedge their energy costs. We're not talking only about gasoline. Oil prices push pricing of other energy resources such as natural gas and electricity because when one energy source gets expensive, both business and consumer users lean on other resources, boosting their use and making it easier for producers to raise prices.

In the next chapter, we'll look more closely at stocks as an investment.

42 | *Understanding Stocks*

Stocks are shares of ownership in a company. When you buy a share of a company, you own a piece of the company equal to the ownership value assigned to that share.

So why do companies issue stock? To raise capital for a variety of purposes, including expansion. There are other ways a company can raise money—they can issue bonds or they can take out a loan. But stock is a way to raise money without incurring debt.

Why do investors buy stock? Because they expect the value of their investment to rise more than other investment alternatives.

HOW DO YOU EVALUATE A STOCK?

This is the question that everyone argues about and there is so much more to learn than we have room for here. The answer is part numbers, part knowledge, and part art. And nobody does it exactly the same.

Here are some questions and tools to get you started:

Start with what the company does. Is the company a leader in its field? Does it have a product or service that positions it to be a leader someday? Is it able to charge a good price for this product or service and is it a popular choice among consumers or businesses that buy it?

Is it a respected brand within its industry? A company's brand is more than its name; it is the value the name suggests. When someone mentions the company's name, it should suggest that its products, management, and standing in the community and its industry are good.

How is its management? We hear so many horror stories about corporate management that we almost believe that good managers don't exist. In truth, they exist many places, but you'll have to look closely. Does the company you're looking at have management with experience in this field and proven talent? We're not just talking about the man or woman at the very top. Quality management has many layers, all productive and creative.

How are its sales? Sales are also called revenues. This is the amount of money coming in the door before the company pays workers, benefits, taxes, and other hundreds and thousands of individual operating expenses. Institutional investors—another term for Wall Street insiders—pore over the company's numbers closely and decide whether sales are on target or not. If you're interested in a particular company, see what the experts are saying about their sales.

How are its earnings? This actually may be the more important question. Have you heard that old saying, "It's not what you make but what you keep"? Earnings are a very good indication of how a company really manages itself. If a company has good earnings after paying all of its necessary expenses, taxes, and operating costs, that means it's keeping a close watch on where the money is going. This is what shareholders want. Keep in mind, however, that you'll see some pretty wide variations in earnings at younger companies because they're getting their footing. If their management, products, and operations are solid, this is exactly the kind of company you might want to take a chance on at the start.

What measurements do I watch? Financial experts have pages and pages of indicators they use to measure the investment attractiveness of companies. One of the first ones you should become aware of as an individual is the price-to-earnings ratio, which measures the ratio of a stock's current price to its earnings. Why should you care? Because the P/E ratio shows when the price of a stock is getting excessively ahead of the earnings the company is actually producing. So suppose the stock you have your eye on is selling at $30 a share. Earnings over the last 12 months were $1 a share. (Some analysts use projected earnings instead.) You divide 30 by 1 and find that your stock has a P/E ratio of 30.

Remember the tech wreck in 2000? Stocks were trading at 40, 50, even 100 times earnings back then—and many made a very quick fall to earth. Is there an ideal P/E? Again, this is up for discussion, but many people looking for stock bargains like to aim for a 20 P/E or lower.

WHO DO YOU TRUST FOR ADVICE?

The answer is that you need to learn a considerable amount by yourself to judge the quality of the information and advice you're given on stocks. Some ways to learn:

- Start reading a leading national business newspaper like the *Wall Street Journal* or *Barron's*.
- Watch business wrap-up shows on TV each night or when you get time.
- Join an investment club that focuses on education not the money.
- Take the time to talk with a financial advisor like a CERTIFIED FINANCIAL PLANNER™ professional.

HOW TO BUY STOCKS

Typically, stocks are bought through a brokerage firm, and you'll have to pay trading fees to purchase them. However, certain companies sponsor dividend reinvestment plans (DRIP) that allow individuals to buy stock directly through the company, with a small fee to a transfer agent. The advantage of DRIPs is that small investors can come on board for relatively small amounts of money, and sometimes DRIP stock is sold at a discount to current market price. They're worth checking out if you feel strongly about owning an individual stock.

For individuals who don't want to do all that work and would prefer to diversify with the help of investment professionals, the solution may be mutual funds. We'll explore mutual funds in the next chapter.

43 | *Understanding Mutual Funds*

Over the past 30 years, mutual funds have risen to prominence as individuals have taken on more responsibility for retirement saving and other investing goals.

Mutual funds pool the money of people with similar investment goals. All mutual funds have a theme—preserving capital, increasing current income, maximizing long-term growth, or combining growth and income. There are other goals too—even socially conscious investing.

Mutual funds are run by managers who spend their days examining various companies, securities, and other investments for hidden value. Investment theorists argue that professionally managed mutual funds have two big advantages over the holding of individual investments. Funds offer diversification because they feature a wide variety of holdings, not just one. Also, they offer liquidity, since with a phone call, you can cash in your investment at will.

However, many experts argue that funds have their problems. Professional management doesn't always mean good management, because some very highly paid managers don't pick very well. On top of that, they charge fees— management, marketing, and otherwise—

that can significantly eat into your profits or further a loss.

TYPES OF FUNDS

Your first exposure to mutual funds was probably in your company 401(k) or your organization or agency's 403(b) plan. Funds are also a key component in self-directed IRAs. People in these kinds of plans are given a choice among several major fund categories:

Stock funds. These funds obviously own stocks of companies, and the funds tend to be classified by the size of the companies they own. Large-cap funds tend to be the biggest companies out there while small-cap funds are young firms poised for growth.

Bond funds. These funds are invested in bonds of governments or companies, and are also divided into various categories based on the bonds' structure. Unless the fund is invested in high-risk bonds, bond funds tend to be a fairly conservative investment choice.

Balanced funds. These funds typically mix stocks and bonds to act like an individual portfolio designed for maximum diversification based on the individual's life stage. It is important to examine whether the fund manager's idea of balance fits your investment strategy.

International/global funds. These funds invest in overseas companies, sometimes in a mixture with U.S. companies of similar type. These funds can be more volatile based on where the companies are located, but they can offer the potential for more growth when U.S. stocks are stagnant.

Sector funds. Have a favorite industry? You can invest in a sector fund and focus on companies in that industry alone. People who invested in technology funds in the late 1990s were very happy, but when 2000 rolled around, they became very sad. The right bet in a sector fund can be very rewarding; the wrong one reminds us all why we should never put all our eggs in one basket.

Index funds. For many people, the decision to buy an index fund was a good one in a hot market and a relatively safe one in a bad market. Index funds try to buy representative amounts of stock in a particular index with the goal of matching the overall market step-by-step.

Because what they do isn't terribly complex, their fees tend to be lower than most funds, and thus can represent a better value for investors.

GETTING A GRIP ON FUND FEES

Mutual funds charge management fees, and investors need to be aware of what they are before they put their money down. That's why you need to read the prospectus or check a reputable source like www.Morningstar. com. The key issue here is the expense ratio, an amalgam of different fees charged by the fund. It includes:

- **The investment advisory fee or management fee.** This fee is used to pay the manager or managers of the fund. Fund managers generally do pretty well. This fee is about 0.5–1 percent annually of the fund's assets. The bigger the fund, whatever the percentage of the management fee, the more the manager or managers make.
- **The 12b-1 fee.** This is a marketing fee that gets a lot of heat. If you can find a well-performing fund without one, buy it.
- **Administrative cost.** Mutual funds have recordkeeping expenses and other charges tied to keeping customers informed about how their fund is doing. The most cost-conscious funds keep these expenses below 0.2 percent.

Morningstar and other resources can help you determine the expense load—an overall number—for your fund and whether it's high or low within the category of funds you want to invest in.

OTHER FEES THAT COST YOU MONEY

Load. This is a sales charge separate from what we discussed above. A load is a sales charge paid by the investor to compensate brokers who sell you the fund. If you're investing in the company 401(k), ask your human resources person what they're doing to limit fees that are passed on to your fellow employees. If you're investing by yourself, aim for quality "no-load" funds that are sold directly to the consumer. Here are key loads to watch for:

- **Front-end load.** These are pretty steep—often around 5 percent.
- **Back-end or deferred load.** These are charged when you sell. They're also known as B shares.
- **Level loads.** These funds charge an initial load that is typically smaller than annual loads charged thereafter.

HOW TO BUY MUTUAL FUNDS

Most mutual funds today can be bought directly unless you are buying from retirement accounts already set up at established brokerages. Then you'll have to pay their commission on top of any fees the mutual fund typically charges new investors.

Do everything you can to buy direct.

In the next chapter, we'll examine bonds and how they work.

44 | *Understanding Bonds and Government Securities*

Bonds turn individuals into moneylenders. How so? Corporations, governments, and nonprofit entities need to borrow to keep running. They would prefer to borrow from investors than from banks. Individuals and large institutions like the idea of an investment that pays them a guaranteed amount at a guaranteed time.

It's a marriage made in heaven.

Bonds are called "fixed-income" securities because the income stated on the bond won't vary, even if it's sold. No matter who owns the bond, they'll earn the same amount.

TYPES OF BONDS

- **Treasuries.** The U.S. Treasury Department sells bonds in a variety of maturities (for a look at what the government sells, go to www.savingsbonds.com). U.S. government bonds are called Treasuries because they are sold by the Treasury Department. They are guaranteed by the U.S. government and are free of state and local taxes on the interest they pay.
- **Quasi-government bonds.** Organizations like the Federal National Mortgage Association (Fannie

Mae), the Federal Home Loan Mortgage Corp. (Freddie Mac), and the Government National Mortgage Association (Ginnie Mae) sell bonds backed by the full faith and credit of the U.S. to fund home ownership. Sallie Mae, the nation's leading provider of student loans, sells various securities to back those loans.

- **Corporate bonds.** Corporate bonds often pay more than government bonds because companies face more risk than governments. High-yield bonds, also known as junk bonds, are corporate bonds issued by companies whose credit quality is below investment grade. Some corporate bonds are called convertible bonds because they can be converted into stock if certain provisions are met.

- **Municipal bonds.** Munis aren't Treasuries, but they're public debt issued by municipalities to fund operating or capital expenditures. Munis are generally considered a safe investment in healthy economies when tax revenues adequately support the government issuing the bonds, but remember Orange County, California's bankruptcy in 1994? The county treasurer invested more than $7 billion in public pension money in junk bonds, and when the market went south, so did all that money. The important point here is that the strength of the investment is only as strong as the government's ability to pay its debts, so make sure the health of that debt is secure.

  When evaluating a municipal bond investment, always check news reports on the city or county's bond rating from Moody's Investors Service (Moodys.com) or Standard & Poor's (www2. standardandpoors.com). There's risk involved. Of course, there are also great tax advantages involved, since they are free of federal, state, and local income tax, which makes it easier to swallow the relatively low returns on these bonds.

BOND LINGO

- **Par value** is what an investor will be paid once the bond matures if the investor keeps it that long. Essentially, it's the principal.
- **Coupon rate** is the amount of interest that the bondholder will

receive expressed as a percentage of the par value. Thus, if a bond
has a par value of $1000 and a coupon rate of 10 percent, the person
holding the bond will receive $100 a year. The bond will also specify
when the interest is to be paid, whether monthly, quarterly, semian-
nually, or annually.

- **Maturity date** is the date when the bond issuer has to return the
principal to the lender (the person who purchased the bond). After
the debtor pays back the principal, it is no longer obligated to make
interest payments. Sometimes, companies call (buy them back before
they mature) their bonds to wipe that debt off the books. Munis can
also be called, but federal government bonds can't.

FIGURING OUT THE BOND YIELD

$$\text{Current Yield} = \frac{\text{Annual Dollar Interest Paid}}{\text{Market Price}} \times 100$$

Commit the above formula to memory. This will allow you to compare
the yield on a bond with the potential yield of other investments. Why
not just refer to the coupon rate? Because that gives you an idea of return
if you hold the bond to maturity. If you plan to buy or sell it now, current
yield is a snapshot of reality.

HOW TO BUY BONDS

Federal bonds can now be bought on the Internet at no charge, which is a
big step forward. Again, go to www.savingsbonds.gov for an overview.
Corporate and municipal bonds generally need to be purchased through
an investment broker.

In the next chapter, we'll explain commodities.

45 | *Understanding Commodities*

Are you concerned that bonds have run their course as interest rates start to climb, and that the returns for stocks in the coming decade may be below their historical average, as some observers predict? How about adding a little pork belly to your investment portfolio? Or soybeans, copper, gold, timber, cattle futures, or oil?

In 2006, the buzz was all about gold and oil. Yet investing in commodities because they're "hot" is the wrong reason to buy them, caution financial planners. The compelling reason to consider commodities is the long-term diversification role they can play in portfolios, even modest ones. But before buying commodities, it's important to understand them as investments, how they fit into portfolios, and how you might invest in them.

WHAT ARE COMMODITIES?

Commodities are essentially the raw materials societies use: agricultural products such as wheat, cattle, and coffee; energy products such as oil and gas; and natural resources such as timber, silver, and the most glittering commodity of all, gold. These tangible investments are in contrast to what's been the predominant investment of the last 20 to 30 years—intangible financial investments such as stocks and bonds.

Commodities tend to do well during inflationary times, while stocks and bonds tend to abhor inflation. The fact that commodities typically perform differently than stocks and bonds is the major reason many investment experts like them in portfolios.

Studies have shown that the addition of commodities can reduce volatility and increase returns. For example, a study that appeared several years ago in the *Journal of Financial Planning*[1] examined the benefits of mixing multiple asset classes in a portfolio. The four assets it studied were domestic large-cap stocks, international stocks, real estate investment trusts, and commodities. The study looked at the four asset classes alone and in equally weighted combinations of two, three, or all four classes.

During the period studied, from 1972 to 1997, commodities by themselves had the lowest average returns and the highest volatility of the four assets. Yet of the top five portfolio combinations showing the best performance and the lowest volatility, commodities were included in every single one of them. The study noted specifically that the commodities performed counter-cyclically to the other asset classes, thus reducing the "downside risk" when the other assets faltered during bear markets.

If you do include commodities in your portfolio, the general recommendation is to keep it small—around 5 to 10 percent of the portfolio's total value.

HOW TO BUY COMMODITIES

The easiest and generally the best way for most investors—particularly those with modest portfolios—is to invest through commodities-based mutual funds. Some are broad-based funds that track major commodities indexes; others concentrate on specific sectors such as energy or other natural resources. The advantage here is that you don't have to invest a lot to add commodities to your portfolio, and you have professional management working for you in a very challenging investment arena. But before buying, see what exposure to commodities your current mutual funds might already have, so you don't overexpose this sector.

A second way is to buy individual shares of commodity companies, such as gold mining firms, oil companies, or forest product businesses. Or you can buy commodities directly, primarily precious metals such as gold or silver. But with direct investing you usually face steep transaction and storage costs, and have less liquidity. And with individual stocks and precious metals, you can't diversify your portfolio as efficiently as a mutual fund basket of commodities can.

The last option is buying commodity futures, generally considered the riskiest way to invest in commodities. With futures, you buy the rights to a shipment of something such as wheat or hogs for a particular price at a particular "settlement" time. Profits or losses are based on price changes leading up to the settlement (most investors sell their contracts before actually receiving the shipment). And because futures are commonly bought with borrowed money, it's easy to quickly lose a lot of money should you guess wrong.

Now that we've explored some ways to invest, the next chapter will look at developing an overall investment strategy.

ENDNOTE

1. Roger C. Gibson, CFA, CFP®. "The Rewards of Multiple-Asset-Class Investing," *Journal of Financial Planning.* March 1999.

46 | *Putting It All Together*

A winning investment strategy isn't the easiest thing in the world to create. Some people have the stamina and the interest to develop a solid strategy that they are prepared to stick with for the long haul. Others need help from trained experts. Yet it's worth reviewing some key concepts necessary to making an investment strategy work for a lifetime.

INVEST WITH A PLAN

Much of the riskiest investing, overbuying, and panic selling during the late 1990s and early 2000s would have been avoided if individual investors had created their own investment plan for achieving *long-term* specific goals, such as retirement or a college education. For example, someone who can reach an investment goal by earning a modest average annual return is less apt to jump into higher-risk investments than someone with no plan except to always "go for the highest return."

Smart investors draw up an investment policy statement (IPS) that specifically outlines realistic return goals, what types of investments they will and won't invest in, what mix of investments, and so on. This IPS serves as a reminder of their goals and strategies, and guides them through market declines and restrains them during boom times.

For some investors, this lesson already comes too late. Panicked investors bailed out of the stock market or drastically cut back, and will likely get back in only after they're "convinced" that the market is rebounding. Yet missing out on the stock market gains during the early stages of recovery can dramatically reduce returns, and the longer you wait, the more you miss out.

DIVERSIFY, DIVERSIFY

Investors chased hot tech stocks in the late 1990s and got badly burned come 2000 and 2001. The NASDAQ lost 39 percent of its value just in 2001, and another 21 percent in 2002. Investors also overloaded on company stock, frequently with poor results.

Meanwhile, real estate investment trusts, which performed poorly in 1998 and 1999 when stocks were booming, had banner years in 2000 and 2001, performed so-so in 2002, and had an excellent 2003. Bonds also returned well during the bear market. By adhering to your investment policy statement and spreading out your investment portfolio, you usually can reduce risk, minimize losses, and take advantage of the next surprise winners.

HOLD REALISTIC EXPECTATIONS

As investors painfully learned, those high double-digit annual returns of the late 1990s—one year the NASDAQ jumped 85 percent—aren't average. Average annual returns for the past 75 years have been around 11 percent for large-cap stocks and 12 percent for small-cap stocks, and many observers believe stocks will average 3 to 4 percent below those averages during the coming decade.

SLEEP AT NIGHT

Investors' tolerance for risk tends to track the market—aggressive when the market is hot, timid when it's down. But risk tolerance should reflect your overall investment needs, investment horizon, and how much market volatility you feel comfortable with—regardless of what the market is doing at the moment. Again, a realistic investment plan should keep you focused and help you sleep.

PAY YOUR TAXES

After running up big gains in the late 1990s, some investors were reluctant to sell even as the market began to slide because they didn't want to pay large capital gains taxes. Three years of market decline took care of that tax problem for many of them.

AVOID "REARVIEW MIRROR" INVESTING

Investors tend to focus on the immediate past. When stocks are booming, investors assume they will always boom. When stocks begin to slide, they fear they will slide forever. Instead, look out the front windshield at the long term.

In the next and final part of our book, we'll take a look at planning for the unexpected.

Part XII

Life's Little Surprises

How a Planner Can Help You Plan for the Unexpected

Shashin Shah, CFP®

Shashin Shah, a CERTIFIED FINANCIAL PLANNER™ professional based in Dallas, knows that the best thing a planner can do for a client is to foresee worst-case scenarios and help clients put all the pieces in place in case those scenarios happen.

There are planners who help individuals put key documents together—wills, medical directives, insurance, and asset information and hold a copy in their office in case of emergency, Shah explains. "And there are other planners who make preparations and are brought in to stage-manage a crisis. A planner acts on the wishes of the client, but his or her job is to determine exactly what the client needs."

Such events don't have to be as dire as the sudden or expected death of a loved one. "Part of disaster planning is having not only paperwork in place, but funds to insure an individual if he or she loses a job or disability insurance after an injury," Shah explains. "The emergency fund is the true financial independence plan, and it's critical during times of crisis." Parents should also have a plan in place for events that bring unexpected costs, such as adult children moving back home. "Parents need to talk about whether they'll charge rent or require in-kind compensation of household expenses, because it's a significant financial strain."

A talented planner gets clients to talk about their worst fears and steps back from those concerns to draft a plan that includes as many contingencies as possible. The plan is as unique as the person.

Shah believes that once a crisis plan is developed, it should be revisited every two to three years. "Lives change. People get divorced, they have babies, and they move and change jobs. Every aspect of a crisis plan—wills, insurance, emergency fund, and other issues—should be reviewed at that time."

47 | *Planning for the Unexpected*

It would be terrific if we could plan for every unexpected event in our lives, particularly those that had the potential to cost us a lot of money. But there are various scenarios you really can pre-think in advance.

PLANNING FOR SUDDEN WEALTH

Money fantasies are nice. Some of them even come true—unexpected inheritances, year-end bonuses, and yes, in even one in several hundred million chances, a winning Powerball ticket.

Most of us have fantasized about the fun we'd have with found money if it ever found us. But how many of us have fantasized about what we'd do to make it do the most good for our families, the causes we care about, and ourselves? Keep these ideas in your hip pocket if your ship ever comes in:

Make sure you have good tax, legal, and financial planning advice. This is a good idea even if you *never* receive a windfall. A qualified tax adviser, attorney expert in estate matters, and a financial planner (such as a CERTIFIED FINANCIAL PLANNER™ professional) will ground you in reality before your fantasy comes true. Should a windfall appear, each expert is able to look at your personal situation and assess the risks and strategies necessary to accepting and managing the funds without costly tax or investing mistakes. While inheritances are not in themselves subject to income tax, bonuses and gambling winnings may be taxable at your highest marginal rate or even place some of your winnings in a higher tax bracket. State and local taxes may also apply. The result can take the wind out of your windfall.

Force yourself to think about true necessities before luxuries. The adage "Pay yourself first" also works in the fantasy world. What are the biggest financial problems you'd like to solve today? That might be the best approach to thinking about your reaction to a windfall. Have you always dreamed about buying a home and owning it outright? Shoring up a retirement and health-care strategy that would stand you in good stead no matter what the market did for the rest of your life? How about paying for your kids' college in cash so they won't have to shoulder debt after graduation? As noted, taxes can eat away a significant portion of unexpected wealth, so it is best to focus on long-term goals and set priorities aimed at creating a lifetime of financial health. It makes little sense to have a brand-new Maserati in the driveway if retirement goals are neglected and other family objectives are left unfulfilled.

Consider a plan for helping others. The news media are littered with stories about poor souls who waste sudden fortunes after being preyed upon by friends, family members, and strangers with a "cause." Giving to others—whether part of a wealth management strategy or simple year-end tax strategy—should be planned with the best advice available based on the circumstances. As long as you're fantasizing about wealth, consider fantasizing about the people and organizations you would really want to help with any extra money you had, and commit to getting the right financial and tax advice before writing a single check. With a little effort, charitable gifts can be enhanced while providing improved control and maximum tax advantage.

Know your fellow winners. It's one thing to go in with co-workers or family on a weekly lottery pool on a casual, fun basis. Unfortunately, that friendly group dynamic could change significantly with a big windfall. This is clearly a question for your legal adviser, but some experts suggest that people who regularly gamble together draft a partnership agreement that can be reviewed by a qualified attorney. The partnership might also obtain a Federal Employer Identification Number that enables the winnings and the tax burden to be distributed along agreed-upon lines if it acquires a winning ticket.

Know the tax impact of any court award. If you win money in a court case, you may be sharing it with Uncle Sam. Generally, compensatory damages for personal physical injury or physical sickness are not taxable. However, other types of court-related compensation could be taxable as ordinary income, including:

- Interest on any type of award
- Amounts received to settle pension rights if you did not contribute to the plan
- Compensatory damages for lost wages or lost profits
- Punitive damages
- Compensation for patent or copyright infringement, breach of contract, or interference with business operations; back pay
- Damages for emotional distress in a Civil Rights Act claim

Think about your career. There are many people who say they'll never quit their job if they come into money. But it's an important issue. Money may change relationships, including relationships at the office and your relationship to money. If an amount determined to be adequate for financial independence is reached, life issues may take on an added sense of urgency. A CERTIFIED FINANCIAL PLANNER™ can help determine the amount needed as well as enhance the management of assets and the production of income for life.

TEN WAYS TO PREVENT IDENTITY THEFT

Identity theft is a topic that doesn't stand still because new ways to steal your personal information—and access your money and credit—crop up every day. Keep in mind that the companies keeping your information don't always have to notify you that it has been stolen. Here are some basic ways to keep your information safe.

Beware the "phishermen." Phishing is a process by which scam artists try and get you to divulge your Social Security number, your account numbers, address or other personal information under the guise of a legitimate company you may already be doing business with. It's most common over the Internet, but there's no reason why a phishing request couldn't come by direct mail or over the phone. They'll get your attention by saying there's a problem with your account. Anytime anyone asks you for personal information, check with the company to make sure the request is real. And always save the evidence—it may help put the con artists in jail.

Check your transactions daily. If you download your credit card and bank account information daily into a bookkeeping program—from secure sites, of course—you can immediately spot irregularities. Check them against any paper receipts and statements to make sure amounts are correct.

Protect your mail. If you're not there to pick up the mail when it arrives every day, then consider a locked mailbox. And never have checks mailed to your residence—pick them up at the bank instead.

Watch your passwords. If the only username and passwords you can remember are your e-mail address and your dog's name, then it's either time for memory tricks or creating a list of passwords you use to Internet sites you regularly visit. Keep any password records at home in a safe place. Change your passwords often, and never click the box that allows you to store passwords or credit card information online.

Get your credit report once a year. By law, you're entitled to free copies of your credit report from each of the three major credit rating agencies—TransUnion, Experian, and Equifax. (Available at www.annual creditreport.com.) Don't get them all at once—stagger them a few months apart so you can see if erroneous data appears throughout the year. Also, if you are on active duty with the military, you can place an active duty alert on your credit reports to help minimize the risk of identity theft while you are deployed. Active duty alerts are in effect on your report for one year—if your deployment lasts longer, you can place another alert on your credit report.

Think twice about identity theft insurance. Some companies also offer identity theft insurance that will cover lost pay if you have to straighten out your credit, but realize they will not do the dirty job of restoring your credit—that's up to you.

And since many of the companies selling this insurance are already affiliated with the credit industry, that's good reason for pause. Also, check your home or renter's insurance policy to see if they provide identity theft coverage.

Watch that wireless. If you have wireless service on your laptop, try not to store any financial data on that machine. Scammers who use their wireless access to hack into your data can steal that data electronically. Also, you face the added risk from terrestrial thieves who might want to steal your laptop from a public place. Lastly, when you get rid of that laptop—or any computer—remove every file before you dispose of it—in fact, it might be a wise idea to use software that will "wipe" the hard drive clean of any files previously installed on it.

Stick with a known ATM. Some of those independent ATMs you see in convenience stores, restaurants, and bars may be collecting your data for illegal use. Use ATMs at established banks.

Buy a shredder. Or at least be willing to cut up all envelopes, direct-mail credit applications, and receipts that you would typically throw away.

What if theft still happens? One of the best resources for a step-by-step guide to fighting identity theft is the Federal Trade Commission and its Web site, www.ftc.gov. The FTC provides a complete listing of contacts and procedures for getting to the bottom of identity theft before the event goes from being serious to devastating.

PLANNING FOR A MAJOR INSURANCE LOSS

In the post-Hurricane Katrina era, it's not only good to have a family disaster plan but it's critical to consider the coverage on every insurance policy you have. Remember, once disaster is threatening, you will not be able to get coverage changes or additions.

Here are points to consider in that process:

Medical deductibles and limits. Property can be replaced. Lives can't. In a disaster, you or your family might need to go to an emergency room. Does your current coverage provide for such out-of-network care? If not, how will you pay for it? As part of your evacuation plan, you might set aside available funds in an account with a bank that has a nationwide network of ATMs so you can access ready cash wherever you go. Don't leave everything up to credit cards unless you have to.

Prescription coverage. See what options your health coverage provides for prescription discounts and prescription-by-mail availability so you can have uninterrupted access to important medications wherever you are.

Homeowner's inventory. If you've been routinely paying your annual premiums without checking coverage for collectibles, home office equipment, or additional furniture or assets when you've renovated your home, start making a list of those changes and review them with your agent. Also, take up-to-date photographs of all major belongings in your home, keep those photos in a safe place, and send a copy set to an out-of-state relative.

Home replacement coverage. Go to several providers to estimate how much you would get for maximum replacement coverage in your area. With so many homeowners heavily mortgaged, this coverage is critical. Check and see if your policy is a "guaranteed replacement" or "replacement" type policy.

Water damage and earthquake insurance options. If you live in a flood plain or an earthquake zone, chances are you probably already know you do since that disclosure may be a legal requirement. But review the need for this coverage with your agent.

Disability coverage. Prudent planners always suggest disability coverage. Many people get disability coverage through work; others purchase separate policies. In either case, this type of additional protection could be key if the insured gets injured in a disaster and is perhaps looking at losing a home and a job at the same time.

Hurricane and windstorm coverage. This coverage varies by state and sometimes by individual county. States, including Alabama, Florida, Louisiana, Mississippi, North Carolina, South Carolina, and Texas, offer windstorm coverage pools for people who can't get private insurance through their agents. Residents of some coastal counties in Georgia and New York can get wind and hail coverage through FAIR (Fair Access to Insurance Requirement) plans, which are high-risk pools run by insurance companies. Your insurance agent or state insurance department will have more details.

Auto insurance. Most comprehensive auto coverage will cover wind, flood, or earthquake damage. Obviously, if you've downsized that coverage as your car has gotten older, consider your financial picture. Could you afford the sudden loss of a working automobile in a disaster?

Business-interruption insurance. A good business-interruption policy can cover many business costs for up to 12 months so long as there is proper documentation. If you don't have this coverage, think about whether it might be right for you in a crisis. Structure your policy for the best coverage possible, and have all pertinent income documents (including your most recent IRS filing) in your emergency documents.

Life coverage. Talk to a number of agents about the appropriateness of coverage that will protect your spouse and children with enough money to help them continue their lifestyle and their educational goals. That includes money for ongoing expenses, mortgage payment, and tuition. Your spouse should also consider similar coverage, particularly if he or she is working. You might also consider life insurance for the children, if only for burial coverage.

Create a disaster book. Create a disaster section in your binder or folder of information your loved ones would need in case of your death.

World events and natural disasters make a single go-to guide a sensible item. Such a guide allows family members to access insurance, home, and estate information in a crisis. And make sure it is in the right place with critical papers and items you would need to take with you in an emergency with a copy (or copies) retained out of state with relatives if possible.

PLANNING FOR A CHILD WITH DISABILITIES

Parents who have a child with a physical or mental disability or a child with a potentially chronic illness must financially plan not only for immediate needs, but for the child's entire life. Here are several financial planning issues you may need to consider.

Overall planning. Designing a viable budget is critical because of the often extraordinary medical expenses. It also is vital that you manage your money and create financial strategies that balance your own needs with those of your child. Saving for your own retirement, for example, should not be ignored.

Medical coverage. Try to have your health plan cover the child for as long as possible. Eventually, usually when the child turns 18, federal supplemental security income and Medicaid may cover most—though not all—medical expenses.

Life insurance. You may want life insurance benefits to help support your child after your death. However, keep two issues in mind. First, large amounts of life insurance could make your estate vulnerable to estate taxes, so a life insurance trust might be appropriate. Second, you'll want to be careful about naming the child as beneficiary if the child needs government assistance to meet daily living needs. Insurance benefits would probably make the child ineligible.

Guardianship. All families should name a guardian for their minor children in the event the parents die prematurely. However, a child with a disability probably will need a guardian for life (including a successive guardian should the original guardian not be able to carry out his or her duties). Even if the child is institutionalized, it's generally advisable to have a relative or friend legally able to act on their behalf.

Letter of intent. This document details your child's medical history and your wishes and expectations for the child's future. Experts consider this to be invaluable for caregivers once the child's parents die.

Government assistance. The two most common programs for such assistance are Medicaid and supplemental security income. However, unless you have very low income, a disabled child living at home probably won't be eligible for these programs until he or she turns 18. At that point, only the child's assets and income are counted toward eligibility.

Special needs trust. Also called a supplemental needs trust, this is a way to provide extra income to a child receiving government assistance without making the child ineligible for assistance. Money that's put into the trust by family or friends and relatives can only be used to pay for extras not covered by the government, such as a vacation, dental care, special equipment, education, or a CD player. It cannot be used to pay for basics such as food, clothing, and shelter, unless they are not adequately provided by government assistance. There is no dollar limit to the amount that can be contributed or earned by the trust. Parents can be trustees.

A variation of this strategy is for a charitable organization to set up a single trust for the benefit of several disabled children.

Irrevocable living trust. For children not receiving government assistance, an irrevocable living trust can be set up. Parents fund the trust while they're alive for the benefit of the child. Gifts to the trust reduce the value of their estate and minimize estate taxes. Financial institutions can serve as trustee, as well as friends or a financial planner or attorney, but you'll want successive trustees so you can be sure the child is cared for throughout his or her lifetime.

Estate planning. A will is essential, because if you die without one, the disabled child will inherit. That may disqualify the child for government assistance. Some parents leave all their assets to a sibling of the child, with the understanding that the sibling will use the money to benefit the disabled child. However, you can't legally require the sibling to do that, and the assets will then become vulnerable to the sibling's creditors or the sibling's spouse. Generally, a trust is considered a more secure option. Also, plan for where any assets are to go once the child dies.

Because of the complicated nature of special needs trusts, government benefits, and estate planning, you'll want to work closely with a knowledgeable attorney and your CERTIFIED FINANCIAL PLANNER™ professional.

CREATING A DISASTER PREPAREDNESS KIT

They've been on the market for years—so-called "beneficiary books" and other template-based filing tools that can help an heir, spouse, or executor sort through a person's affairs upon their incapacitation or death. There's no question that these tools make a lot of sense—but they're not only for the retirement set.

It's worth the time to develop a consolidated, orderly plan for the unthinkable.

Any individual with assets should create an easy-to-find, easy-to-understand file of financial information and keep that data in a safe, accessible place at home, with their attorney or CERTIFIED FINANCIAL PLANNER™ professional and possibly with a trusted friend or relative who lives a safe distance away from the aforementioned locations.

This information may be organized in a pre-purchased kit, a school binder, or in scanned documents stored on a computer disk:

- Birth, death, marriage certificates (make a note to the holder of this file that they should immediately order at least ten official copies of each in case they are executor or are asked to help an executor)
- Divorce decrees with all relevant settlement information
- Location of wills, trusts, and any power of attorney information
- Advanced health-care directives
- Adoption papers, if applicable
- Key identification numbers, including driver's license, passport, and employee identification data
- Recent bank and brokerage statements
- Detailed funeral and burial wishes

- Location of cash that may be used to handle emergency expenses
- Recent medical records that may be good to have on hand if the individual is incapacitated
- Copies of residential deeds and mortgage data
- Car title, lease, loan information, and license plate data
- All insurance policy (health, disability, and life) and agent contact information
- Photocopies of credit and debit cards, front and back (displaying the individual's signature)
- A current copy of the individual's home financial software program reflecting up-to-date financial data
- The locations for all critical paper documents and stocks and bonds
- Where safe-deposit, lockbox, and filing cabinet keys are
- Contact information for the individual's human resources department at work
- Location of tax returns for the last three years
- All relevant contact numbers for executors, financial advisers, trustees, guardians, attorneys, and any other pertinent individuals
- All user IDs and passwords for online accounts, including access to computer
- Guidelines on what to do about orphaned pets, including set plans for who will adopt them and pay for their care

In organizing all this information, it makes sense for the individual to put himself or herself in the shoes of the people they've selected to handle things in a crisis. Since these individuals may be capable but still frazzled or upset, it's essential that this information be simple to navigate and updated as often as possible. Some guidelines in organizing the documents:

Start with a simply written table of contents. When someone dies or is incapacitated, loved ones are typically distracted. They may forget details they've been told. That's why a detailed index of this data (with page numbers or folder labels) is so critical. Many people think that putting together a comprehensive binder or box of information is all they need to do, but a simple summary is particularly appreciated at stressful times.

Set a time each year to review and revise this information. Some experts advise individuals to update their wills and other estate preparations every five years or as often as change takes place. This crisis information should be updated more often—optimally, every year. A person's address, relationship, job status, and financial details can certainly change within a given year—that's why record keeping needs to keep pace with this information.

Keep the team informed. It's never easy to talk about death or illness with loved ones, but individuals need to make time to show their chosen family members and professionals this crisis kit, preferably where all this information is kept. If family members or advisers have questions or suggestions on how to better present this data, those ideas should be incorporated as time goes on.

PROTECTING YOURSELF AGAINST AN AUDIT

It's that letter no one wants to get.

In 2006, the Internal Revenue Service planned to conduct about one million audits, up 37 percent from 2001. The agency says it will target roughly 200,000 filers earning over $100,000—nearly double the number of four years earlier.

Even if you aren't that wealthy, the increasing number of self-employed individuals may also be part of the government's expanding tax dragnet. In any event, it's always smart to be vigilant against the expensive and stressful possibility of a tax audit. A qualified tax professional can assist you in the preparation of your return to minimize the chances of questions on your return.

There are three types of audits:

- **Correspondence audits** happen when the IRS sends a letter asking for clarification on relatively simple items. It's usually handled and completed through the mail.
- **Office audits** are conducted on the IRS's turf. You meet with an

examiner who wants to see documentation intended to answer their specific questions. It's wise not to volunteer any other information beyond what they ask.

- **Field audits** are the stuff of TV cop shows. That's when the IRS comes to your home and starts nosing around to see why that Jaguar is sitting in the driveway of someone who reported $28,000 in income last year. These tend to be pretty serious.

However, the government looks for particular signs and signals that may put you in the audit pile. The following measures won't guarantee that you'll avoid an audit, but they're key issues that the IRS focuses on when deciding which returns to target:

Goofing the basics. This is an obvious point, but remember to sign the return, add the Social Security number, and double-check the math. Fill out every applicable line on the return, or better yet, get a tax preparer to do it since professionally prepared returns tend to be easier to read and understand because you're paying qualified people to get it right. The bottom line—sloppy returns tend to draw scrutiny.

Rounding can be a problem. Precise numbers suggest precision. It's always best to use the precise number you need for an item than rounding up or down— rounded numbers tend to draw attention from the IRS, even if you're trying to be conservative.

Note sales of stocks or bonds carefully. Anytime you sell stocks or bonds, the IRS and the taxpayer receives a 1099 noting the sale price. Your tax professional can show you the proper way to account for these sales on your return. Also remember that income items such as interest, dividends, and other sources of income are matched with the return from documents that are already on file with the IRS.

Scores are everywhere. In case you didn't know, the IRS— like the lending industry— assigns you a score. It's called the Discriminate Information Function (DIF), a computer program that compares, among other things, the deductions you're taking against others in your income bracket. It's the way an increasingly technology-driven IRS is screening for suspicious returns. One of the best ways to avoid a high DIF score is to report all income—don't let yourself think that any amount is not worth reporting.

Itemized deductions. You should claim every deduction the law entitles you to, but a good tax professional can advise you of reasonable limits that are less likely to trip your return. In particular, the IRS looks for overblown charitable deductions—make sure you make cash contributions by check or credit card so there's a record, and that all donations above $250 have receipts or other acknowledgement from the charity. If you do get audited, you need to prove the original value of the items donated and their fair market value.

Keep scrupulous mileage records. If you use your vehicle for work or business, keep a notebook or chart in the car so you can enter mileage information as soon as you complete the trip. The records should list beginning and ending odometer figures, location, and reason for the trip. Keep the same records for mileage claimed for medical expense and charitable purposes.

Watch that home office. Even though the government loosened restrictions on home office deductions in 1999, make sure you can substantiate that business area of your home if you're asked.

As you've reached the end of this book, it's entirely possible that you may have questions or more things you want to learn. Here's a great way to start. Go to www.fpanet.org, the Web site of the Financial Planning Association, and learn about what a financial planner can do for you. Then visit PlannerSearch.org to find a financial planner in your area who fits your specific needs and goals. Good luck!

Appendix: Web Sites

BANKRUPTCY

- **www.abcworld.org:** The American Board of Certification is a state-by-state listing of certified attorneys in bankruptcy law.
- **www.nfcc.org:** The National Foundation for Credit Counseling lists nonprofit consumer credit counseling agencies nationwide.

BONDS

- **www.savingsbonds.gov:** The U.S. Treasury's official site for purchasing individual and institutional Treasury securities.

COLLEGE SAVINGS

- **www.SavingforCollege.com:** Up-to-the minute information on 529 plans, Coverdell education savings accounts, financial aid, and other college affordability strategies. Includes a consistently updated state-by-state 529 plan comparison tool.
- **www.FinAid.org:** This Web site was started in 1994 as a public service and is a great resource for information about student financial aid on the Web.

- **www.CollegeBoard.com:** A great resource for financial aid and college pricing information.

CREDIT CARDS

- **www.bankrate.com:** Bankrate, Inc., is the Web's leading aggregator of financial rate information.

DEBT

- **www.annualcreditreport.com:** This site accesses all three credit bureaus, Experian (www.experian.com), Equifax (www.equifax.com), and TransUnion (www.transunion.com). You have free access to each of these credit reports once a year.

DIVORCE

- **www.TheLilacTree.org:** An Evanston, Illinois-based organization for women contemplating or going through divorce.

FINANCIAL PLANNING

- **www.fpanet.org:** The Financial Planning Association's Web site. Stop here for a general overview of what planners do and planning issues of interest to consumers.
- **www.plannersearch.org:** This site is part of the Financial Planning Association (www.fpanet.org). It enables you to find a planner by name, location, and specialty.
- **www.cfp.net:** The Web site of the Certified Financial Planner Board of Standards, which provides disciplinary records on financial planners.
- **www.nasaa.org:** North American Securities Administrators Association's Web site provides further disciplinary details on planners who market securities as part of their practice.
- **www.naic.org:** National Association of Insurance Commissioners for disciplinary details on planners who market insurance products.
- **www.sec.gov:** The Securities and Exchange Commission.

IDENTITY THEFT

- **www.ftc.gov:** The Federal Trade Commission, which takes as its mission consumer protection.

INSURANCE

- **www.eHealthInsurance.com:** Web site that allows you to price individual health insurance.
- **www.digitalinsurance.com:** Web site that allows you to price group insurance.
- **www.hsainsider.com and www.healthdecisions.org:** Two sites that can help you research health savings accounts.
- **www.fema.gov:** Flood insurance details.
- **www.earthquakeauthority.com:** California Earthquake Authority.
- **www.ambest.com:** A.M. Best's insurance rating system.

MUTUAL FUNDS

- **www.morningstar.com:** Morningstar's rating service for both stocks and mutual funds.

REAL ESTATE

Associations:
- **www.Realtor.org:** National Association of Realtors
- **www.coophousing.org:** National Association of Housing Cooperatives

Construction Assistance:
- **www.rsmeans.com/calculator/index.asp:** RS Means Project Cost Estimator
- **www.hanleywood.com:** Hanley Wood, provider of specialized paid reports on specific home renovation and construction projects

Credit Sites:
- **www.myfico.com:** Credit reports

Economic Information:
- **http://uclaforecast.com:** UCLA Anderson Forecast
- **www.census.gov/hhes/www/housing/census/histcensushsg.html:** U.S. Census Bureau/Census of Housing

Financial/Tax Planning:
- **www.fpanet.org:** Financial Planning Association
- **www.sec.gov/edgar.shtml:** Securities and Exchange Commission EDGAR database to look up all public securities filings

For 1031 Exchanges:
- **www.1031.org**

Foreclosure Information:
- **www.RealtyTrac.com:** RealtyTrac.com

Mortgage Trends:
- **www.hsh.com:** HSH Associates, Financial Publishers

RETIREMENT
- **www.aarp.org:** The Web site of the American Association of Retired Persons (AARP), probably the best resource for retirement-related news, retirement financial planning, health-care, and other retirement-related issues.

SMALL BUSINESS
- **www.nfib.org:** National Federation of Independent Business.
- **www.sba.gov:** U.S. Small Business Administration.

TAXES
- **www.irs.gov:** The Internal Revenue Service's Web site. Its search function can help you locate information on any tax issue.

Glossary

401(k) plan—An employer-sponsored, salary reduction and qualified retirement plan that allows employees to defer paying current federal income taxes on a portion of their annual compensation. Contributions and earnings grow tax-deferred until withdrawn. Withdrawals are taxed at the employee's income tax rate at the time of withdrawal.

403(b) plan—A salary reduction plan for employees of nonprofit organizations and government entities such as schools, hospitals, and educational organizations. Similar to the operation of a 401(k), contributions and earnings are tax-deferred until the money is withdrawn from the plan.

529 plan—A tax-advantaged education savings plan operated by a state or educational institution. These plans are categorized as either prepaid or savings, and each has separate characteristics.

Accrued interest—Interest that accumulates on the unpaid principal balance of a loan.

Adjusted Gross Income (AGI)—All taxable income less IRS-allowable adjustments to income. This figure is from U.S. IRS tax forms.

Administrator—Someone appointed by a court to settle an estate when there is no will.

After-tax return—The return from an investment after the cost of taxes has been recorded.

Amortization—The process of gradually repaying a loan over an extended period of time through periodic installments of principal and interest.

Annuity—An insurance-based contract that provides future payments at regular intervals in exchange for a lump-sum premium paid when the annuity is purchased. They're a strategy for lifetime income in retirement.

Asset—Anything owned that has monetary value.

Asset allocation—An ongoing process of balancing assets within a portfolio to limit risk.

Award letter—An official notification from a college's financial aid office listing all the financial aid awarded to the student. The award letter will include information about the cost of attendance and terms and conditions for the financial aid.

Beneficiary—The person or party named by the owner of a life insurance policy or investment accounts to receive the proceeds in the event of the owner's death.

Capital gain or loss—The difference between the sales price and the purchase price of a capital asset. When that difference is positive, the difference is referred to as a capital gain. When the difference is negative, it is a capital loss.

Cash equivalents—Short-term investments such as U.S. Treasury securities, certificates of deposit, and money market fund shares, that can be readily converted into cash.

Cash value—The savings element of a permanent life insurance policy, which represents the policy owner's interest in the policy.

CERTIFIED FINANCIAL PLANNER™ **practitioner**—A credential granted by the Certified Financial Planner Board of Standards, Inc. (Denver, Colorado) to individuals who complete a comprehensive curriculum in financial planning and ethics. CFP®, CERTIFIED FINANCIAL PLANNER™ and federally registered CFP (with flame logo)® are certification marks owned by the Certified Financial Planner Board of Standards, Inc. These marks are awarded to individuals who successfully complete the CFP Board's initial and ongoing certification.

Certified Public Accountant (CPA)—A license granted by a state board of accountancy to someone who has passed the Uniform CPA Examination (administered by the American Institute of Certified Public Accountants) and has fulfilled that state's educational and professional experience requirements for certification.

Coinsurance or co-payment—The amount an insured person must pay for a covered medical and/or dental expense if his or her insurance doesn't provide 100 percent coverage.

Commodities—Grains, food products, livestock, oils, and metals that are traded on national exchanges. These exchanges deal in both "spot" trading (for current delivery) and "futures" trading (for delivery in future months).

Common stock—A unit of ownership in a corporation. Common stockholders participate in the corporation's profits or losses by receiving dividends and by capital gains or losses in the stock's share price.

Compounding—Earning interest not only on the original principal amount, but also on accumulated prior interest.

Consolidated Omnibus Budget Reconciliation Act (COBRA)—COBRA is a federal law requiring employers with more than 20 employees to offer terminated or retired employees the opportunity to continue their health insurance coverage for 18 months at the employee's expense. Coverage may be extended to the employee's dependents for 36 months in the case of divorce or death of the employee.

Cosigner—A person who signs a promissory note in addition to the borrower and is responsible for the obligation if the borrower does not pay.

Cost basis—The tax cost of securities, which determines the profit when sold.

Creditworthy—An individual with no negative credit history per the criteria established by the lender.

Current yield—The ratio of the coupon rate on a bond to the dollar purchase price expressed as a percentage. Thus, if you pay par or 100 cents on the dollar for your bond, and the coupon rate is 6 percent, the current yield is 6 percent. However, if you pay 97 cents for your 6 percent bond, the current yield would be 6.186 percent (.06 divided by 97). If you paid 102 cents for a 6 percent bond, the current yield would be 5.88 percent (.06 divided by 102).

Deduction—An amount that can be subtracted from gross income, from a gross estate, or from a gift, thereby lowering the amount on which tax is assessed.

Defined benefit plan—A qualified retirement plan under which a retiring employee will receive a guaranteed retirement fund, usually payable in installments. Annual contributions may be made to the plan by the employer at the level needed to fund the benefit. The annual contributions are limited to a specified amount, indexed for inflation.

Defined contribution plan—A retirement plan under which the annual contributions made by the employer or employee are generally stated as a fixed percentage of the employee's compensation or company profits. The amount of retirement benefits is not guaranteed; rather, it depends upon the investment performance of the employee's account.

Disclosure statement—Statement of the total cost and amount of a loan, including the interest rate and any additional finance charges.

Diversification— Investing in different companies, industries, or types of assets to reduce risks in an investment portfolio.

Dollar-cost averaging—Periodic purchases of stocks or other investments that in the best-case scenario allow investors to register investment gains as prices head up and shield themselves from greater risk as investments head down.

Employee Retirement Income Security Act (ERISA)—ERISA is a federal law covering all aspects of employee retirement plans. If employers provide plans, they must be adequately funded and provide for vesting, survivor's rights, and disclosures under federal law.

Employee stock ownership plan (ESOP)—A defined contribution retirement plan in which company contributions must be invested primarily in qualifying employer securities.

Estate tax—Upon the death of a decedent, federal and state governments may impose tax on the value of an estate left to heirs.

Executor—Someone designated in a will or by the probate courts to carry out the wishes of someone who has died.

Expected family contribution (EFC)—The amount a family is expected to contribute to a student's education. EFC is calculated based on family earnings, net assets, savings, size of family, and number of family members in college.

Financial aid—College financial assistance in the form of scholarships, grants, work-study, and loans for education.

Free Application for Federal Student Aid (FAFSA)—The form that must be completed by students and parents applying for Federal Title IV student aid. All parents should consider filling out this form even if they have no immediate need for financial aid, because they may need it later if there is a family financial emergency.

Gift aid—College financial aid, such as grants and scholarships, which don't need to be repaid.

Gift taxes—A federal tax levied on the transfer of property as a gift and paid by the donor. The first $12,000 a year offered by the donor to recipient is tax-exempt.

Grants—College financial aid awards that do not have to be repaid. Grants are available through the government, state agencies, and colleges.

Individual retirement account (IRA)—A personal tax-deferred investment account to save for retirement. Contributions to a standard IRA may be deductible, and investments (including earnings and gains) generally are not taxed until distributed to you. Contributions to a Roth IRA are not deductible, but qualified distributions are not taxable.

Inflation— An increase in the price of products and services over time. The government's main measure of inflation is the Consumer Price Index.

Interest rate—The cost of borrowing money, expressed as a percentage of the amount borrowed for a period of time, usually one year.

Intestate—The condition of an estate left by a decedent without a valid will. State law then determines who inherits the property or serves as guardian for any minor children.

Joint tenancy—Co-ownership of property by two or more people in which those who survive one of the owners automatically assume ownership of a decedent's interest.

Keogh plan—A retirement plan designed for self-employed individuals that allows up to $44,000 of self-employed income (as of 2006) to be deducted from compensation and set aside into the plan.

Liability insurance—Insurance coverage that offers protection against claims resulting from the finding that a property owner has caused bodily injury or property damage to another party.

Living trust—A trust created by a person during his or her lifetime.

Load—A sales or redemption charge, usually imposed by a mutual fund.

Load fund—A mutual fund that carries a sales charge.

Lump-sum distribution—The disbursement of the entire value of a profit-sharing plan, pension plan, annuity, or similar account to the account owner or beneficiary. Lump-sum distributions may be rolled over into another tax-deferred account.

Marginal tax bracket— The range of taxable income that is taxable at a certain rate. Currently, there are six marginal tax brackets—10 percent, 15 percent, 25 percent, 28 percent, 33 percent, and 35 percent.

Marital deduction—A tax code provision that allows all assets of a deceased spouse to pass to the surviving spouse free of estate taxes. It's also called the unlimited marital deduction.

Money market fund—A mutual fund that specializes in investing in short-term securities.

Municipal bond—A debt security issued by municipalities. The income from municipal bonds is usually exempt from federal income taxes and can be exempt from state income taxes in the state in which the municipal bond is issued.

Municipal bond fund—A mutual fund that specializes in investing in municipal bonds.

Mutual fund—A collection of stocks, bonds, or other securities purchased and managed by an investment company with pooled funds from many investors.

Net asset value—The price at which a mutual fund sells or redeems its shares. The net asset value is calculated by dividing the net market value of the fund's assets by the number of outstanding shares.

No-load fund—A mutual fund that does not pass a sales charge along to investors.

Pell grants—A federal college grant program that awards free money (don't have to pay it back) solely on demonstrated financial need to every eligible undergraduate student who hasn't already earned a bachelor's or professional degree. The amount of the Pell grant depends on financial need, college costs, and whether the student is attending college full time or part time. The funds can be used for tuition, fees, and living expenses.

Perkins loans—Federally insured college loans funded by the government and awarded by the school. The loans feature a low interest rate and are repayable over an extended period.

Portfolio—All the investments held by an individual or a mutual fund.

Preferred stock—A class of stock with claim to a company's earnings, before payment can be made on the common stock, and that is usually entitled to priority over common stock if the company liquidates. Generally, preferred stocks pay dividends at a fixed rate.

Prenuptial agreement—A legal agreement arranged before a marriage that establishes who brought what property into the marriage and how it will be divided in case of divorce.

Prepaid tuition plan—A college savings plan that is guaranteed to rise in value at the same rate as college tuition. For example, if a family purchases shares that are worth half a year's tuition at a state college, they will always be worth half a year's tuition, even ten years later when tuition rates will have doubled.

Price/earnings ratio (P/E ratio)—The market price of a stock divided by the company's annual earnings per share. A widely regarded yardstick for investors.

Principal—The amount of money invested excluding earnings.

Probate—The court-supervised process in which a decedent's estate is settled and distributed.

Profit-sharing plan—An agreement under which employees share in the profits of their employer.

Qualified domestic relations order (QDRO)— At the time of divorce, this order would be issued by a state domestic relations court and would require that an employee's ERISA retirement plan accrued benefits be divided between the employee and the spouse.

Qualified retirement plan—A pension, profit-sharing, or qualified savings plan established by an employer for the benefit of the employees in compliance with IRS rules.

Replacement cost—The cost of replacing property without a reduction for depreciation. People shopping for homeowner's insurance should insist on replacement cost as a measurement for damage to their property.

Rollover—A method by which an individual can transfer the assets from one retirement program to another without the recognition of income for tax purposes. The requirements for a rollover depend on the type of program from which the distribution is made and the type of program receiving the distribution.

Roth IRA—A nondeductible IRA that allows tax-free withdrawals when certain conditions are met. Income and contribution limits apply.

Simplified employee pension plan (SEP)—A type of plan under which the employer contributes to an employee's IRA. Contributions may be made up to a certain limit and are immediately vested.

Spousal IRA—An IRA designed for a couple when one spouse has no earned income. The maximum combined contribution that can be made each year to an IRA and a spousal IRA is $8,000 (in 2005 through 2007) or 100 percent of earned income, whichever is less. This total may be split between the two IRAs as the couple wishes, provided the contribution to either IRA does not exceed $4,000.

Subsidized Stafford loans—Need-based college loans in which interest does not accrue and payments are deferred until after students stop attending school full time.

Umbrella policy—Umbrella coverage is insurance coverage that extends the terms of a regular insurance policy once coverage limits for the regular policy have been reached. Specifically, umbrella coverage is for people who want protection against a large jury award that is not covered in their standard policy.

Universal life insurance—A type of life insurance that combines a death benefit with a savings feature which accumulates tax deferred at current interest rates. Under a universal life insurance policy, the policyholder may increase or decrease his or her coverage under certain rules without purchasing a new policy.

Variable universal life insurance—Life insurance that combines a death benefit with a savings feature that accumulates tax-deferred at current interest rates. However, under this insurance, the cash value can be placed in a variety of subaccounts with different investment objectives. Fees are charged on these subaccounts, so be careful.

Vesting—The qualification date for minimum company benefits at an assigned time in an individual's seniority with the company or organization.

Whole life insurance—This is a type of life insurance that features a death benefit and accumulates cash value tax-deferred at a particular interest rate. Whole life insurance is also referred to as "ordinary" or "straight" life insurance.

Will—A legal document that declares a person's wishes concerning the disposition of property, the guardianship of his or her children, and the administration of the estate after his or her death.

Yield—In general, the yield is the amount of current income provided by an investment. For stocks, the yield is calculated by dividing the total of the annual dividends by the current price. For bonds, the yield is calculated by dividing the annual interest by the current price. The yield is distinguished from the return, which includes price appreciation or depreciation.

Index

405

The Encyclopedia of Financial Planning

The Encyclopedia of Financial Planning